Angola's Colossal Lie

African History

VOLUME 4

The titles published in this series are listed at *brill.com/afh*

Angola's Colossal Lie

Forced Labor on a Sugar Plantation, 1913–1977

By

Jeremy Ball

BRILL

LEIDEN | BOSTON

Cover illustration: Forced Labor on a Sugar Plantation, 1913–1977

Library of Congress Cataloging-in-Publication Data

Ball, Jeremy, author.
Angola's colossal lie : forced labor on a sugar plantation, 1913-1977 / by Jeremy Ball.
pages cm. -- (African history ; volume 4)
ISBN 978-90-04-30174-0 (pbk. : alk. paper) -- ISBN 978-90-04-30175-7 (e-book)
1. Forced labor--Angola--History--20th century. 2. Sugar workers--Angola--History--20th century. 3. Sugarcane industry--Angola--History--20th century. 4. Sugar--Manufacture and refining--Angola--History--20th century. I. Title. II. Series: African history (Brill Academic Publishers) ; v. 4.

HD4875.A838B35 2015
331.11734096730904--dc23

2015023731

ISSN 2211-1441
ISBN 978-90-04-30174-0 (paperback)
ISBN 978-90-04-30175-7 (e-book)

This book is printed on acid-free paper.

For os mais velhos [*the old ones*], *who shared their memories*

Contents

Note on Currency

In 1911, in the wake of the Republican Revolution, the Portuguese government adopted the *escudo*, divided into a hundred *centavos*, to replace the *milréis* (a thousand *reis*). A thousand *escudos* equaled one *conto*, a unit of account rather than of currency. Between 1928 and 1958 the government made the *angular*—which was pegged at parity with the *escudo*—the currency in Angola. In 1958, as part of its efforts to unify the empire, the colonial government reintroduced the *escudo* to Angola and discontinued use of the *angolar*.

MAP 1 *Angola*
CHASE LANGFORD

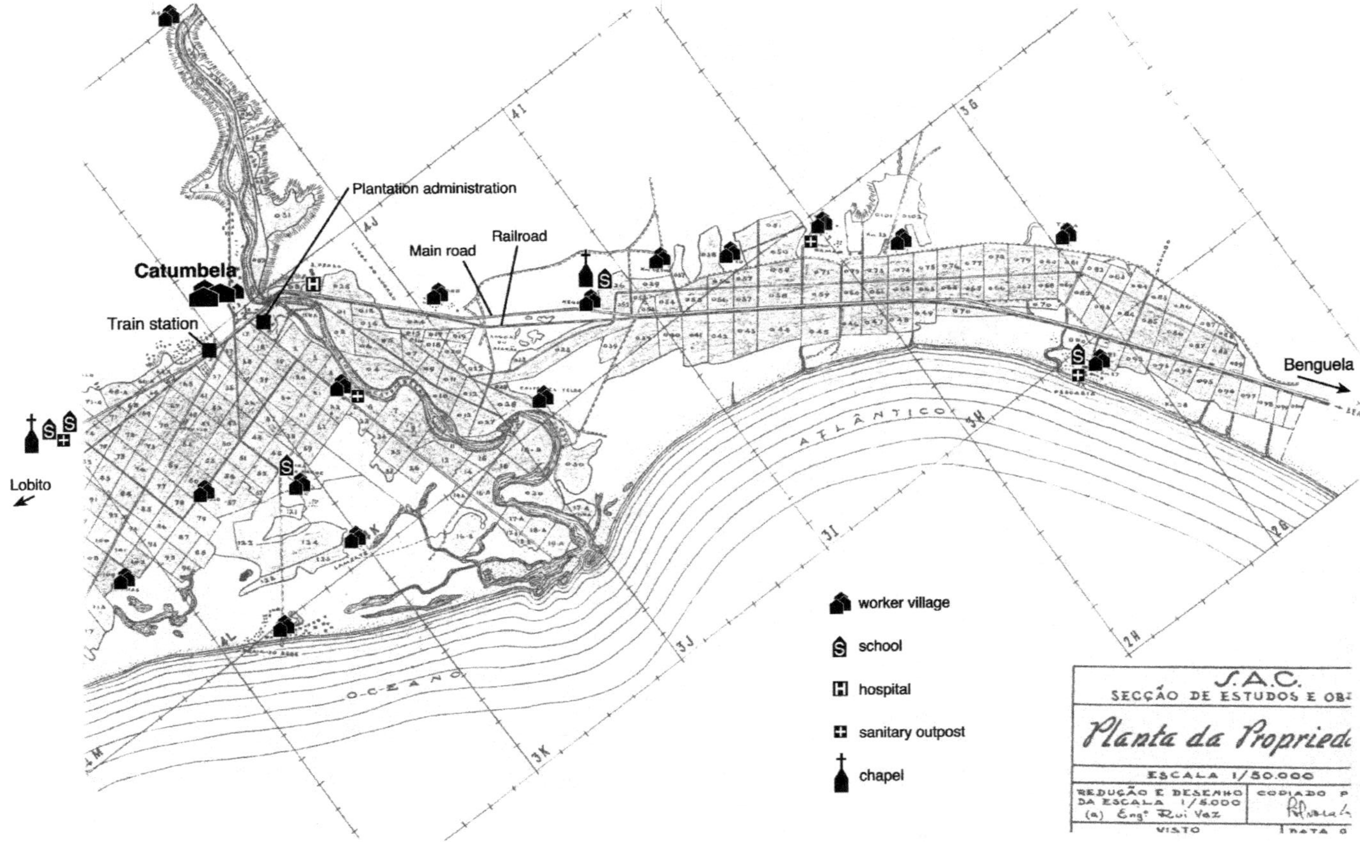

MAP 2 *Sociedade Agrícola Do Cassequel, 1960*
CHASE LANGFORD

Acknowledgements

I am deeply grateful to my advisors and colleagues at UCLA, where this project began. As my dissertation advisor, Ned Alpers offered encouragement and support at critical times. William Worger, Judith Carney, and Patrick Geary all offered advice and commented on drafts in ways that improved my thinking. Over the years, I have also benefitted from conversations about Portuguese colonialism and Angolan history with several scholars. In particular, Pedro Aires Oliveiro, Jill Dias, Landeg White, Carlos Damas, Manuel Ennes Ferreira, Maria da Conceição Neto, Rosa Cruz e Silva, Douglas Wheeler, Roquinaldo Ferreira, Marissa Moorman, Todd Cleveland, and Marcelo Borges all provided insightful feedback at different stages of the project. For their support in Angola, I am particularly thankful to José Pires, Orlando and Albertina Monteiro, Precioso Maria Chaves, and Kito Marcelino. A special thank you to Manuel Domingos for his work translating interviews from Umbundu to Portuguese and for his friendship during the months of travel in Angola. I also wish to thank two of my earliest teachers from Boston College, David Northrup and Carol Hurd Green, who first inspired my intellectual interest in Africa and aspiration to become a college professor and researcher.

Conducting archival and oral history research in Angola and Portugal is expensive. I am grateful for the generous financial and institutional support that made possible my extended stays in Lisbon, Luanda, and Catumbela. A Fulbright IIE award (2000–2001) paid for my research in Lisbon and the Calouste Gulbenkian Foundation (2001) supported initial research in Angola. A Young Africanist Award from the Woodrow Wilson International Center for Scholars (2002) provided financial support and an environment conducive to writing at a crucial time. A second Fulbright grant (2006) supported additional oral history interviews in the Angolan interior. Dickinson College, my academic home since 2005, provided a full-year sabbatical and research funds to return to Lisbon (2012). The Dickinson College Research and Development Committee also provided necessary subvention support for the project.

Archival work was key to *Angola's Colossal Lie*, and I am thankful to the archivists at the Arquivo Histórico de Angola (Luanda) and in Lisbon, the Biblioteca Nacional, the Sociedade de Geografia, the Arquivo Histórico Ultramarino, the Arquivo do Banco Espírito Santo, the Centro de Intervenção para o Desenvolvimento Amílcar Cabral (CIDAC), and the Arquivo de Fotografia de Lisboa.

Finally, this book would not have been completed without the unwavering support and love of my wife, Amy Wlodarski. Thank you for believing in the project and providing me the time and intellectual space to write and re-write.

Illustrations

Maps

Tables

Images

Abbreviations

ADRA	Acção para o Desenvolvimento Rural e Ambiente
AHA	Arquivo Histórico de Angola
AHBES	Arquivo Histórico do Banco Espírito Santo
AHP	Arquivo Histórico-Parliamentar
AHU	Arquivo Histórico Ultramarino
AMS	Arquivo Mário Soares
ANTT	Arquivo Nacional de Torre do Tombo
BN	Biblioteca Nacional
CFB	Benguela Railway Company
CIDAC	Centro de Informação e Documentação Amílcar Cabral
CWIHP	Cold War International History Project
FAPLA	The People's Armed Forces for the Liberation of Angola
FNLA	National Front for the Liberation of Angola
FO	Foreign Office
GES	Espírito Santo Group
ILO	International Labor Organization
MPLA	Popular Movement for the Liberation of Angola
NSA	National Security Archive
PRO	Public Records Office
SAC	Sociedade Agrícola do Cassequel
UNITA	National Union for the Total Independence of Angola
USNA	United States National Archives
WNLA	Witwatersrand Native Labor Association

Glossary

A bem da nação	For the good of the nation.
Aguardente (de cana-de-açúcar)	Rum; also known as *cachaça.*
Ambaquista	African merchant(s) and traders who spoke some Portuguese and dressed in European clothes.
Assimilado	Assimilated person. Under the *indigenato* system instituted in the 1920s, *assimilados* were those mixed race and African individuals who met the colonial government's criteria for citizenship.
Cacimbo	The cool period on the Angolan coast between June and September.
Caixa	Box. Documents at the AHU and the AHA are organized in *caixas.*
Chefe de posto	Colonial official in charge of a *posto;* head of the administrative post.
Cipaio (*pl. cipaios*)	African policeman, generally employed in garrisoning the posts and collecting hut tax.
Contratado	An individual fulfilling a term of forced labor, labeled euphemistically by colonial authorities as "contract labor."
Cubata	Thatched mud hut.
Curador dos indígenas	Guardian of the natives. Duties included overseeing contracts for forced labor and hearing workers' complaints. Rarely a full-time position, the duties of the *curador* were usually assigned to a local administrator.
Empreitada	A task or job. *Contratados* at Cassequel worked by *empreitada.*
Funge	Angolan staple porridge made from either maize or cassava.
Garapa	Sugar-cane juice distributed to workers at Cassequel.
Guia(*s*)	Work gang(s).
Imposto indígena	Native tax. Under the *Indigenato* all *indígenas* had to pay an annual tax to the government in Portuguese currency.
Indígena	Indigenous person. The vast majority of the population that could not prove *assimilado* status were referred to as *indígenas*. They had no rights under

	colonial law and were subject to forced labor. The *indigenato* system was abolished in 1961.
Kimbo	African homestead, or small village.
Liberto	Emancipated slave.
Mão-de-obra indígena	Native labor.
Mestiço	Person of mixed racial descent.
Muçeques	Shantytowns outside Angola's cities and towns.
Palmatórias	A *palmatória* is a wooden paddle with holes in the striking surface; it was used for corporal punishment.
Poder popular	People's power. A form of political organization adopted by the MPLA as strategy and slogan after independence.
Posto	Portuguese colonial administrative post.
Régulo	African headman.
Roça	Plantation on the island of São Tomé.
Roçeiros	Plantation owners on the island of São Tomé.
Seculo	Portuguese rendering of the Umbundu word *sekulu. yimbo*, meaning village leader.
Serviçal (serviçais, pl.)	Servant(s).
Soba	African chief. A Portugalization of the Umbundu word "*soma*."
Sobado	A constellation of villages recognizing the authority of a single *soba*.
Voluntário(s)	Voluntary worker. At Cassequel, denoted those workers on the plantation of their own volition.

Introduction

For more than half of the twentieth century, a system of forced labor existed in Portuguese-controlled Angola. The International Labor Organization (ILO), which spearheaded the 1930 Forced Labor Convention, defined forced labor as "all work or service, which is exacted from any person under the menace of any penalty and for which the said person has not offered himself voluntarily."[1] Portugal refused to sign the Forced Labor Convention until 1959 and finally abolished forced labor in 1962 in an effort to stave off demands for independence from Angolan nationalists. Portuguese officials insisted that its colonial labor regime instilled the value of hard work in its African subjects and ensured the development of Angola. Conversely, those Angolans forced to serve terms as *contratados* [contract labor] for periods lasting anywhere from six months to several years remember the system's inherent abuse and humiliation. According to Luís Massuna, who served as a *contratado* in the 1950s.

> In that time we worked for the *chefe de posto*...who paid us that unjust salary, whilst the rest of the money remained with him. Hence, one time I asked the administrator why if we worked, the money to be paid to us remains here [with the administrator]? The administrator thought about it, and said, "When you have a dog...and this dog goes hunting and brings home an animal, do you give the meat or the bone to the dog?" We said, "I give him the bones." "Hence," the administrator said, "you are like the dog, because you go to work."[2]

Contratados who remembered forced labor more than forty years after its abolition also commented frequently on the system's humiliation.

The historical record of colonial Angola rarely gives voice to the perspectives of African workers such as Massuna. Instead, the Portuguese colonial administration constructed a self-serving narrative about development, or "civilizing," that ignored African voices while celebrating Portuguese sacrifices and efforts to bring the benefits of Western civilization to Africans. This study is about the system of forced labor: how it operated, how it is remembered by former *contratados*, and its impact on the development of Cassequel, a large agro-industrial sugar plantation founded in 1913 and nationalized by an independent Angolan government in 1976.

1 Article 2 of the Forced Labor Convention 1930, International Labor Organization (ILO), http://www.ilo.org/ilolex/cgi-lex/convde.pl?C029 (accessed January 16, 2015).

2 Author interview with Luís Massuna, May 10, 2006, Mussanji (Quilengues), Angola.

 | DOI 10.1163/9789004301757_002

Focusing on Cassequel addresses a significant lacuna in Angolan historiography. No comprehensive studies have been made of a colonial-era business in Angola and how it transitioned to independent Angola. This study analyzes the relationship between Cassequel's Portuguese stockholders and successive governments. For much of its history, members of the powerful and well-connected Espírito Santo family controlled Cassequel while wielding considerable political and economic influence in Portugal. Portuguese sugar policy generally reflected their interests.[3] This study highlights how the political and economic policies of Salazar's Estado Novo [New State] nurtured the interests of Portuguese corporations such as the Espírito Santo Group and promoted their ability to invest in and repatriate profits from Angola.

In addition to producing semirefined sugar in Angola, Cassequel's owners took over sugar refining in Portugal and thus achieved vertical integration, from the planting of the cane to the output of refined sugar. In 1932, Cassequel received the Angolan monopoly for the distillation of industrial and absolute alcohol from molasses. Cassequel mixed its industrial alcohol with gasoline to create a biofuel sold throughout Angola as "Cassecol" and exported to Portugal and beyond. Over time, Cassequel's Espírito Santo owners bought large sisal and cattle ranches, and a local fishery, in addition to further investment in insurance and banking. In 1973, Cassequel acquired Angola's other major sugar plantation and achieved a monopoly of Angolan sugar production. Protected markets, guaranteed prices, and access to forced labor made Cassequel a veritable gold mine for its owners for many decades.

Focusing on Cassequel highlights the changing relationship between business and labor. Until 1962 the parties existed in a position of profound inequality. Cassequel relied on forced labor. After the abolition of forced labor in 1962, working conditions improved as the company focused on attracting voluntary workers. The end of Portuguese colonialism as a result of a military coup in April 1974 and the subsequent granting of independence in the midst of a fractious civil war in November 1975 led to the nationalization of Cassequel and the new government's refusal to pay indemnities to stockholders because it accused the Espírito Santo family of colluding with the colonial regime and the South African invasion in 1975. Nationalization led to the departure of most of Cassequel's highly skilled managers and technicians. Coupled with workers' demands for higher salaries and a deteriorating economic system, Cassequel (renamed *Primeiro de Maio* after International Workers' Day) limped along with diminishing harvests and production until the government closed the company in 1991.

---

3 Gervase Clarence-Smith, *The Third Portuguese Empire, 1825–1975: A Study in Economic Imperialism* (Manchester, UK: Manchester University Press, 1985), 150–51.

This study, by reviewing events up to 1977, goes beyond common end dates in Angolan history: 1961 (the start of the war for independence) or 1975 (independence). Examining the independence era provides insight into how the Popular Movement for the Liberation of Angola (MPLA)'s centralized economy affected a private company such as Cassequel: its owners, managers, and workers. Considering the first years of independence also provides an opportunity to discuss splintered memory in postcolonial Angola. War and the MPLA's doctrinaire Marxist political and economic policies left no room for opposition or debate.

This study is both a labor and business study. My framing argument is that Cassequel's owners and managers created a highly profitable sugar plantation by using their close connections to the Portuguese government to insure protected markets, guaranteed prices, a monopoly of biofuel production, vertical integration, and access to plentiful forced labor. This successful business model began to unravel with the abolition of forced labor in the early 1960s, which led to rising labor costs and costly mechanization. Nationalization eroded one of Cassequel's key assets: its trained, highly skilled technicians, who decamped for better-paid work abroad. Top-down, doctrinaire management squashed further innovation and—coupled with a lack of parts and central government's nonpayment of salaries—led to Cassequel's diminishing output and eventual closure.

(Re)Constructing Angolan Labor and Business History

Labor has been central to Angolan history since at least the fifteenth century, when Portuguese traders bought the first slaves from the King of Kongo. For the next four centuries, Angola supplied slaves throughout the Atlantic world—from continental Europe to Brazil and including the first African slaves to arrive in seventeenth-century Jamestown.[4] Portugal established a small colony at Luanda Bay beginning in 1575 essentially to service this trade in slaves. The colony developed slowly, in fits and starts, and by the early nineteenth century, it included a Portuguese-controlled zone along the Kwanza River Valley and around the south-central town of Benguela, which had been founded in 1617. During the gradual end of the Atlantic slave trade from 1836 to 1861, and especially from the mid-1870s forward, Portuguese policy makers initiated campaigns of conquest in the Angolan interior. The establishment in

4 See, for example, Lisa Rein, "Mystery of Va.'s First Slaves Is Unlocked 400 Years Later," *Washington Post*, September 3, 2006, p. A01.

1875 of the Geographical Society of Lisbon galvanized Portuguese enthusiasm for African exploration and colonial conquest. The 1878 abolition of slavery in Angola and the European "scramble for Africa" from the 1880s reinvigorated Portuguese efforts to expand their empire in central Africa. By 1891 the borders of present-day Angola had been agreed upon, and Portugal possessed a territory of more than 480,000 square miles.[5]

With their territorial claims recognized in Europe, Portuguese leaders set out to make the colony profitable. To do so, they devised methods for ensuring continued access to African labor after the abolition of slavery. Colonial policy makers agreed that establishing plantation agriculture—funded by Portuguese capital and worked by African laborers—would be a sure way to ensure Angola as an economic boom to Portugal. The "native problem," discussed at length in colonial reports and in the settler newspapers of Angola's coastal ports, was a euphemism for the inability of the state and the settlers to control the African labor they so desperately needed to realize profits. During the first decade of the twentieth century, settlers in Angola's coastal zones complained that the Portuguese government's lack of firm control in the interior regions made it difficult to find sufficient African workers willing to work for the offered wages.[6] In response to these concerns, and to keep at bay the covetous eyes of neighboring colonial powers, Portugal extended its hegemony over most of the interior by 1920. The following year Portuguese officials divided Angola into eleven administrative districts, and the military structure of districts was eliminated, a sign of the transition from military to civil administration. The high commissioner, the highest political authority in Angola, ruled through the district governors of the eleven civil districts, which were divided into sixty-five *conselhos* or *circunscrições* and directed by administrators.[7]

Occupation of the Angolan interior gave colonial administrators access to African labor, and because individuals refused to migrate in sufficient numbers to perform grueling manual labor for little pay, colonial administrators devised methods—both direct and indirect—to enforce a system of forced labor on their African subjects.[8] Able-bodied men were sent against their will to work for private employers at coastal fisheries, sugar plantations, and the coffee

5 Douglas L. Wheeler and René Pélissier, *Angola* (New York: Praeger Publishers, 1971), 51.

6 See, for example, David Birmingham, "The Coffee Barons of Cazengo," *Journal of African History*, (vol. XIX, no. 4, 1978), 523–38.

7 Lawrence W. Henderson, *Angola Five Centuries of Conflict* (Ithaca, NY: Cornell University Press, 1980), 19.

8 For a comparative case study of forced labor in Asante, see Gareth Austin, *Labour, Land and Capital in Ghana: From Slavery to Free Labour in Asante, 1807–1956* (Rochester, NY: University of Rochester Press, 2005).

plantations of northern Angola for periods lasting from ten to eighteen months. High death rates and widespread resentment among these *contratados* and their communities characterized this forced labor. Men, women, and children were also impressed into forced labor for public purposes, including the construction and maintenance of the colony's road system. This labor system took a heavy personal toll on individuals and families. In his poem "Contratados," Angola's first president, the poet and medical doctor Agostinho Neto, writes of the resilience, courage, and longing of *contratados* who even in despair sing:[9]

Long months separate them from their own	*Largos meses os separam dos seus*
and they go filled with longing	*e vão cheios de saudades*
and dread	*e de receio*
but they sing	*mas cantam*
Tired	*Fatigados*
exhausted by work	*esgotados de traballhos*
but they sing	*mas cantam*
Filled with injustice	*Cheios de injustiças*
silent in their innermost souls	*caladas no imo das das suas almas*
and they sing	*e cantam*

Poems, along with music and oral narratives, provide much of our understanding of forced labor's impact on generations of Angolans.

In 1926, a military coup overthrew Portugal's First Republic and in 1933 installed the Estado Novo [New State], an authoritarian and conservative regime that had opposed many of the reforms of the First Republic. The Estado Novo would remain in power until its overthrow, again by the military, in 1974. The leaders of the Estado Novo—and particularly António Salazar, who was minister of finance and colonies before serving as prime minister from 1933 to 1968—instituted a more centralized colonial administrative system. Salazar canceled earlier attempts by the First Republic to devolve some power to administrators and settlers in Angola and he used protective tariffs and laws limiting foreign capital to entice wealthy Portuguese businessmen to invest in Angola. As far back as 1913, wealthy bankers such as José Espírito Santo had responded to profitable investment opportunities in Angola while supporting the greater colonial effort.

9 Agostinho Neto, *Sacred Hope* (Dar es Salaam: Tanzania Publishing House, 1974), 46. Translated into English by Marga Holness.

Leaders of the Estado Novo such as Armindo Monteiro, minister of colonies between 1931 and 1935, enhanced an imperial mythology that made the colonial mission a central tenet of Portuguese nationalism. It was the Estado Novo that codified the classification of the Angolan population into categories of *indígena* [native] and *não-indígena* [nonnative]. Under this system, known as the Indigenato, *indígenas* formed a legally separate population, distinct from Europeans and *assimilados* [Africans judged by Europeans to have assimilated European culture]. White colonists were automatically citizens, whereas Africans had to prove they were assimilated or civilized by passing an examination. By the 1950s only thirty thousand Africans—less than 1 percent of the 4.5 million Africans in Angola—were legally assimilated and thus eligible for citizenship. In effect this policy codified a caste system with a small, mostly white elite and a large African underclass denied the rights of citizenship.[10]

In the 1950s, as African nationalism and international criticism of Portugal's colonial labor policy spread, the government pressured employers to improve working conditions in order to attract a voluntary work force.[11] In 1960, violent protests and attacks against Portuguese colonial rule initiated a nationalist war of independence. Portugal responded with decisive military repression, enacted a series of reforms to eliminate some of the most hated aspects of Portuguese colonialism, and embarked on a massive development plan to grow the Angolan economy and improve living conditions. In 1961, Portugal abolished the Indigenato by revoking the Statute of Natives (Estatuto dos Indígenas, Decreto-Lei 39.666, May 20, 1954) and giving full rights of citizenship to all Angolans. This reform made available to all Angolans the identity card that had formerly been the symbol of citizenship, one restricted to whites and *assimilados*.[12] In 1962, leaders of the Estado Novo finally abolished forced labor.

Throughout the New State period, the state provided generous incentives to Portuguese corporations—which were closely allied with the regime—to invest in Angola. Incentives included monopolies, relatively easy transference of profits to Portugal, preferential access to forced labor, and negotiated minimum prices for goods. These policies benefited metropolitan capital and explain

10 Lawrence W. Henderson, *The Church in Angola: A River of Many Currents* (Cleveland: The Pilgrim Press, 1992) 295–296.

11 For an analysis of the transition from coercive methods of obtaining labor to capitalist labor markets, see John Sender and Sheila Smith, *The Development of Capitalism in Africa* (London: Methuen, 1986).

12 Henderson, *The Church in Angola*, 295–296. Also see, Mário Moutinho, *O Indígena no Pensamento Colonial Português* (Lisboa: Edições Universitários Lusófonas, 2000).

why, on the eve of independence, Portuguese conglomerates such as the Espírito Santo Group provided such support to the government and made so few overtures to nationalist groups in Angola.

During the period of late colonialism (1962–1975), Angolan workers no longer faced government coercion, and large employers like Cassequel improved working conditions to attract an entirely volunteer workforce. Many former workers remember this period as a time of relative prosperity. The ongoing war for independence also took a toll on the Portuguese army, which faced revolutions in Mozambique and Guinea-Bissau, and on April 25, 1974, the army overthrew the Estado Novo in a bloodless coup. The new government initiated peace talks with Angola's three nationalist movements. In spite of a power-sharing arrangement, civil war broke out among the three movements before the handling over of Angolan independence on November 11, 1975. Thus, after four centuries in Angola, the Portuguese left without relinquishing power to a successor government. By May 1976, the MPLA, with the help of Soviet and Cuban aid, defeated its political rivals, the US-backed National Front for the Liberation of Angola (FNLA) and the South African–backed National Union for the Total Independence of Angola (UNITA). The MPLA reorganized the Angolan economy by nationalizing nearly all of the country's private industry, including Cassequel. The new government targeted Portuguese conglomerates such as the Espírito Santo Group for retribution, while protecting large amounts of foreign capital, notably in the burgeoning oil industry.

Historiography

It may be true that the "historian can obtain little more than glimpses into the sordid world of labor recruitment" in twentieth-century Angola.[13] However, there have been several important studies, most written in the exposé style, dating to the early 1900s. Examples include Henry W. Nevinson's *A Modern Slavery* (1906) and William A. Cadbury's *Labor in Portuguese West Africa* (1910).[14] The issue of forced labor in Portuguese Angola continued to be cited by foreign missionaries during the 1910s and 1920s, and in 1924, an American

13 Frederick Cooper, *Decolonization and African Society: The Labor Question in French and British Africa* (Cambridge: Cambridge University Press, 1996), 34.

14 A former Portuguese *curador dos indígenas* [guardian of the natives] for the island of Príncipe, Jerónimo Paiva de Carvalho, contributed an important study based on his personal experience with *Alma Negra: Depoimento Sobre a Questão Dos Serviçais de S. Tomé* (Porto: Tipografia Progresso, 1912).

professor of sociology at the University of Wisconsin—Madison, Edward Alsworth Ross, visited Angola on behalf of the Temporary Slavery Commission of the League of Nations to investigate labor conditions. His *Report on the Employment of Native Labor in Portuguese Africa* (1925) chronicled Portuguese labor abuses including forced labor in the Angolan interior.[15] Predictably, Portuguese officials hid behind a banner of nationalist pride and labeled Ross a communist agitator. In his report, Ross advocated for an abolition of forced labor, and his report reflected a growing divide between free labor advocates, who wanted a Forced Labor Convention to ban the practice, and colonial powers such as Portugal, who insisted on their right to use forced labor.[16] Ross's findings influenced thinking behind the 1930 Forced Labor Convention and the 1936 Recruiting of Indigenous Workers Convention adopted by the League of Nations; Portugal ratified neither convention.

The next investigative report to focus attention on forced labor in Angola came twenty-two years after the Ross Report, when a senior Portuguese legislator and former diplomat named Henrique Galvão submitted his *Relatório sobre problemas dos nativos nas colónias Portuguesas* [Report on Native Problems in the Portuguese Colonies] (1947) to an in-camera session of the Portuguese National Assembly.[17] The Galvão Report, like the Ross Report, assessed the brutality of forced labor and the subsequent decision of large numbers of people to migrate from Angola to neighboring colonies. Within his report, Galvão described the labor system in Angola as a "colossal lie," noting that the reality of forced labor and oppressive colonialism significantly contradicted the official rhetoric about "educating" and "civilizing" Angolans. Portugal's authoritarian leader António de Oliveira Salazar immediately squashed the Galvão Report.[18]

In 1955, historian and activist Basil Davidson published *The African Awakening*, which included analysis of labor practices in Angola and reiterated many of the conclusions reached by Ross and Galvão.[19] Davidson stated unequivocally his

15 Edward Alsworth Ross, *Report on the Employment of Native Labor in Portuguese Africa* (New York: The Abbott Press, 1925).

16 Daniel Roger Maul, "The International Labour Organization and the Struggle Against Forced Labour from 1919 to the Present," *Labor History* (vol. 48, no. 4, November 2007), 481.

17 Henrique Galvão, "Exposição do Deputado Henrique Galvão, á Comissão de Colónias da Assembleia Nacional, em Janeiro de 1947." Arquivo Histórico-Parliamentar, Assembleia da República. For a useful overview, see Luís Farinha, "Do Império Português à Descolonização: Henrique Galvão e o império." *História* (ano XXII, número 21, Janeiro 2000), 18–28.

18 An abridged English version is published as an appendix in Henrique Galvão, *Santa Maria: My Crusade for Portugal* (Cleveland: The World Publishing Company, 1961).

19 Basil Davidson, *The African Awakening* (London: Jonathan Cape, 1955).

opposition to Portuguese colonialism, and his book reads more as a political statement than as an historical account. In 1967 historian James Duffy published a more objective account of Portuguese labor policy in Angola, *A Question of Slavery: Labor Policies in Portuguese Africa and the British Protest, 1850–1920*, and a number of analytical studies followed.[20] For example, Gervase Clarence-Smith's article "Slavery in Coastal Southern Angola 1875–1913," provided a regional case study of labor in the far south of Angola.[21] In the 1970s, two more studies published respectively in 1978 and 1979 exposed the exploitative nature of Portuguese administration: Gerald Bender's *Angola under the Portuguese: The Myth and the Reality* and Lawrence W. Henderson's *Angola: Five Centuries of Conflict*. These scholars challenged Portuguese scholars of colonial labor from the 1950s who emphasized the labor reforms of late colonialism and the social welfare provided to Africans by colonial employers, studies such as Afonso Mendes's *O Trabalho Assalariado em Angola* and Fernando Diogo da Silva's *O Huambo: Mão-de-Obra Rural no Mercado de Trabalho de Angola*.[22]

Since the mid-1970s, there have been several studies of plantation and migrant labor in Southern Africa. Collectively these studies explain how colonial powers and European settlers sought to control and profit from Africans' labor. Charles van Onselen, William Worger, and Leroy Vial and Landeg White emphasize the process of recruitment and conditions in workers' compounds and the ways colonial employers controlled Africans' lives.[23] In the past decade a growing corpus of Angolan labor studies has emerged. Emmanuel Esteves's dissertation "O Caminho de Ferro de Benguela e o impacto econômico, social e cultural na sua zonas de influência 1902–1952" (Porto, 1999) analyzes the types and conditions of work performed for the building and operation of the railway, as well as its broader economic and social impact. Because the railway attracted voluntary workers from across the same central plateau region as Cassequel,

20 James Duffy, *A Question of Slavery: Labour Policies in Portuguese Africa and the British Protest, 1850–1920* (Oxford: Oxford University Press, 1967).

21 Gervase Clarence-Smith, "Slavery in Coastal Southern Angola 1875–1913," *Journal of Southern African Studies* (ol. 2, no. 2, 1976), 214–23.

22 Afonso Mendes, *O Trabalho Assalariado em Angola* (Lisboa: Instituto Superior De Ciências Sociais e Política Ultramarina, n.d.); and Fernando Diogo da Silva, *O Huambo: Mão-de-Obra Rural no Mercado de Trabalho de Angola* (Luanda: Fundo de Acção Social no Trabalho em Angola, n.d.).

23 Charles van Onselen, *Chibaro: African Mine Labour in Southern Rhodesia 1900–1933* (Johannesburg: Ravan Press, 1976); William Worger, *South Africa's City of Diamonds: Mine Workers and Monopoly Capitalism in Kimberley 1867–1895* (New Haven: Yale University Press, 1987); and Leory Vail and Landeg White, *Capitalism and Colonialism in Mozambique* (Minneapolis: University of Minnesota Press, 1980).

Esteves's analysis provides a useful comparison to my focus on forced labor. Todd Cleveland's dissertation "Rock Solid: African Laborers on the Diamond Mines of the Companhia de Diamantes de Angola (Diamang), 1917–1975" (University of Minnesota, 2008), focuses on the work performed by forced and voluntary workers and the gendered organization of labor in the mines and company encampments of Diamang in northeastern Angola. Cleveland provides particular insight into the gendered division of work at Diamang, where, unlike Cassequel, women and families accompanied forced laborers. In 2012, Eric Allina published *Slavery by Any Other Name: African Life under Company Rule in Colonial Mozambique* (Virginia UP), a study of how people experienced life and labor under the Mozambique Company between 1888 and 1942. Alhough Allina's study focuses on a concession company and a slightly earlier period, his insights into the functioning of colonial capital and labor provide instructive comparisons to how capital and labor worked at Cassequel in Angola.

Perhaps the best-known published work in English to focus on the Ovimbundu of Angola's central plateau during the twentieth century is Linda Heywood's *Contested Power in Angola: 1840s to the Present*. Heywood provides a comprehensive analysis of Portuguese colonial administration and its impact on the indigenous political and economic system of the Ovimbundu of the central plateau. Heywood details the workings of forced labor recruitment at its source and its impact on Umbundu communities and families. My work follows workers to their destination, thus providing a fuller understanding of workers' experiences. Heywood makes another significant contribution to Angolan historiography because she takes her study beyond independence (the usual end date for modern Angolan histories) to explain how nationalism, the post-independence civil war, and the creation of an authoritarian state affected the Ovimbundu.

A recent dissertation by Angolan historian Maria Neto, "In Town and Out of Town: A Social History of Huambo (Angola) 1902–1961" (University of London, 2012) provides further insight into the legal division between native and citizen under Portuguese colonial law. Neto's analysis of social change in Huambo adds to our understanding of how urbanization, the railway, white settlement, and the entrenchment of colonial administration led to social change among the Ovimbundu. Miguel Bandeira Jerónimo's monograph, *Livros Brancos, Almas Negras: A "Missão Civilizadora" do Colonialismo Português c. 1870–1930* unpacks Portugal's civilizing rhetoric—and the contradictory reality on the ground—within a wider imperial debate over labor and the so-called civilizing mission.[24]

24 Miguel Bandeira Jerónimo, *Livros Brancos, Almas Negras: A "Missão Civilizadora do Colonialismo Português c. 1870–1930"* (Lisboa: Imprensa de Ciências Sociais, 2009).

Although there are no published histories of single Angolan businesses, Gervase Clarence-Smith's *The Third Portuguese Empire, 1825–1975* provides important context for understanding Portugal's colonial economic policy and its broad consequences in Angola. Clarence-Smith explains how successive Portuguese governments extracted wealth from Angola to enrich metropolitan investors and bolster the Portuguese economy. Valentim Alexandre's chapter "A questão colonial no Portugal oitocentista" in Valentim Alexandre and Jill Dias's *O Império Africano 1825–1890* argues that policy makers reserved Angola for Portuguese capital and commerce, while selling off concessions to foreign capital in other Portuguese colonies.[25] My work on Cassequel supports the arguments made by Clarence-Smith and Alexandre about the nature of Portuguese business in Angola. For the initial independence period after 1975, the definitive work on economic policy is Manuel Ennes Ferreira, *A indústria em tempo de guerra (Angola, 1975–91)*. Maria Rodrigues Coelho's "Rupture and Continuity: The State, Law and the Economy in Angola, 1975–1989" adds further analysis of the MPLA's economic policies and how they led to a collapse in the impressive economic growth of the 1960s and early 1970s.[26] All of these studies provide context for Cassequel's founding, development, and nationalization in 1976.

I also draw on the historiography of African nationalism, independence, and the Cold War to contextualize Cassequel's nationalization and the conflicted memories of former employees. Interviews with former Cassequel employees and two memoirs—Sócrates Dáskalos's *Um Testemunho para a História de Angola do Huambo ao Huambo*[27] and Gonçalo Inocentes, "As Cheias do Rio Catumbela"[28]—influenced my argument that foreign intervention fueled the MPLA's doctrinaire economic and political policies and led to a demonizing of anyone who did not support the party.[29]

---

25 Valentim Alexandre and Jill Dias (eds.), *O Império Africano Séculos XIX e XX* (Lisboa: Edições Colibri, 2000).

26 Manuel Ennes Ferreira, *A indústria em tempo de guerra (Angola, 1975–91)* (Lisboa: Edições Cosmos Instituto da Defesa Nacional, 1999) and Maria Antonieta Martins Rodrigues Coelho, "Rupture and Continuity: The State, Law and the Economy in Angola, 1975–1989" (PhD diss, University of Warwick School of Law, 1994).

27 Sócrates Dáskalos, *Um Testemunho para a História de Angola do Huambo ao Huambo* (Lisboa: Vega, 2000).

28 Gonçalo Inocentes, "As Cheias do Rio Fagulha," (unpublished manuscript, 2012).

29 There are several important studies of Angolan independence and the civil war that followed, including: John Marcum's *The Angola Revolution, Volume II: Exile Politics and Guerrilla Warfare (1962–1976)* (Cambridge, MA: The MIT Press, 1978); Fernando Andresen Guimarães, *The Origins of the Angolan Civil War Foreign Intervention and Domestic Political Conflict* (New York: St. Martin's Press, 1998); Piero Gleijeses, *Conflicting Missions: Havana,*

My study contributes to this Angolan labor, business, and economic history in several important ways. The focus on the Cassequel Sugar Plantation allows for an analytical assessment of how political and economic policy provided the conditions and inducements for Portuguese businessmen to invest in Angola, and why those colonial investments became closely tied to elite Portuguese nationalism. The case study of a major, Portuguese-owned company during the colonial era is unique, and my analysis explains both Cassequel's development over time and how its management shifted to an entirely voluntary labor force after the abolition of forced labor in 1962. Moreover, historian D.K. Fieldhouse points out that there have been few detailed studies of how European-owned companies in the colonies viewed independence.[30] This study addresses this lacuna and argues that the Espírito Santo Group's support for continued Portuguese colonialism resulted from its close ties to the *Estado Novo* in Portugal. This intimate connection to the center of Portuguese power explains why the Espírito Santo Group failed to make overtures to the MPLA and decided to support UNITA in the civil war. Finally, my work contributes a unique and rarely heard perspective on forced labor from former *contratados*. These individuals and their communities directly experienced forced labor, and their memories of that system provide an important and rarely documented archive. Interviews with former administrators provide another rarely documented perspective—generally silenced in the historical narrative that privileges the MPLA as the only legitimate liberators—about late colonial reforms and independence. Ending the study with Cassequel's closure in 1991 allows for evaluation of the MPLA's economic and political agenda and how these policies affected the lives of Cassequel's employees.

Finding Cassequel

Even today, the old sugar plantation Cassequel—stretching out between the port towns of Lobito and Benguela, and surrounding the old trading town of Catumbela—dominates the dry coastal plane connecting the Atlantic and the coastal mountains of south-central Angola.[31] Many of its buildings, painted in

---

Washington and Africa, 1959–1976 (Chapel Hill: University of North Carolina Press, 2002); and John Stockwell, *In Search of Enemies: A CIA Story* (New York: W.W. Norton, 1978).

30 D.K. Fieldhouse, *Merchant Capital and Economic Decolonization: The United Africa Company 1929–1987* (Oxford: Clarendon Press, 1994), 337.

31 The Angolan government renamed Cassequel *Primeiro de Maio* [First of May] after independence, but local residents continued to refer to the old plantation as Cassequel in 2007.

a uniform (and now faded) pink, dot the main highway. Even though tens of thousands of migrants and refugees from Angola's nearly three-decade-long civil war now live in the hills ringing the plantation's fertile plain, it is still possible to see clusters of the thatched huts that were built in the 1950s to house *contratados*. The most striking feature of the region, and the reason sugarcane flourished, is the Catumbela River, which bifurcates the plantation lands of Cassequel before emptying into the Atlantic Ocean. An impressive system of irrigation ditches—parts of which were dug by slave labor in the late nineteenth century and maintained and expanded by generations of *contratados*—carries water to the remote recesses of the plantation. Travelers in the early twentieth century often commented upon the lush and verdant appearance of Cassequel's sugarcane fields and palm-lined irrigation channels. Even today, the intense greenery of banana groves and maize fields presents an image of a well-tended garden.

Cassequel's built environment encoded the company's hierarchy. Atop a hill, above the Portuguese fort built in 1836 to enforce Portuguese hegemony along Benguela's coastal plain, sit the handsome houses of Cassequel's Portuguese administrators, engineers, and doctors. These houses—also in pink—are surrounded by pockets of palm trees and flowering bushes and look out over the river, the plantation lands, Catumbela, and the Atlantic Ocean in the distance. In 2006, the homes still retained their elite societal status in that several belonged to generals in the Angolan Army, who are among Angola's postcolonial elite. Below the hilltop residences, clustered along the tree-lined streets of Catumbela, sit the well-built homes of Cassequel's solidly middle management: mechanics, secretaries, accountants, and other Portuguese employees. As their homes demonstrate, these workers belonged to a privileged racial and economic category within colonial Angolan society. By the 1950s, some of these workers would have been *mestiços* and black Angolans with the coveted legal *assimilado* status, which exempted them from forced labor and entitled them to skilled positions such as mechanic or nurse.

Even in its current dilapidated state, Cassequel is impressive. Its stately headquarters building along the main highway linking Lobito and Benguela, its hundreds of buildings, and its now-defunct factory with jutting smoke stack and massive machinery (looted and deteriorating) personify a colonial past. The surviving thatched huts in which Cassequel's five thousand African workers—voluntary and forced—lived stand in marked contrast to the lovely neighborhoods for Portuguese employees. Remnants of the potable water stations and medical clinics the company built in these worker villages can still be seen.

The uniform pink color of Catumbela's buildings symbolized the symbiotic relationship between town and company. Although the town predates

Cassequel, the company came to dominate the town by the 1940s. Cassequel's employees made up the majority of the town's citizens, and the company underwrote much of the town's infrastructure, including its potable water and electricity. Catumbela reflected a Portuguese aesthetic, with its white stone sidewalks (*calçadas Portuguesas*), workers' cottages, Catholic Church, cinema, and plazas. The urban planning reflects the dominant role of Angola's Portuguese settler population during the colonial era. Even twenty years after the company's closure, and more than thirty years since independence, Catumbela looks much like the company town it was constructed to be, but now a large welcoming sign on the town limits greets visitors to the region with "Welcome to Catumbela—City of Beer," reflecting the new importance of the town's largest employer, the French-owned Cuca Beer Company's brewery and bottling plant.

We might consider the task of "finding Cassequel" as a metaphor for historical inquiry into its past and the ramifications of that past on its present makeup. Cassequel consists of multiple layers: colonial, nationalist, Angolan, and Portuguese. Uncovering these layers entails a process of historical inquiry into the sources that remain: both the documentary record sealed in an old company vault and the memories of those who still remember. Henrique Galvão characterized the labor system in Angola as a "colossal lie." Cassequel's own well-ordered edifices belied the brutality of the labor system on which the company relied.

Sources

Because of the international nature of colonialism, this study required travel to various archival centers. In Geneva, I visited the library of the International Labor Organization to read reports of its investigations and hearings about Portuguese colonial labor policy. These investigations before the reforms of 1962 all documented forced labor. Trips to the Public Records Office in Kew (UK) and the National Archives in College Park, Maryland, yielded insightful analysis of conditions in colonial Angola written by British and American diplomats. Online I accessed two valuable sources for the Cold War: the National Security Archive based at the George Washington University and the Cold War International History Project based at the Woodrow Wilson International Center for Scholars.

In Lisbon, I spent several months reading documents in the Arquivo Histórico Ultramarino (AHU), Portugal's colonial archive, which contains important (but spotty) materials on twentieth-century Angola. Unfortunately, a large part of the twentieth-century material has not yet been catalogued, which makes research a challenge. The most useful materials I found in the AHU were reports from various years from the Negócios Indígenas, or Native Affairs Department. The half-dozen annual reports contain important data about the numbers of *contratados* from each district in Angola and include statistics such as the number of *fugidos* [runaways] from various employers, including Cassequel. The AHU also houses governors' reports and reports from district administrators; it bears repeating that the African voice in such documents is basically absent.

Several additional archives in Lisbon provided valuable information, including the Arquivo Nacional de Torre do Tombo, which houses the Salazar Archive, an important repository for information about Cassequel's major shareholders, the Espírito Santo family. Portugal's parliamentary archive, the Arquivo Histórico-Parliamentar, has an original copy of Henrique Galvão's 1947 Report on Native Labor, as well as a file marked confidential on Galvão. Across the street from the Arquivo Histórico-Parliamentar is the Arquivo Mário Soares, which contains correspondence and reports from the period of the 1974 revolution in Portugal, including minutes of government meetings about colonial policy. The Centro de Informação e Documentação Amílcar Cabral (CIDAC) contains a rich collection of pamphlets and policy statements written by the nationalist movements in the former colonies. CIDAC has, for example, the best collection of MPLA documents available as well as newspapers, dissertations, and books. Two other important resources in Lisbon are the Biblioteca Nacional (National Library), which has a very good collection of Angolan newspapers, and the Sociedade de Geografia, which houses an important collection of colonial administrative reports, maps, and an accessible collection of statistical surveys and annual *boletims* [official government reports about governance] from both Angola and Portugal.

In Angola the national archive, the Arquivo Histórico de Angola (AHA), contains boxes of materials from the various provinces within Angola. These boxes, or *caixas*, include administrative reports that provide information about labor recruitment, the payment of salaries, corporal punishment, and methods of dealing with runaway *contratados*. The AHA also contains a useful collection of photographs and postcards. Significantly, this study draws extensively on what's left of Cassequel's archive, which managed to survive nationalization and civil war locked away in a walk-in safe in Catumbela. The survival of this archive is especially noteworthy because of the paucity of existing company archives from Angola's colonial and postindependence eras. As a result of the chaotic and violent transition to independence, the archives of major companies were often destroyed in the fighting, stolen by looters, or damaged by neglect. Cassequel's archive includes collections of confidential letters, annual reports for most of the years between the mid-1920s and 1974, correspondence between the administration in Catumbela and the board of directors in Lisbon, various reports on different aspects of plantation management, and photographs.[32] Since my initial research in Catumbela in July and August 2001, the bulk of this archive has been bought by the Arquivo Histórico do Banco Espírito Santo (AHBES) in Lisbon. The AHBES, in addition to these recently acquired materials, contains correspondence from various members of the Espírito Santo family who served as chairs of boards of directors for both the Espírito Santo Bank and Cassequel.[33] The archival sources I consulted generally reflected the concerns and priorities of colonial administrators and company management.

Oral history offers another possible means of documenting former workers' understanding of colonial-era labor, whether forced or voluntary. Until recently, such an approach remained limited as a result of the ravages of civil war, which restricted access to the interior, where most of the informants reside. The end of violence in 2002 resulted in greater access to all of Angola and thus to wider populations of octogenarians who suffered under the forced labor system. The memories of how these individuals experienced forced labor enrich our understanding of the system's human cost.

Uncovering the African perspective of work at Cassequel before 1961 required that I travel to former centers of recruitment, such as Balombo, Bailundo, and Chinguar, to contact former *contratados*. Given the lack of widespread social media available to most Angolans in 2006, traveling to the centers of forced labor recruitment seemed like the best method for locating *mais velhos/as* [old ones] who experienced the system. Most *contratados* returned to their home villages after completing their service, so it is logical that many lived their lives in their home regions. Of course, this technique for locating interviewees precluded interviewing those no longer living in their home districts. Working with Angolan linguist and historian Manuel Domingos, I conducted a dozen group interviews with as few as four to as many as a couple dozen *mais velhos/as* who served as *contratados* or forced labor, building and maintaining roads during colonial times. In total, we conducted 56 substantive in-depth interviews with former *contratados* and 10 with women who served as

32 The author accessed the uncatalogued archive in a walk-in safe at Cassequel's former headquarters in Catumbela, Angola, in 2001. The archive of the Espírito Santo Bank subsequently purchased the documents from local government authorities in Catumbela, and the documents now reside in Lisbon.

33 In late 2014, the Portuguese government took over the Banco Espírito Santo, which could not cover loans made in Angola. The new, government-owned bank is called Novo Banco.

forced labor constructing roads. In addition, I estimate that roughly an additional 100 or so observers/participants listened to and sometimes contributed to the group interviews. Most group interviews took place outdoors and were open to the whole community. Contacting the *mais velhos/as* required seeking permission first from provincial authorities, then from the district administrator in each of the four provinces where we conducted interviews: Benguela, Huambo, Bié, and Huila. Angolan officials welcomed the opportunity to assist the oral history project by facilitating access to those *mais velhos/as* who serve as the repository of the past. In a few instances administrators offered their own perspectives on Angolan and local history while others noted with pride the presence of a foreign researcher as proof of the peace dividend since the end of Angola's decades-long civil war in 2002. Never did we offer any remuneration for conducting interviews, although in almost all the group interview we bought a case of soda to be shared amongst participants and observers.

Technically, introductions to district administrators had to be made in person, as many areas lacked communication technologies such as the Internet or even telephones. In the case of Bié, for example, the assistant governor called the municipal authorities in the town of Chinguar over a two-way radio, as there was no telephone link, to authorize that "all assistance be afforded to the American historian" in locating and arranging interviews. The local municipal administrator then called in the head *soba* [chief] for the area, who works for the government, and instructed him to invite *mais velhos/as* to participate in an oral history project. Interviews generally took place in a local *onjango* [a covered, open-air gathering place]. We recorded the interviews with a tape recorder. In every village we visited, multiple generations gathered to hear their elders making history in dialogue, and giving this interviewer the sense that the occasion of the interview was truly momentous.[34]

Interviews about a labor system that ended nearly half a century ago present unique historiographic challenges in that forty years of intermittent war affects how and what individuals remember about forced labor and the colonial era. Anticolonial propaganda, especially in the early years after Angolan independence in 1975, might have affected how these *mais velhos/as* remember their past. The group settings of most interviews may also have contributed to the reiteration of a dominant memory about the colonial past as exploitative and repressive, without providing space for alternative interpretations, although interviewees disagreed on some points such as the extent to

34 Della Pollock, ed., *Remembering Oral History Performance* (New York: Palgrave Macmillan, 2005), 2.

which the Portuguese developed Angola.[35] Bureaucratic constraints of having to receive government permission and using government officials to provide interviewees also raises questions about the objectivity of interviewees and their ability to speak freely without fear of retribution. Angola in the 2000s was not a society open to contradictory opinions and interpretations. In all of our group interviews conducted in interior recruitment districts, a government representative, usually the *soba*, listened and sometimes answered questions. Occasionally, as recollections of forced labor came to a close I asked about the civil war years and how people survived. I noted that few wanted to discuss the war years. I assume this reticense resulted from the trauma of those years in combination with the presence of a government (MPLA)-appointed *soba* in attendance.

Fortunately for the study, the topic of colonial forced labor is not politically controversial. Even in informal, off-the-record discussions in these former recruitment districts, I never heard anyone speak well of forced labor. People did speak well of other aspects of Portuguese colonialism, however. Many voiced admiration and appreciation for Portuguese culture and the extent to which Portugal developed Angola. Interviews reflect the biases and interpretations of individuals, and point to the fact that memory is an imperfect and subjective source. When used critically and in conjunction with other historical methods, however, it can provide valuable insight not only into the past but also into the present.[36] In this study, interviews provide an invaluable window into how individuals experienced forced labor and colonialism and how they responded to labor reforms, the war for independence, and the MPLA's restructuring of Angolan society. These sorts of personal feelings and subjective experiences do not appear in statistics and reports, and they enrich the historical record.

Gender imbalance within existing accounts is another compelling factor in favor of the collection of oral narratives in that women's experiences are rarely documented in official sources and often differ significantly from those of men. Oral history affords one of the few means of accessing women's memories of forced labor on the roads and caring for the family during their

35 Popular Memory Group, "Popular Memory: Theory, Politics, Method," in *Making Histories: Studies in History-Writing and Politics*, edited by R. Johnson, G. McLennan, B. Schwarz, and D. Dutton (Minneapolis: University of Minnesota Press, 1982), 210–211.

36 For more on the subjectivity of oral history see Alessandro Portelli, "The Peculiarities of Oral History," *History Workshop* (no. 12, Autumn 1981). See also Richard Roberts, "History and Memory: The Power of Statist Narratives," *International Journal of African Historical Studies* (vol. 33, no. 3 2000), 513–522.

husbands' long absences as *contratados*. The setting—two male interviewers asking women about their experiences—also raises important questions about methodological constraints of the study. Will women speak freely about their experiences with male interviewers? Did sexual exploitation cause such shame that it prevents women from discussing what occurred in a public setting? To what extent have gender relations evolved since independence, and how will this change, or lack thereof, affect women's memories? Originally, our interview questions did not include women because they did not serve as *contratados* at Cassequel. However, as our group interviews progressed, women observers offered insights into what it meant to stay on the home front while their husbands and sons served as contract labor. For this reason, we arranged in Bailundo and then in Quillengues, to interview women in separate group sessions. In total, we conducted 10 in-depth interviews with *mais velhas*. The constraints imposed by two male interviewers and group settings surely limited the extent to which interviewees shared about sexual exploitation.

In general, forced labor affected the lives of Angolan women in two concrete ways. First, women and children contributed to the construction and maintenance of highways. During periods lasting several weeks, women performed unpaid, heavy labor carrying loads of dirt and rock to repair the dirt roads crisscrossing Angola. Portuguese and African foremen oversaw roadwork and not infrequently demanded cooking and sexual services from these same women. Second, and more germane to this study, the forced removal of men, generally far from home with extremely limited means for communication, forced their wives, sisters, and mothers to maintain the homestead on their own. In addition to the emotional stress that accompanied separation, long absences meant that men could not contribute toward the family's daily maintenance. In some cases, men did not return from forced labor, whether as a result of death or flight. In the case of death, women received no financial compensation, which led to extreme poverty, hunger, and/or a loss of land and standing in the community.

Conversely, interviews with a half dozen former *voluntários* in and around Catumbela provided access to contrasting experiences of Cassequel during the colonial era. Most spoke with pride about the company, its prosperity, and their own contributions to the company's advancement. These interviews took place against the backdrop of a shuttered Cassequel and a relatively bleak economic outlook for many of these workers and their families. Interviews with former Portuguese administrators likewise presented an almost idyllic image of Cassequel as both a benevolent and productive employer and a compelling place to live and raise a family. Narrators' responses to questions about labor, nationalization, and independence indicated that memory of Cassequel is not monolithic, but rather conditional upon one's position within both the company and colonial society. The "Portuguese" and "Angolan" narratives diverged considerably on several key points of interpretation about the past. In response to questions about the MPLA's postindependence economic policy, former Portuguese administrators lambasted what they described as an unwarranted confiscation of Cassequel by the Marxist and authoritarian MPLA. They pointed to Cassequel's subsequent deterioration and closure as proof of independent Angola's failed economic policies and political chaos. Former Angolan *voluntários*, on the other hand, spoke about the euphoria of independence and subsequent hardships resulting from civil war. Some interviewees blamed *poder popular* [People's Power] for economic hardship, whereas others simply held the civil war responsible for their poverty.[37] Most interviewees did not want to talk about the war and changed the subject when asked specific questions.[38]

Assessing archival and oral sources provides the opportunity to interrogate general assumptions about colonial Angolan labor, business operations, and the impact of independence and nationalization on one Angolan community. One such assumption is that colonial businesses earned vast profits at the expense of workers. This study supports this conclusion, although with the important caveat that between 1962 and 1975 Cassequel made impressive strides in improving working conditions, which benefitted thousands of Angolans. These reforms lowered Cassequel's profit margins and provided a quality of life for workers that has arguably not been replicated since independence. Former voluntary workers who labored at Cassequel in the late 1960s and 1970s remember the company with fondness and in many cases stressed nostalgia for a productive company that cared for its employees. These voices were more difficult to hear in the political context of Angola in the 2000s because of a lack of freedom of speech. It is clear that Cassequel was much more than an exploitative monopoly owned by capitalist cronies of António Salazar (as stated by the MPLA legislation confiscating Cassequel states). Cassequel did rely on forced labor for most of its history, but it also employed thousands of voluntary workers and its owners built one of colonial Angola's most impressive and profitable companies over decades.

---

37 For an economic analysis of independent Angola, see Manuel Ennes Ferreira's *A indústria em tempo de guerra (Angola, 1975–91)*.

38 For more about the constraints on free speech and criticism of the MPLA in contemporary Angola see, Lara Pawson, *In the Name of the People: Angola's Forgotten Massacre* (London: IB Tauris, 2014).

Chapter Synopses

Chapter 1 provides historical background to the economic development of the sugarcane industry and the town of Catumbela. The politics of colonial labor policy frames the explanation of the transition from slavery to forced labor in the late nineteenth and early twentieth centuries. These political and economic developments created the conditions for the founding of the Cassequel Sugar Plantation in 1913. A discussion of labor policy reveals that colonial attitudes toward forced labor were not monolithic. Tensions existed among policy makers, colonists, foreign critics, and Angolans over the legality and morality of forced labor and its role in developing Angola for Portugal and spreading Portuguese culture among Angolans. The chapter ends in 1920 as Portugal consolidated its hegemony over Angola.

Chapter 2 examines the period 1921 to World War II. The overthrow of the First Republic by a military coup in 1926 led in 1932 to the installation of the Estado Novo, a political regime marked by its authoritarianism and a belief in Portugal's historic and future role as a colonial power. To understand Cassequel's rapid development during this period, I explain the political and economic context of Angola, especially the financial crisis of the 1920s, the overthrow of Portugal's First Republic and the implementation of the Estado Novo. Against this backdrop Cassequel's production soared, along with its reliance on forced laborers known as *contratados*. Cassequel's company correspondence and Edward Alsworth Ross's 1924 report on Angolan labor for the Temporary Slavery Commission of the League of Nations provide insight into the experiences of *contratados*.

Chapter 3 focuses on the post-World War II period up through the year of African independence in 1960. The chapter argues that the emerging international human rights discourse and the Cold War changed attitudes towards colonialism. Leaders of Portugal's Estado Novo altered the constitution to make the African colonies provinces of metropolitan Portugal and theorized a new ethos of colonialism called *luso-tropicalismo*, which emphasized a multiracial Portuguese nationalism. The bulk of the chapter recounts and contextualizes how former *contratados* interviewed in 2006 remember their servitude in the post-World War II era before the 1961 abolition of forced labor. These testimonies provide personal insights into the quotidian details of forced labor.

Chapter 4 examines the political context for the labor reforms at Cassequel following the 1961 outbreak of the Angolan nationalist war for independence. Correspondence among Cassequel's administration, board of directors, and colonial authorities provides insight into how and why policy makers decided to abolish forced labor in 1961. Investigations conducted by the ILO detail this shift between 1961 and 1970. The chapter ends in 1973 on the eve of the revolution in Portugal, which brought down the Estado Novo and ushered in negotiations for Angolan independence.

Chapter 5 focuses on the independence era, 1974–1977, and its legacy in contemporary Angola. I argue that the chaotic transfer of power to an independent Angola, exacerbated by a domestic civil war fueled by Cold War rivals, led to Cassequel's nationalization and a significant decline in production and deterioration of working conditions. Interviews with former workers and administrators, recently declassified government assessments, and a range of newspaper and secondary sources, provide insight into conditions on the ground at Cassequel, renamed Primeiro de Maio [First of May] in 1976.

The Epilogue discusses what happened to former workers after Cassequel's closure in 1991. Poverty and the concentration of land ownership in the hands of a few beg the question: Did the revolution deliver a better life? I conclude with a consideration of the importance of memory in the postwar period, for Cassequel is a contested place of memory. For some, namely those who served as forced labor, it represents a tragic place, reminiscent of hard work and colonial humiliations; for others, namely Portuguese skilled workers, Cassequel evokes memories of comfort and pride on the one hand and lost opportunities and bitterness toward independence on the other. Consideration of these disparate memories, in addition to the documentary record, provides an opportunity to understand contemporary Angola.

CHAPTER 1

Sugarcane, *Aguardente*, Forced Labor and the Founding of Cassequel Sugar Plantation, 1899–1920

In 1914, the British consul to Angola visited Cassequel Sugar Plantation, which had been founded the previous year by a Portuguese entrepreneur and colonist named António da Costa backed by Lisbon-based investors. Consul Hall undertook the journey to the south-central-coast port of Lobito and the neighboring sugar plantation at Catumbela, to see for himself whether the Portuguese authorities had, as they claimed, ended the practice of a system of forced labor that critics described as akin to slavery.

Consul Hall traveled the ten miles inland from the port of Lobito to Cassequel aboard the Benguela Railway and disembarked at the Catumbela station, nestled among verdant sugar canefields. At the plantation, he met António da Costa and presumably other Portuguese and European managers and engineers busy at work in the new factory. His interactions with workers confirmed what his hosts had already told him: the workers at Cassequel work voluntarily and are under no compulsion. The consul reported that management kept track of workers' hours on a piece of cardboard. The description is worth citing at length not only because of its detail, but also because it is one of the few extant descriptions of payment to voluntary workers at an Angolan sugar plantation in the 1910s.

> Each of them carried on him, either hung by a thong round his neck or tied up into some part of his clothing, a small cardboard ticket, along the top edge of which was written a number, corresponding to a number in the register, and his name; the rest of the card was ruled into squares, thirty-six in number, representing six weeks of six working days each. About midday white officials go round the plantation putting a mark in a square to represent half a day's work done, and making a similar note in a book for the purpose. At the end of the day each laborer presents his card at the office and the date of the day is written in the square already marked. I saw both these operations going on. When the card is filled, or at shorter intervals (on this point I did not get exact information), the owner receives the corresponding wages and has a new card, with his original number on it, issued to him.[1]

1 "Letter from Consul-General H. Hall to Sir Edward Grey," received July 17, 1914, FO 367/1956, PRO, 2. For a comparable situation from Tanganyika, see John Iliffe, *Tanganyika Under German Rule, 1905–1912*. (Cambridge: Cambridge University Press, 1969), 135–139.

 | DOI 10.1163/9789004301757_003

According to Consul Hall, voluntary workers enjoyed leeway over the number of days worked.[2]

The Consul's descriptions of the flexibility afforded to voluntary workers, known locally as *voluntários*, reflected one modus operandi with local workers in 1914 during a period when Cassequel's managers struggled to find a sufficient number of workers to meet a growing need for labor. And yet, unbeknownst to Cassequel's British visitor, forced labor did persist on the plantation. Although *voluntários* made up a significant percentage—generally as much as half—of Cassequel's workforce, plantation authorities also used other sources to meet the labor demands of tending, collecting, and processing two biannual sugarcane harvests. This source was government-supplied forced laborers, known as *contratados*, or contract workers, because of the "contract" each worker agreed to at the government post in the interior where he began his term of service. Because of the complexity of the situation at Cassequel, which consisted of diverse labor categories (including voluntary and forced African workers as well as skilled foreign workers) one must consider the political, legal, and economic factors influencing labor decisions at Cassequel and in colonial Angola before 1914.

Before Cassequel's founding in 1913, the sugar processed from Catumbela's verdant sugarcane fields went toward the production of *aguardente* [rum]. *Aguardente* production dates to the eighteenth century, when it became an important product for the lucrative trade with independent Umbundu[3] kingdoms of the interior.[4] This trade in locally produced *aguardente* boomed during the nineteenth century; in 1892 the colonial governor of Benguela described *aguardente* production as the most valuable industry in his district and one of the most important trade items used by colonial merchants in barter trade with the trade caravans of the Ovimbundu that carried rubber to the coast.[5] The Umbundu kingdoms of the Benguela Plateau controlled the nineteenth-century trade routes from the interior to the coastal ports of Catumbela and Benguela. The Ovimbundu consolidated into twenty-two kingdoms in the eighteenth century, and by the late nineteenth century three of the largest—Viye, Bailundo, and Ciyaka—dominated trade with the coast. In the 1890s

2 This arrangement may have been common during the 1910s but seems to have ended sometime in the following two decades.

3 A note on orthography: *Ovimbundu* (pl.) is the name of the people (sing. *Ocimbundu*). *Umbundu* is the name of the language, of the culture, and the form of the descriptive adjective.

4 Guilherme Gomes Coelho, *Relatórios dos Governadores das Provincias Ultramarinas, Districto de Benguella, 1887* (Lisboa: Imprensa Nacional, n.d.), 15.

5 Francisco de Paulo Cid, *Relatórios dos Governadores das Provincias Ultramarinas, Districto de Benguella*, 1892 (Lisboa: Imprensa Nacional, 1892), 23.

world rubber prices escalated and Angolan rubber exports skyrocketed, creating an economic boom in the coastal trading town of Catumbela. Unlike the rubber trade in the neighboring Congo Free State, Angolan rubber—especially the root rubber (*landolphia*) being carried to the coastal towns of Catumbela and Benguela—was collected and transported to the coast by African traders, mostly Ovimbundu, whose interior kingdoms remained outside Portuguese control until 1902.[6] African traders bartered their rubber, slaves, ivory, and wax for a range of European manufactures, including *aguardente* distilled from coastal sugarcane plantations.

To cash in on the lucrative rubber trade, colonists relied on a mix of free and slave labor. Until Portugal extended its hegemony into the interior and actively suppressed the domestic Angolan slave trade, coastal planters acquired slaves from the same Umbundu caravans carrying rubber to the coast. It was because of this dependence on slave labor that most colonists opposed Portugal's 1878 abolition of slavery in Angola. In practice, most colonists disparaged the principle of free labor as impossible and unworkable. To address these criticisms, the Portuguese government appointed a high-level commission to study and write a new labor law for the colonies. António Enes, a former member of the Portuguese parliament in the 1880s who had served briefly as Minister for Marine and Overseas, headed up the panel. Enes argued that work would uplift the African savage and would lead to the development of a superior, Luso-African civilization. As we will see, these were ideas long championed by Portuguese defenders of slavery and reasserted in the late nineteenth century by proponents of the philosophy of the white man's burden.[7] Enes's commission produced the new labor law of 1899, which enshrined the principle of forced labor and sent a clear message to colonists that the government would help to supply the requisite forced labor to make colonial agriculture productive and profitable. The commitment to forced labor occurred during a period when Angolan agriculture was relatively weak and there was virtually no industry. The government hoped that the availability of government-regulated forced labor would help to end the domestic trade in slaves and attract the capital and know-how necessary to bring about the rapid development of Angola.[8]

---

6 For more on the Angola rubber trade see, Jeremy Ball, "'A Time of Clothes': The Angolan Rubber Boom, 1886–1902," *Ufahamu* (vol. 28, no. 1, Fall 2000), 25–42; Rosa Cruz e Silva, "O Impacto da Borracha de 'Segunda' no Comercial-Catumbela Benguela, 1890–1910," *Fontes e Estudos* (no. 1, November 1994), 63–78; and Maria da Conceição Neto, "Comércio, Religião e Política no Sertão de Benguela: O Bailundo de Ekwikwi II (1876–1893)," *Fontes e Estudos* (no. 1, November 1994), 101–118.

7 James Duffy, *Portuguese Africa* (Cambridge, MA: Harvard University Press, 1959), 238.

8 Douglas L. Wheeler and René Pélissier, *Angola* (New York: Praeger Publishers, 1971), 62.

Debates about African labor took place during a period of expanding Portuguese hegemony in Angola. Portuguese colonialism there dated to the founding of Luanda in 1576 and Benguela in 1617. For two-and-a-half centuries, the colonial nuclei around these two coastal trading centers focused on the slave trade to the Americas, and Portuguese authority extended barely beyond the cities' immediate hinterlands and the Kwanza River Valley south of Luanda. Following the gradual abolition of the Atlantic slave trade from Angola (1836–1861), Portuguese policy makers sought to develop trade and agricultural production in Angola. After abolishing slavery in Angola in 1878, Portuguese leaders pursued a policy of territorial expansion from the coast to the interior highlands. Proponents of territorial expansion in the colonies envisioned a new era of Portuguese prosperity buoyed by new colonial markets for Portuguese products and profitable colonial exports. Portuguese elites also associated imperial expansion with a revival of national greatness; thus, Portuguese nationalism became closely tied to imperialism.[9]

The Umbundu kingdoms of the central highlands, with their centralized kingship and control over lucrative trade routes, became targets of Portuguese territorial expansion between 1890 and 1902. After the Portuguese conquest, indigenous authorities were subordinated to Portuguese colonial administrators, and the Ovimbundu became subject to forced labor for the expanding plantation agriculture of the coast.

In 1910, Portugal's constitutional monarchy fell amid political strife, and a republic took its place. The First Republic pledged to develop Angola and reformers in Angola and Portugal rallied behind the new government's modernizing rhetoric. In 1911, the First Republic banned the manufacture of *aguardente* in Angola in an effort to curb the sale of alcohol to Africans. The ban devastated Angolan sugarcane planters; as a concession, the government encouraged the production of semiprocessed sugar in Angola by halving tariffs paid on up to 6,000 tons of Angolan sugar entering Portugal for a period of fifteen years. These incentives encouraged Portuguese entrepreneurs to invest, and the Angolan sugar industry was born. Both of central Angola's major sugar companies—the Sociedade Agrícola do Cassequel (Cassequel) in Catumbela and the Companhia do Açúcar de Angola in Dombe Grande—were founded during this period.[10] This chapter argues that the codification of forced labor coupled

9 Wheeler and Pélissier, *Angola*, 59.

10 For a good overview of sugar and rum production in Angola, see Gervase Clarence-Smith, "The Sugar and Rum Industries in the Portuguese Empire, 1850–1914," in B. Albert and A. Graves, eds., *Crises and Change in the International Sugar Economy, 1860–1914* (Norwich & Edinburgh: ISC Press, 1984), 226–235; and Clarence-Smith, "O proteccionismo e a produção

with tariff-protected sugar markets and a sympathetic and supportive government, led to the development of a lucrative sugar industry at Cassequel. By providing economic incentives and appealing to nationalist sentiment, the Portuguese government brought elite business interests on board the colonial project. The chapter ends in 1920, when the Portuguese military subjugated the last pockets of African resistance to colonial hegemony and introduced civil government throughout Angola, including an individual tax for every African man called the *imposto indígena* [native tax].[11] The tax, as we will see, served dual purposes: to raise revenue for the colonial treasury and to produce *contratados* for the colony's plantation sector.

Colonial Labor Legislation

In the late nineteenth century, Angola underwent a tumultuous transition from slavery to forced labor. To fully appreciate the context of this transition, it is important to remember Angola's centuries-old participation in the Atlantic slave trade. For centuries, the settlements of Luanda and Benguela served as ports of embarkation for millions of slaves headed to the Americas.[12] The trade networks funneling slaves to these two ports reached far in to the interior of west-central Africa, well beyond the twentieth-century borders of Angola. After the gradual abolition of the Atlantic slave trade from Angolan ports (1836–61), the slave trade from the interior continued to supply the colony's small but growing coastal plantations. In 1858, Portugal's prime minister, the Marquês de Sá da Bandeira, decreed that Africans in Angola presently held in slavery would become free in twenty years time. During that twenty-year period no African could be enslaved and children born of slaves would be free.[13] From 1869 forward they would enjoy an interim status as *libertos* [freemen], a classification not well defined and less clearly enforced. In 1878, new legislation, the *Regulamento para os contratos de serviçais e colonos nas províncias*

de açúcar na África Central e Equatorial (Angola, Moçambique, Zaire, Zimbabwe), 1910–1945," *Revista Internacional de Estudos Africanos* (no. 4 e 5, Janeiro-Dezembro 1986), 159–189.

11 For an excellent analysis of the juridical status of *indígenas* and colonial "pacification" campaigns, see Mário Moutinho, *O Indígena no Pensamento Colonial Português 1895–1961* (Lisboa: Edições Universitárias Lusófonas, 2000).

12 For statistics on slave embarkations from Luanda and Benguela, see *The Trans-Atlantic Slave Trade Database*, http://www.slavevoyages.org/tast/index.faces [accessed January 20, 2015].

13 Duffy, *Portuguese Africa*, 77.

da Africa [regulation for the contracts of servants and masters in the African provinces], stipulated that freed slaves would henceforth become *serviçais* [sing. *serviçal,* servants]. The new law enshrined the idea of free labor, but in response to colonists' arguments that free labor would ruin the colony's agricultural sector, further regulations stipulated that individual Africans judged to be vagrants by colonial officials would be legally required to work. These new labor regulations tempered the abolition of 1878 with the principle of forced labor.[14]

Debates over free and forced labor reflected two intellectual currents in Portuguese society.[15] The liberal humanist current had its roots in the Enlightenment and preached free labor and the development of the colonies and its peoples.[16] The colonial current justified forced labor and reflected a colonial worldview that only the economic exploitation of Angola's natural and human resources would guarantee the continued economic viability of Portugal's African colonies. This thinking reflected what historian João Pedro Marques explains as a history of *tolerationism* in Portuguese society towards slavery. Marques argues that the absence of a strong abolition movement in Portuguese society rested on an idea of the inherent barbarity of Africans and a belief in the appropriateness of the Portuguese civilizing mission.[17] Opponents of free labor argued that Africans would never go to work for Portuguese interests in sufficient numbers to make Angola profitable; without forced labor, opponents argued, Angola's plantation agriculture would not be viable, and the colony would become an economic drain on Portugal.

In an effort to appease colonists' vocal criticisms of the principle of free labor (embedded in the 1878 labor legislation as unworkable) and to formulate a new and comprehensive colonial labor policy, the Portuguese government appointed a blue-ribbon commission headed by António Enes in 1898. Enes had already written the book *Moçambique*, which became one of the basic texts of Portugal's modern colonial policy.[18] The government charged the commission with the task of formulating a policy "to ensure the most practical and

14 João Pedro Marques, *Sá da Bandeira e o Fim da Escravidão: Vitória da Moral, Desforra do Interesse* (Lisboa: Instituto Ciencias Sociais, 2008), 124.

15 For the most thorough analysis of the debate over abolition in Portugal see Marques, *Sá da Bandeira e o Fim da Escravidão*.

16 Cláudia Castelo, *Passagens para África: O Povoamento de Angola e Moçambique com Naturais da Metrópole (1920–1974)* (Lisboa: Edições Afrontamento, 2007), 43–44.

17 João Pedro Marques, *The Sounds of Silence: Nineteenth-Century Portugal and the Abolition of the Slave Trade* (New York: Berghahn Books, 2006), 50. Translated by Richard Wall.

18 António Enes, *Moçambique: Relatório Apresentado ao Govêrno* (Lisboa: Agência Geral das Colónias, 1893).

efficient means to obligate the natives to regular employment."[19] As Enes himself averred:

> If we do not learn how, or if we refuse, to make the Negro work and cannot take advantage of his work, within a short while we will be obliged to abandon Africa to some one less sentimental and more utilitarian than we, less doctrinaire in legislating and more practical in administrating: and our final abandonment will not even benefit the native, because Portugal is, and will continue to be after imposing the obligation to work, the most benign and humanitarian sovereign of all those who have raised their flag over the African continent.[20]

Enes and the commission argued that the state had the duty and right as "sovereign of semi-barbarous populations" to "force them [Africans] to work in order for these rude negroes of Africa to improve themselves, to acquire a happier kind of existence."[21] Accordingly, Portuguese officials used "scientific" arguments then in vogue among European intellectuals to argue that Africans were inferior and thus could not be expected to make what Europeans considered to be the rational decision to work for wage employment. Oliveira Martins, a leading Portuguese intellectual of the late nineteenth century, ridiculed missionary and philanthropic arguments that there were no racial limits to a person's capacity to develop.[22]

Commissioners also argued forced labor would make the African colonies profitable for Portugal at a time of chronic budget deficits and insecurity about whether more powerful colonizing powers would respect Portuguese sovereignty in central Africa. Colonial policy makers saw Angolan productivity as

---

19 António Enes e outros, "O Trabalho dos Indígenas e o Crédito Agrícola: Do relatório elaborado pela Comissão encarregada de estudar o problema de trabalho dos indígenas em 1899," *Antologia Colonial Portuguesa, Vol. 1* (Lisboa: Agência Geral das Colónias, 1946), 25–55.

20 António Enes e outros, "O Rrabalho dos Indígenas e o Crédito Agrícola," 28–29.

21 Ibid., 27.

22 Oliveira Martins, *O Brasil e as Colónias Portuguesas* (1st ed. 1880). Reprinted in Alexandre, *Origens do Colonialismo Português Moderno (1822–1891)* (Lisboa: Sá da Costa, 1979), 212. For a comprehensive overview of the development of Western racism, see George M. Fredrickson, *Racism: A Short History* (Princeton, NJ: Princeton University Press, 2002). On the influence of science on British and French thinkers, see Michael Adas, *Machines as the Measure of Men: Science, Technology, and Ideologies of Western Dominance* (Ithaca: Cornell University Press, 1989), 210–236.

the "only practical solution to the national crisis."[23] According to Enes: "We need the labor of the natives, not only to improve the condition of these workers; we need them for the economy of Europe and for the progress of Africa."[24] The commission concluded that if Portuguese leaders did not want to force Africans to work for colonial interests, then they should abandon Africa altogether.

The commission's 1899 labor code states that "all natives of Portuguese overseas provinces are subject to the obligation, moral and legal, of attempting to obtain through work the means that they lack to subsist and to better their social condition. They have full liberty to choose the method of fulfilling this obligation, but if they do not fulfill it public authority may force a fulfillment."[25] The law established Africans' legal and moral obligation to work and the state's duty to regulate contracts between individual Africans and private employers.[26] The state also insisted on its right to forced labor for public purposes such as road building and public works. Indeed the practice of forced labor for public purposes was common practice among colonial powers in Africa during the early twentieth century. To justify forced labor for public purposes such as road building, a prominent Portuguese colonial official named Eduardo Costa cited other colonial powers and African law as evidence in a 1903 article:[27]

> In the first place, requisitioning work exists in the most advanced civilizations, such as in the French colonies, and not so long ago in British colonies; in the second place, because it is one of the customs of the native populations that the *regulos* requisition [people] for works of public utility, or still for their own personal profit.[28]

Where controversy among colonizing powers did arise was over the legality and morality of forced labor for private enterprises. After 1899, the legalization

23 Enes e outros, "O Trabalho dos Indígenas e o Crédito Agrícola," 28. On the economic crisis afflicting Portugal during this period, see Eugénia Mata e Nuno Valério, "Uma nova época de estagnação (1891–1914)," in Eugénia Mata e Nuno Valério, *História Económica de Portugal: Uma Perspectiva Global* (Lisboa: Editorial Presença, 1994), 162–178.

24 Enes e outros, "O Trabalho dos Indígenas e o Crédito Agrícola," 29.

25 Cited in James Duffy, *Portuguese Africa*, 155.

26 Ibid.

27 In 1930, Portugal, France and Belgium abstained from approving the Forced Labor Convention over whether the state should have the right to force colonized people to work for private employers.

28 Eduardo Costa, "A Administração civil nas nossas colonias africanas," *Boletim da Sociedade de Geographia de Lisboa* (Lisboa: Impensa Nacional, 1903), 626.

of forced labor for private enterprise in Angola and on the Portuguese islands of São Tomé and Príncipe in the Gulf of Guinea contributed to international debate about what constituted free labor. There was little agreement beyond the idea that slavery, narrowly defined to mean the legal right to own another person, was unacceptable. Free labor advocates campaigned for an international legal framework to define and guarantee free labor; they cited egregious abuses in the Congo, Angola, and São Tomé and Príncipe, where under the guise of regulated forced labor, individuals were denied their freedom and subjected to conditions analogous to slavery.[29] Despite widespread concern over labor issues, however, there existed little agreement about whether colonial powers had the right to use forced labor, whether for public or private purposes. Colonial powers insisted that the uncivilized nature of African societies required the use of forced labor. Even the International Labor Organization (ILO), which was founded under the Paris Peace Treaties of 1919 and regarded the struggle against forced labor as one of its topmost priorities, conceded to the insistence of the European powers not to apply "universal" labor standards to colonies so that labor regulations contained exemptions for colonial possessions.[30] European powers argued that the same standards could not be applied to "civilized" populations, such as those in Europe, and "uncivilized" colonial peoples.

In Angola, a small number of courageous journalists wrote stirring editorials about what they described as "labor stealing" and "outright slavery" under the guise of regulated forced labor. These men were primarily based in Luanda and described themselves as *naturais* (Angolan-born). Most of these men would have been described in colonial society as *assimilado* (of African heritage and assimilated to Portuguese culture) and/or *mestiço* (of mixed African and Portuguese heritage). From 1870 to 1926, the press in Portugal and Angola was relatively free, and so these men used newspapers such as *O Futuro d'Angola* and *O Cruzeiro do Sul* to advocate for reform.[31] They railed against Portuguese racism and disrespect for African culture. Journalist José de Fontes Pereira (1823–1891) cited the expression "*com preto e mulato nada de contrato*" [with

29 Daniel Roger Maul, "The International Labour Organization and the Struggle against Forced Labour from 1919 to the Present," *Labor History* (vol. 48, no. 4, November 2007), 477–500. For more on the international boycott of "slave cocoa" in São Tomé and Príncipe, see Henry W. Nevinson, *A Modern Slavery* (first published New York: Harper, 1906; reprinted New York: Schocken, 1968).

30 Maul, "The International Labour Organization and the Struggle against Forced Labour from 1919 to the Present," 480–481.

31 For an insightful analysis of the Angolan press in the early twentieth century, see Wheeler and Pélissier, *Angola*, 84–108.

mulattoes and blacks, no need for contracts] in a 1882 editorial in *O Futuro d'Angola* as an example of this disdain.[32] In 1901 a group describing themselves anonymously as *Os Naturais* [Angolan-born] responded to a March 26 editorial in the *Gazeta de Loanda* (a paper that reflected colonists' views) that questioned the humanity of Africans. The collection of essays, published in Lisbon under the title *Voz D'Angola Clamando no Deserto, Offerecida aos Amigos da Verdade Pelos Naturaes* [Voice of Angola Crying Out in the Desert, Offered to Friends of Truth by the Angolan-Born], stated categorically the authors' opposition to what they viewed as increasingly virulent race hatred [*ódio de raça*] in the colonial press.[33] Many of the *naturais* denounced accusations in the *Gazeta de Loanda* editorial, such as "the black does not work; the black is not completely a man."[34] In a powerful rhetorical reversal, the *naturais* questioned the humanity of the colonial work regimen:

> The black is a miserable instrument of shameful interests, which impose on him a cruel regimen of the whip, injuring him with intellectual blows and physical force, until criminal excess sends him to the grave. The black prefers prison to this kind of tyrannical, inhuman, violent and barbarous kind of work.[35]

The authors of *Voz D'Angola Clamando no Deserto* argued for equality before Portuguese law for all assimilated Angolans and they criticized colonists whom they denigrated as "poor whites" with no more civilization than the "uncivilized black" (*preto boçal*).[36] These defensive insults reflected the complex political and social hierarchy of early twentieth-century Angolan society, with Portuguese civilization being the apogee and African civilization the nadir. The *naturais* wanted an end to discrimination based on color and the delivery of social and economic development as promised in Portugal's colonial rhetoric. The writers called Portugal to task for the state of Angola and Angolans after four hundred years of Portuguese rule. As one wrote, "Portuguese Africa is despised, enslaved, without light, and abandoned in a criminal fashion by its conquerors to an ignorance for which it is not responsible."[37] These arguments anticipated

---

32 Cited in Wheeler and Pélissier, *Angola*, 100.

33 Wheeler and Pélissier, *Angola*, 106.

34 *Voz D'Angola Clamando no Deserto Offerecida aos Amigos da Verdade Pelos Naturaes* (Lisboa: Edições 70, 1984 [1st ed. Lisbon, 1901]), 14.

35 Ibid., 17.

36 Ibid., 71.

37 Ibid., 76.

foreign critics of Angolan forced labor who would question Portugal's capacity to effectively govern a colonial empire.

An international campaign against forced labor in Angola and São Tomé and Príncipe (henceforth, "the islands") gained momentum by 1909 after nearly a decade of published exposés on the issue, including a 1906 book titled *A Modern Slavery* by a British journalist named Henry Nevinson.[38] An estimated 67,000 *serviçais* had been shipped to the islands between 1888 and 1908.[39] Critics, primarily from Britain, described the forced labor system that brought individuals from the Angolan interior to work the cacao plantations of the islands as a virtual slavery and intentionally dubbed the cacao they produced "slave cocoa." At the time, São Tomé and Príncipe were the world's leading source of cacao, and their plantations created a great deal of wealth for their Portuguese owners and the Portuguese treasury. A 1913 article in the Lisbon press described São Tomé as the most prosperous of Portugal's colonies because of its "cacao-gold."[40] The slogan "slave cocoa" clearly aimed to unsettle Britons who drank hot cocoa as part of their regular diet. This campaign followed in the footsteps of the earlier, British-led movement to remove Belgium's King Leopold II from the Congo Free State. In 1906, in response to the publication of Nevinson's book, a group of leading Portuguese citizens formed the Sociedade de Propaganda to counter the negative publicity being generated by the slave cocoa campaign and to disseminate positive stories about Portugal in order to improve Portugal's image abroad.[41] The government of Portugal quietly acknowledged that the forced labor system bringing workers from the Angolan interior to the islands resulted in a life-long servitude akin to slavery, and in 1909 suspended the shipment of *serviçais* to the islands.

The slave cocoa campaign and the declaration of Portugal's First Republic in 1910 encouraged a small but influential group of free labor advocates in Lisbon to establish the Anti-Slavery Society of Portugal in 1911. These free labor advocates shared a liberal humanist and philanthropic worldview and their ranks included the influential future governor of Angola, José Norton de Matos

38 Henry W. Nevinson, *A Modern Slavery* (first published New York: Harper, 1906; reprinted New York: Schocken, 1968). Nevinson first wrote about conditions in Angola for *Harper's Magazine*.

39 Lord Hailey, *An African Survey Revised 1956: A Study of Problems Arising in Africa South of the Sahara* (London: Oxford University Press, 1938), 1372.

40 "A Campanha Chocolateira Alta Traição," *A Capital* (April 15, 1913), 1.

41 For an overview of the *Sociedade de Propaganda*, see Douglas L. Wheeler, "Remembering Portugal," *Portuguese Studies Review* (vol. 5, no. 2, 1996–97), 13–15.

(1912–1915 and 1921–1923), who as governor fought for more regulation of forced labor in an effort to protect Africans against egregious abuses.

The First Republic appointed José Norton de Matos governor of Angola in 1912. In his memoirs, Norton de Matos reflected that "When I arrived as Governor-General in Angola in the middle of 1912, I found in the province a system of native labor that, with rare exceptions, could not be called free."[42] Norton de Matos set out to implement reforms in order to create a modern colonial administration that would regulate forced labor for private employers with government-sanctioned contracts between individual *contratados* and employers. He understood that if Portugal did not regulate forced labor, it risked losing its extensive African colonial territories to ambitious colonial powers such as Britain and Germany. These fears dated to 1890, when the British sent gunships into the Portuguese port of Lourenço Marques in Mozambique as a warning to Portugal to withdraw land claims along the Shire River in what is today Malawi. This British ultimatum forced Portugal to give up dreams of a *mapa da côr rosa* [pink map] or a line of contiguous territory linking Portuguese Angola and Mozambique during the scramble for Africa.[43] This recent history influenced how many Portuguese reacted to the British-led campaign against slave cocoa, which felt so bitter to many of them.[44]

Norton de Matos's first reform created the Negócios Indígenas [Native Affairs Department]. The legislation establishing the Negócios Indígenas put all subjects relative to native affairs under the authority of the secretary of the Native Affairs Department.[45] This was a considerable responsibility, especially

42 José Norton de Matos, *A Província de Angola* (Porto: Edição de Maranus, 1926), 126. John T. Tucker, a prominent missionary in the central highlands, made the same assessment. See John T. Tucker, *A Tucker Treasury* (Winfield, BC: Wood Lake Books, 1984), 163.

43 Douglas Wheeler, "Aqui é Portugal!: The Politics of the Colonial Ideal during the Estado Novo, 1926–1974," in *Portugal na Transição do Milénio* (Lisboa: Fim de Século, 1998), 383–384. For a thorough overview and analysis of the ultimatum and the public reaction against Britain and the monarchy, see Nuno Severiano Teixeira, *O Ultimatum Inglês: Política Externa e Política Interna no Portugal de 1890* (Lisboa: Alfa, 1990).

44 Simão de Laboreiro, *A Circunscrição Civil Da Ganda Relatório do Administrador, 1914–1915* (Loanda, Angola: Imprensa Moderna, 1916), 50. The state's right to coerce labor was mandated in the 1899 labor regulations and then reaffirmed by a decree of May 27, 1911. This in turn was replaced by the General Native Labor Regulations for the Portuguese Colonies, approved by Decree No. 951 of October 4, 1914, which also substantially maintained the obligation to work and the measures to be taken to ensure compliance with it in the form laid down in 1899.

45 Portaria Provincial No. 135, January 30,1914, *Boletim Oficial de Angola*, (no. 5, 1914).

given the fact that the department had insufficient funding.[46] The new department's responsibilities included (1) organizing a census of the native population, (2) studying and compiling customs of individual tribes (3) understanding political and economic organization of native societies (4) understanding native law, and (5) compiling statistics about native employment and overseeing contracts between employers and employees. Regulating each of these elements of "native affairs" reflected an effort to improve the efficiency and fairness of native administration and to deepen colonial officials' understanding of African culture. An ethnographer named José de Oliveira Ferreira Dinis served as the first secretary of native affairs and *curador* (guardian) for the province of Angola.[47] The position of the *curador* dates to the 1878 *Regulamento para os contratos de serviçais e colonos nas províncias da Africa* and reflected the paternalistic rhetoric of Portugal's self-proclaimed civilizing mission in Africa. The *curador* served as a guardian of his African subjects, and his responsibilities in this capacity included recruiting labor, overseeing contracts, and receiving contract-related complaints from both employer and employee. Dinis argued that the colony needed a clear definition of the term *indígena* [native]. In other words, who should be classified as an *indígena*? Portuguese colonial policy held up assimilation to Portuguese culture as an ideal, so what should distinguish an African who had assimilated Portuguese culture, known in Angola as an *assimilado*, from an *indígena*? Dinis proffered a potential definition in his 1913 report: "*Indígena* is the individual of color (black or mulatto) that satisfies all of the following criteria: (a) was born in the province; (b) does not speak fluent Portuguese; (c) has the habits and customs of a native."[48] Attempts such as this one to codify legal definitions reflected wider efforts to regulate and control Angolans.

Under Portugal's colonial administration of Angola, the smallest administrative division was the *posto*, of which there were 287 in 1921. Each *posto* was headed by a *chefe de posto* [district administrator]. Individual *chefes de posto* held multiple positions, including *curador*.[49] With very rare exceptions, all these officials were white and most came from Portugal. Dinis conceded that

46 Colónia de Angola: Repartição Central dos Negócios Indígenas, *Relatório de 1942*. Relatórios do Curador e Negócios Indígenas, AHU, Maço 1661, Sala 3, 12.

47 Portaria Provincial No. 372, April 17, 1913, *Boletim Oficial de Angola* (no. 16, 1913), 28–29.

48 José de Oliveira Ferreira Dinis, Secretário dos Negócios Indígenas da Província de Angola *Relatório do Ano de 1913* (Luanda, Angola: Imprensa Social, 1914), 28–29.

49 See, for example, Jerónimo Paiva de Carvalho, *Alma Negra: Depoimento Sobre a Questão Dos Serviçais de S. Tomé* (Porto: Tipografia Progresso, 1912). Carvalho was a former *curador* on the island of Príncipe.

in the past, *curadores* had done little in their role as guardians, but he argued in his 1913 report that with increased power and financing the *curador* would be able to guarantee that employers met their contractual obligation to individual *contratados*.[50] These contractual obligations included the provisions of adequate food and the termination of the contract on a specified date.

As Norton de Matos and Dinis set out to end the worst abuses of colonial administration, Luanda's *naturais* journalists published editorials in their newspaper *Voz d'Africa* [Voice of Africa] decrying colonial law as guaranteeing "a monopoly of one race over another."[51] The same piece described the law as "a hypocritical mask" covering up unfettered exploitation of Africans' labor. Throughout the first half of the twentieth century, groups of Angolan *assimilados* and *mestiços*, working within colonial structures and discourses, advocated for more rights and opportunity. In opposition, individual colonists and colonial officials such as Dinis, for example, warned against the "false belief" that Africans could be Portuguese citizens.[52]

In 1913, Norton de Matos laid down his administration's rules on *mão de obra indígena* [native labor]. He insisted that male *indígenas* deemed vagrants by colonial officials and those who could not pay their individual tax [*imposto indígena*] had the moral and legal obligation to do contract work for a private employer.[53] Legally, the individual *contratado* had the right to choose among employers, but in practice this rarely occurred.[54] Decree 154 of October 1, 1913, stipulated that labor contracts be entered in notebooks containing detailed information about each *contratado*, including name, employer, age, home district, parents' names, duration of the contract, place of work, salary, signature of the employer and colonial administrator of the worker's home district.[55] The long list of regulations addressed criticism from leaders of the slave cocoa campaign and attempted to implement a policy of African development along the lines articulated by nineteenth-century reformers such as the Marquês de Sá da Bandeira.

Decree 154 also regulated the obligations of both employer and employee. For example, employers were required to provide clean housing, working hours were limited to ten hours per day, and the employer had the duty to

---

50 Dinis, *Relatório do Ano de 1913*, 66.

51 "Partido Nacional Africano," *A Voz d'Africa* (no. 4, anno 1, October 15, 1912), 1.

52 Dinis, *Relatório do Ano de 1913*, 6. For the French situation, see G. Wesley Johnson, ed., *Double Impact: France and Africa in the Age of Imperialism* (Westport, CT: Greenwood Press, 1985).

53 Decree 154 of October 1, 1913, *Boletim Oficial de Angola*, quoted in Dinis, *Relatório do Ano de 1913*, 71–72.

54 Ibid., 70.

55 Ibid., 69.

repatriate the *contratado* at the end of his contract.[56] The employee had the duty to complete the stipulated length of the contract (usually between 6 and 12 months) and to fulfill the daily labor tasks. Additional reforms—such as medical support to pregnant African women, inspections of African neighborhoods for health risks, and Department of Health inspections into the food, lodging, clothing, working hours, and treatment of *contratados*—were never implemented.[57] In 1913 Norton de Matos ordered that civil servants, including policemen, study the African language in their area of service.[58] In spite of the reforms, the Native Affairs Department remained small, underfunded and stranded in Luanda throughout the 1910s and 1920s. There was no investigative unit. In practice each *chefe de posto* acted as *curador* in his district, adding to an already full job description by the terms of which a *chefe de posto* served simultaneously as judge, postmaster, treasurer, president of the municipal council, and head of the military. Norton de Matos succeeded in creating a system of government-supplied forced labor to private employers, but the government carried out virtually no practical enforcement of contractual protections for individual *contratados*. Much of the failure of the regulatory structure resulted from colonists' resistance to reform and regulation.[59] In the Luanda press, settlers lamented controls on forced labor and argued that if the reforms took effect, it would be impossible to develop the colony.[60]

Colonists were not the only ones to use newspapers to pressure Norton de Matos. The *assimilado* newspaper editors of *A Voz d'Africa* issued a challenge to Norton de Matos in a 1912 editorial lambasting the lack of labor regulation and labor conditions that they described explicitly as slavery:

> In Angola Slavery! Slavery! A message from the sons of Angola to the Government of the Portuguese Republic…it is a fact that no scrupulous person with a healthy conscience is able to negate that slavery exists in this province. They buy and sell people exactly as they buy and sell animals… The various regulations elaborated, the decrees and the laws promulgated on the subject have not stopped the buying and selling of men, women, and children.[61]

---

56 Ibid., Section 13d, 72.

57 Dinis, *Relatório do Ano de 1913*, 97.

58 For a copy of a test of the Umbundu language administered to policemen on January 22, 1914, see "Districto de Benguela," Caixa 4071, AHA.

59 Diniz, *Relatório do Ano de 1913*, 75.

60 Ibid., 75.

61 *A Voz d'Africa* (no. 5, anno 1, November 1, 1912), 2.

In 1913, the reformist governor shut down *A Voz d'Africa* because of its critical editorial page.

The imposition of taxes, alongside the conquest of territory and extension of Portuguese hegemony, served as an indirect method to deliver forced labor to colonial employers.[62] Taxes paid by Africans to the Portuguese crown began with the vassal treaties of the sixteenth century.[63] The first *cubata* [hut] tax in Portuguese-controlled areas dates to 1886.[64] Each African head of household paid a set amount for each of the huts belonging to his household. Usually a man had a hut for each of his wives, so wealthier men paid more in taxes. In fiscal year 1907–08, the government collected 40 *contos* in tax revenues from the hut tax, "a modest amount that will grow in increments."[65] In the early twentieth century, the tax meant more than just revenue. "It is axiomatic," Governor Henrique de Paiva Couceiro wrote in 1910, that "the tax will play an important role in producing work."[66] In other words, individuals unable to pay their hut tax will either voluntarily go to work for a colonial business or be sent into forced labor, where they will earn the necessary money to pay their tax. In 1920, the colony dropped the hut tax and adopted an individual tax [*imposto indígena*].[67] To ensure tax collection and exercise control over Africans' labor, the government began issuing *cadernetas de trabalho* [passbooks]. The *caderneta* recorded the individual man's biographical information, his home *posto*, and his work and tax history. In the words of one colonial administrator, "The principal objective is the control of how the native fulfills his work obligation."[68]

After Norton de Matos's departure in 1915, colonists increasingly relied on *chefes de posto* to supply forced laborers for agricultural and other enterprises. Without the pressure exerted by the governor to safeguard contractual obligations to *contratados*, colonial administrators served primarily the employers who paid a commission for each *contratado* delivered. A decree issued on April 18,

62 José de Oliveira Ferreira Dinis, "Da Política Indígena em Angola: Os impostos indígenas," *Boletim da Agência Geral das Colónias* (no. 47, ano V, Maio de 1929), 136.

63 For a history of different tax systems in Angola before the twentieth century, see Sebastião Lopes de Calheiros e Meneses, *Relatório do Governador Geral da Provincia de Angola: Referido ao anno de 1861* (Lisboa: Imprensa Nacional, 1867).

64 Dinis, "Da Política Indígena em Angola: Os impostos indígenas," p. 147.

65 Henrique de Paiva Couceiro, *Angola: Dous Annos de Governo Junho 1907–Junho 1909* (Lisboa: A Nacional, 1910), 222.

66 Ibid., 222.

67 Dinis, "Da Política Indígena em Angola: Os impostos indígenas," 156.

68 "Circular N. 7/116, Secretária de Colonização e Negocios Indígenas, to the Administrador da Circunscricao Civil de Huambo," December 29,1921, Concelho do Huambo, Caixa 466, AHA.

1918, paid *chefes de posto* 10 *centavos* per recruited worker. A later decree, issued in December 1918, provided that no direct remuneration was to be granted to the authorities, but that at the end of each man's contract the employer would pay 50 *centavos* into a state fund that was to cover expenses and pay gratuities to chiefs showing special diligence in supplying laborers. A third order issued in March 1920 ignored the preceding one, as it raised the amount payable to *chefes de posto* to 20 *centavos* per worker for contracts up to one year and to 50 *centavos* per worker for longer agreements.[69] Whatever the exact wording of the law, in practice administrators earned money for supplying workers, either in the form of payments from employers or a percentage of workers' salaries or both.[70] *Contratados* had little to no recourse for securing their wages. What happened to the wages then depended on the individual official. Most deducted the *imposto indígena* and a commission from the paltry wages and returned what was left to the *contratado*. Likewise, the extent to which a forced worker had the ability to choose his employer depended on the *chefe de posto*. If he was lucky a *contratado* might be given a choice among a few employers, but most often *contratados* were simply told where they would be fulfilling their forced labor. People impressed as *contratados* generally accepted resignedly.[71]

One of the major destinations of *contratados* from the central highlands in the 1910s and 1920s was the Cassequel Sugar Plantation in Catumbela. Before examining labor practices at Cassequel, we will learn about Cassequel's founding in 1913 and its emergence by the 1920s as one of Angola's most important agro-industrial enterprises.

From Water to Rum: A Place Called Kasekele

The name *Cassequel* first appeared to this historian during a research trip to the Arquivo Histórico Ultramarino [Historical Archive of the Overseas] in

69 Hutcheon, Angola August 12, 1922, Dispatch No. 41, FO 371/7211, Public Record Office. This was, of course, not a new theory in Angola. The classic Portuguese statement of the need for forced labor as a result of the "lazy native" can be found in António Enes e outros, "O Trabalho dos Indígenas e o Crédito Agrícola: Do relatórioelaborado pela Comissão encarregada de estudar o problema de trabalho dos indígenas em 1899," *Antologia Colonial Portuguesa*, Vol. 1 (Lisboa: Agência Geral das Colónias, 1946), 25–55.

70 For example, in 1922 Cassequel sent *escudos* 131 in wages to the *Capitão Mor* of the District of Alto Quanza to distribute to returning contract workers. "Angariamento contratos de serviçães indígenas," Districto de Benguela, Pasta 133, Caixa 2115, AHA.

71 Adrian C. Edwards, *The Ovimbundu under Two Sovereignities: A Study of Social Control and Social Change among a People of Angola* (London: Oxford University Press, 1962), 43.

Lisbon to examine the Angola collection. The name appeared in a series of contract books listing the names, home districts, parents' names, and *sobado* [chieftancy] of *contratados* heading to Cassequel on contracts lasting between nine and twelve months. A little subsequent research revealed that Cassequel was a major sugar plantation and refinery based in Catumbela. During that same trip, I came across a book commemorating the wonderful work of the Fundação Ricardo Espírito Santo in preserving and restoring Portuguese decorative arts. In the book's introduction, a French journalist referred to the wealth generated by Cassequel for the foundation's founder, Ricardo Espírito Santo (1900–1955), one of the leading Portuguese bankers of the mid-twentieth century: "Besides serving as president of the Association of Banks, Ricardo Espírito Santo would serve as president of Sacor—Portugal's sole oil refinery. He founded many commercial enterprises, but it was perhaps Cassequel Sugar Company…that brought him the greatest prosperity."[72] These two discoveries led to further research in Angola in order to uncover more about the history of Cassequel and its relationship to the powerful Espírito Santo banking family.

Cassequel is the Portuguese spelling of the San word *Kasekele*, the *kimbo* [town] on the banks of the Catumbela River where a seminomadic population of San hunter-gatherers known as the Vassekel lived until the nineteenth century.[73] The Catumbela river mouth had long been an entrepôt for trade, in particular the export of slaves to the New World, which had dominated the local export trade from the seventeenth century. Then, in 1836, when the government of Portugal officially abolished the trans-Atlantic slave trade and built a fort overlooking the Catumbela River to enforce Portuguese power over the region, Portuguese traders established the town of Asseiceira near the mouth of the Catumbela River.[74] By the end of the nineteenth century, locals called the growing town Catumbela, after the adjacent river.[75] In the 1840s, the autonomous African peoples living in the Catumbela area staged an unsuccessful revolt against the expropriation of their lands to recently arrived colonists.[76]

---

72 Christine Garnier, "Em casa de um homem do renascimento," in Alexandra de Béthencourt, ed., *Fundação Ricardo do Espírito Santo Silva* (Lisboa: Fundação Ricardo do Espírito Santo Silva, 1999), 21. For more on the Ricardo Espírito Santo Foundation consult the Foundation's website, http://www.fress.pt/.

73 José Redinha, *Distribuição Etnica da Província de Angola* (Luanda: Centro de Informação e Turismo de Angola, 1965), 20.

74 Aida Freudenthal, José Manuel Fernandes, Maria de Lurdes Janeiro, eds., *Angola no século XIX Cidades, Território e Arquitecturas* (Lisboa: Mem Martins, 2006), 46.

75 Fernando Batalha, *A Urbanização de Angola* (Luanda: Museu de Angola, 1950), 16.

76 Aida Freudenthal, *Arimos e Fazendas: A transição agrária em Angola* (Luanda: Edições Chá de Caxinde, 2005), 134.

What had been community land, controlled by lineage heads, became privately owned land belonging to colonists. The Land Law of 1856 operated according to Portuguese land laws and did not recognize community land controlled by lineage heads. These laws clearly benefited colonists, who claimed land concessions up to 1,000 hectares.[77] Settlers wanted this land because of its location along the river, along which traders from the interior traveled to bring trade goods to market. The site also provided easy access to ocean trade and the fresh water of the river provided the needs of the inhabitants and made possible extensive agriculture and the tapping of groves of palm trees for palm oil.[78] Africans forced off their land became landless workers for Portuguese colonists or migrated out of the area.

From the 1860s through the 1890s, Catumbela developed its market and was frequented by caravans of Umbundu traders who transported wax, ivory, slaves (known euphemistically as *libertos* or *serviçais* after abolition in 1878) and rubber down the escarpment, following footpaths that ended in Catumbela. Catumbela housed several trading firms and grew to look like a provincial Portuguese town with tree-lined streets, a square for negotiation between caravans and Portuguese and Luso-African traders, a town hall (Câmara Municipal), a Catholic church, and the presidio atop a small hill overlooking the river and town.

During the first decade of the twentieth century, the Portuguese were busy consolidating their authority in the surrounding district of Benguela, in part because many people continued to live outside of Portuguese authority.[79] To the southeast the Portuguese faced fierce resistance from the Kwanyamas, who fought off colonial encroachment until a decisive military defeat in 1915.[80] In the interior districts of Huambo and Bié, Portuguese authority was more or less assured after Portuguese forces defeated the 1902 Ovimbundu rebellion.[81]

In 1904, Nevinson described the Catumbela's spatial characteristics:

> Katumbella itself is an old town, with two old forts, a dozen trading-houses and a river of singular beauty, winding down between the

77 Freudenthal, *Arimos e Fazendas*, 144.

78 Freudenthal, *Arimos e Fazendas*, 106.

79 Henrique de Paiva Couceiro, *Angola (Dous annos de Governo Junho 1907–Junho 1909) Historia e Commentarios* (Lisboa: A Nacional, 1910), 72.

80 René Pélissier, *Les Guerres grises: Résistance et révoltes en Angola, 1845–1941* (Orgeval: Pélissier, 1977).

81 For an overview of the 1902 Ovimbundu rebellion see Douglas Wheeler and C. Diane Christensen, "To Rise with One Mind: The Bailundo War of 1902" in Franz-Wilhelm Heimer, ed., *Social Change in Angola* (München: Weltforum Verlag, 1973), 53–92.

> mountains. It is important because it stands on the coast at the end of the carriers' foot-path, which has been for centuries the principal trade route between the west and the interior.... The path ends, vulgarly enough, at an oil-lamp in the chief street of Katumbella.[82]

Catumbela grew in importance after the government decided to build a port to serve the Benguela Railway 8 miles to the north at Lobito Bay because of its natural deep-water harbor.[83] Construction on the Benguela Railway began in 1904; by 1909, it extended over 200 kilometers and connected the port of Lobito to the interior regions of Angola, which were undergoing the slow process of incorporation into the governmental structure of the expanding colonial nucleus. The railway helped to put Catumbela on the map, with the construction of a railway station and easier, more efficient access to interior markets. In 1905, the Railway Company dedicated an iron bridge over the river and named it the Dom Luís Filipe Bridge, in honor of the Portuguese Crown Prince. Locals boasted that the railway bridge over the Catumbela River was "Africa's third iron bridge."[84] It is not clear whether the boast was indeed accurate or which iron bridges deserve the designations as Africa's first two iron bridges. In that same year, the Portuguese colonists of Catumbela organized the first town government and the Portuguese government built new postal and telegraph offices.

In 1909, Catumbela had a population of about 2100, of which nearly eighty percent were Africans living in *cubatas* [huts] on the outskirts of the town center in area called Caputo.[85] A local historian estimated that *serviçais* made up roughly one-fourth of the total population (about 500 people).[86] As we have learned, the designation *serviçais* circa 1909 indicated a labor status somewhere in the gray zone between free labor and slavery. Two agencies in

82 Nevinson, *A Modern Slavery*, 42. Nevinson includes a photograph of this oil-lamp between pages 18 and 19.

83 Ibid., 169. In fact, as early as 1843, the colonial government made plans and passed legislation to move the entire city of Benguela to the site of Lobito because of the site's better harbor for large ships. However, the move never happened because of lack of funds. See Batalha, *Urbanização de Angola*, 18. See also João Bernardina B. de Sá, "O Porto do Lobito e o Caminho de Ferro de Benguela como Factores de Desenvolvimento," *Fontes e Estudos Revista do Arquivo Histórico Nacional* (no. 1, Novembro 1994), 79–100.

84 Augusto Bastos, *Monographia de Catumbella* (Lisboa: Tipografia Universal, 1912), 44.

85 Bastos, *Monographia de Catumbella*, 67.

86 Massano de Amorim, "Relatorio sobre incursão de Cá Luiz, nos territorios Belgas e Commercio de Benguella, 1901–1902." AHU, Sala 12, Maço 1106, 20–21.

Catumbela "contracted" *serviçais* for shipment to the islands.[87] There were also approximately 1,200 free Africans living in Caputo and they worked in a range of unskilled and skilled jobs.[88]

Two sugar plantations abutted Catumbela so that visitors traveling by rail or road entered through verdant sugar cane fields. The two plantations São Pedro [St. Peter] and Maravilha do Cassequel [Wonder of Cassequel] depended on irrigation drawn from the Catumbela River, the source of the region's agricultural fecundity. The region's warm and humid weather was ideal for sugarcane, but the relatively arid climate meant that the sugarcane fields had to be irrigated, as sugarcane is a thirsty crop.

São Pedro extended 1,230 hectares along the southern side of the river and in 1909 produced 71 hectares of sugarcane, with 1 hectare of cane capable of producing between four and five *pipas* ["a pipe," a cask used for holding wine with a capacity of 550 liters][89] of *aguardente* in a season. The relatively small amount of land planted in sugarcane probably resulted from a lack of capital to either process more sugarcane or extend the irrigation ditches, or from a lack of labor. São Pedro's workforce consisted of one hundred and fifty *serviçais* and four European employees. The Europeans performed the skilled and managerial positions of field manager, blacksmith, barrel maker, and clerk, whereas the Africans prepared, planted, and harvested the sugarcane, in addition to managing the farm's other crops and animals.[90] Between June 1890 and July 1893, the workers at São Pedro constructed a dam and 7 kilometers of stone-lined irrigation ditches to carry water from the Catumbela River to the cane fields.[91] The irrigation works took three years to construct, with an average of two hundred *serviçais* and two European supervisors working full-time.[92] The total labor cost was *réis* 60,000$000, with the two hundred native workers

87 Another destination for Africans "contracted" in Catumbela was the southern port of Mossamedes. See Clarence-Smith, "Slavery in Coastal Southern Angola 1875–1913." For a defense of the use of *serviçais* in Mossamedes from the colonists' perspective, see Viuva Bastos, *A Escravatura em Mossamedes: Carta Aberta dirigida a S. Ex.ª o Presidente da Republica por um grupo de agricultores, industriaes e commerciantes de Mossamedes* (Lisboa: Typographia do Commercio, 1912).

88 Ibid., 67–69.

89 A "pipa," is a cask used for holding wine with a capacity of 550 liters. Bastos, *Monographia de Catumbella,* 80. See also, "Various relatórios do chefe do Concelho da Catumbela, 1901–1908," Concelho de Catumbela, Caixa 3530, AHA.

90 Bastos, *Monographia de Catumbella*, 80.

91 SAC, "Cartas Recebido 1935–1940," Arquivo do Cassequel.

92 Concelho de Catumbela, Caixa 3530, "Relatórios do chefe do Concelho da Catumbela, 1901–1908," AHA, 81.

earning a final sum of *réis* 47,250$000, which calculates to *réis* $273 per day based on a six-day work week.[93] In comparison, the two Europeans earned *réis* 4$166 per day based on the same work week. To put the wage differentials into perspective, in 1891 in Benguela 1 kilo of palm oil cost *réis* $060, and a year's subscription to the *Boletim Official do Governo Geral da Provincia de Angola* cost *réis* 3$600.[94] Julio Tavares Coutinho and José Joaquim Reis da Conçeição, owners of São Pedro, invested in irrigation systems and machinery for carrying and distilling cane because they believed in the potential growth in the demand for *aguardente*. The works constituted a great financial investment.[95] As we have seen, *aguardente* was one of the trade items most in demand by Umbundu trade caravans bringing rubber from the interior to trade in the markets of Catumbela.

Maravilha do Cassequel (Maravilha) on the northern side of the Catumbela River consisted of between 4,000–5,000 hectares, with only 30 planted in sugarcane in 1909 and the median production per hectare at six *pipas*. Records indicate that twenty years earlier, in 1887, 510 *libertos* [freedmen also known as *serviçais*] worked 38 hectares of sugarcane at Maravilha.[96] The relatively small amount of land planted in sugar cane reflected either a lack of capital or labor. Perhaps the plantation required massive investments to construct more extensive irrigation works.

The Road to Cassequel: Catumbela's Aguardente Crisis

Before Cassequel's founding in 1913 nearly all of the sugarcane grown in Catumbela went toward the production of *aguardente*. It was amidst this *aguardente* prosperity that Portugal's First Republic decided to ban liquor production, including the distillation of *aguardente*, and the sale of hard liquor to Africans in Angola.[97] Sugarcane planters threatened armed revolt

93 Artigo 161, Decreto N.° 951, 14 de Outubro de 1914, *Diário do Governo* (I série, número 187), sets 6 as the maximum number of work days in a week. For the réis/pound sterling exchange rate see, Clarence-Smith, *The Third Portuguese Empire* (London: Manchester University Press, 1985), Annex 2. For an explanation of changes in Portuguese currency, see Jeanne Pennvenne, *African Workers and Colonial Racism*, xvii.

94 *Boletim Official do Governo Geral da Provincia de Angola* (7 de Fevereiro de 1891, no. 6), 98.

95 Bastos, *Monographia de Catumbella*, 81.

96 Gomes Coelho, *Relatórios dos Governadores das Provincias Ultramarinas, Districto de Benguella, 1887*, 14–21.

97 *Diario do Governo* (no. 124, 29 de Maio de 1911). The Republican Revolution of October 1910 reformed the political system, but did not significantly alter the economic status quo. In

and civil disobedience in protest.[98] The ban reflected the commitment of leaders of the First Republic to bring Portuguese colonial administration more in line with French and British colonial polices, which discouraged the sale of hard liquor to African societies. The decision may have also reflected lobbying from Portuguese wine producers who hoped to expand the market for their wine, as the ban exempted wine and beer sales. To overcome planters' resistance, the First Republic passed legislation calling for fines of between *réis* 500$000 and 5,000$000, prison, and confiscation of machinery for planters and distillers who did not comply with the law.[99] To ease the loss of income for the largest, best-financed sugarcane growers, the First Republic set guidelines for the payment of indemnities to planters of sugarcane. Indemnities applied to areas under exploitation in December 1909, and among these, those planted in sugarcane had to have paid the alcohol tax in "some years between 1904 and 1909."[100] Indemnities were paid in government bonds, 30 percent of which were redeemable immediately, 25 percent each of the following two years, and the remaining 20 percent when the cultivator could prove that he had an area under cultivation for the production of sugar at least equal to the area being claimed for indemnities.[101] According to the government assessment published in the *Boletim Official do Governo Geral da Provincia de Angola*, São Pedro owners Conceição and Coutinho were entitled to receive indemnities for 70 hectares.[102] At an indemnity of *réis* 667$529 per hectare, the total equaled *réis* 46,727$030. António Pimenta da Gama Barreto, owner of Maravilha, received indemnities for 52 hectares, totaling *réis* 34,711$508. Considering the amount of capital invested in machinery, labor, and land, and calculating the depreciation caused by inflation, indemnities did not cover money invested. For example, Conceição and Coutinho invested *réis* 60,000$000 to build an irrigation system. Many planters went bankrupt and

---

regard to the colonies the Republican government reformed colonial administration to reflect contemporary ideas about the civilizing mission. For an introduction to the Republican Revolution, see Douglas Wheeler, "The Portuguese Revolution of 1910," *Journal of Modern History* (vol. 44, June 1972), 172–194.

98 Gervase Clarence-Smith, *The Third Portuguese Empire, 1825–1975: A Study in Economic Imperialism* (Manchester: Manchester University Press, 1985), 120.

99 Clandestine distilling and fermenting continued. See, for example, fines paid for the fermenting of quimbombo, a type of beer fermented from sugarcane or corn, Concelho do Huambo, Caixa 480, AHA.

100 *Diario do Governo* (no. 124, 29 de Maio de 1911).

101 *Diario do Governo* (no. 124, 29 de Maio de 1911).

102 *Boletim Official de Angola* (no. 19, 11 de Maio de 1912).

were forced to sell.[103] António Barreto, owner of Maravilha, may have been typical. In 1911, he was fifty-one years old. Rather than starting over, he decided to collect his indemnities and sell his property.[104]

A lack of capital had plagued sugarcane growers in colonial Angola since at least the 1860s.[105] The outlawing of *aguardente* production dealt another blow to small-scale planters, but meant opportunity for entrepreneurs with capital. One such entrepreneur was a Portuguese settler named António da Costa. Da Costa's trading firm, António da Costa, Limited, based in Benguela, traded in sundry agricultural and manufactured products. In 1912, da Costa purchased Maravilha do Cassequel and São Pedro for their prime sugar-growing land, access to water for irrigation, and proximity to both the port of Lobito and the Benguela Railway, and thus access to the protected Portuguese market. In addition to cultivated and fallow land, both plantations possessed valuable infrastructure, including light railways for the carrying of cane, sheds, and offices.[106] In 1913, da Costa valued the lands, buildings, small rail systems, and all improvements at São Pedro and Maravilha at *escudos* 100,000$000 (roughly £22,000).

That year da Costa and seven Lisbon-based investors formed the Sociedade Agrícola do Cassequel. The two primary investors were da Costa[107] and José Maria do Espírito Santo Silva,[108] who began his career in Lisbon selling tickets for the Spanish lottery and in 1884 founded the Casa Bancária Espírito Santo Silva & Co. It is believed that Espírito Santo Silva was the illegitimate son of a prominent Portuguese nobleman, which might explain how he raised sufficient

103 Gervase Clarence-Smith, "The Sugar and Rum Industries in the Portuguese Empire, 1850–1914," in Adrian Graves and Bill Albert, (eds.), *Crisis and Change in the International Sugar Economy, 1860–1914* (Norwich & Edinburgh: ISC Press, 1984), 233.

104 António Barreto's age is listed in "Lista dos cidadaõs residentes n'esta freguezia do Sagrado Coração de Jesus de Catumbella," 8 de Agosto de 1901, Caixa 3530, AHA.

105 Freudenthal, *Arimos e Fazendas*, 185–186.

106 *Boletim Official de Angola* (no. 19, 11 de Maio de 1912).

107 Da Costa invested *réis* 150,000$000, 100,000$000 in property (the fazendas and all property pertaining therein) and 50,000$000 in cash.

108 José Maria do Espírito Santo Silva invested *réis* 95,000$000. The company had a total capital of *réis* 300,000$000. In 1906, José Maria do Espírito Santo Silva made his first investment in a colonial enterprise, a sugar plantation in Mozambique called the Companhia Colonial do Buzi. Espírito Santo, along with Waldemar de Albuquerque d'Orey, and a few others invested the initial capital of 40 contos de réis. For more on the founding of the Banco Espírito Santo and Espírito Santo investments in Africa, see Carlos Alberto Damas, "José Maria do Espírito Santo e Silva, de cambista a banqueiro, 1869–1915," *Análise Social* (vol. XXXVII, Outono de 2002), 871–872. In 1913, José Maria do Espírito Santo Silva also invested an additional 75 contos in his business partner's trading firm, António da Costa, Limitada.

capital to found a bank, one which would grow into one of Portugal's leading banks by the 1920s, when its name changed to the Espírito Santo Bank.[109] Espírito Santo invested his own money in Cassequel, and according to one of his grandchildren, always had a strong interest in his colonial investments.[110] By October 1914—with the capital raised in Lisbon—the new company Cassequel installed a factory to turn sugarcane into semi-refined sugar (Image 1.1). In December 1914 Cassequel processed its first sugar harvest; the following year, its workers processed 1,800 tons of sugar.[111] Da Costa and his partners exported nearly all of this sugar to Portugal, where it received preferential tariff protection. The European demand for sugar had been growing for years, and because of a drop in sugar exports from the Caribbean and South America during World War I Portuguese consumers paid a premium for Angolan sugar.

Cassequel returned substantial profits for its owners during its first two years of operation. After José Espírito Santo's death on Christmas Eve, 1915, Cassequel paid dividends to his heirs in the amount of *escudos* 9,500$00 (£2,111), roughly 10 percent of the family's initial investment in 1913.[112] In 1916 alone, Cassequel paid the incredible dividends of *escudos* 142,500$00 (roughly £31,000).[113]

Cassequel's profitability resulted, in part, from access to a protected market in Portugal. In fact, the Portuguese government offered tariff incentives to the exports of its colonies dating back to 1870, when it decreed that colonial products transported on national ships would pay 50 percent of the tariffs levied on foreign imports.[114] Portugal, like other western European states, incorporated its colonies in a neo-mercantilist relationship aimed to expand markets for its national industries and to import primary products from the colonies.[115] In 1901,

109 For more on the fascinating life of the founder of one of Portugal's most important banks, see Carlos Alberto Damas and Augusto de Ataíde, *O Banco Espírito Santo uma Dinastia Financeira Portuguesa* (Lisboa: Banco Espírito Santo, 2004).

110 Author interview with José Manuel Pinheiro Espírito Santo, August 30, 2002, Lisbon.

111 José do Sacramento e Sousa, *Relatório da Alfândega de Benguela Relativo ao ano de 1915* (Lisboa: Imprensa Nacional, 1918), 70.

112 1 *escudo* (1$00) = 1 *milréis* (1$000). O Decreto-Lei de 22 de Maio de 1911 changed the monetary base from the *réis* to the *escudo*, though as late as 1913 the capital of Cassequel was quoted in *milréis*, not *escudos*.

113 "Inventario Orphanologico de José Espírito Santo e Silva, 1917," Tribunal de 1ª Instância de Lisboa, 3ª vara cível, 3° ofício. This "Inventaria Orphanologico" may be consulted in the "JMESS—Empresas Africanas," AHBES.

114 Alberto Diogo and Jorge Eduardo da Costa Oliveira, "Regime Açucareiro," *Actividade Económica de Angola* (nos 61 a 63, Setembro/Dezembro 1961 e Janeiro/Agosto 1962), 169–186.

115 For a terrific analysis of Portugal's mercantalist relationship with its colonies, see Gervase Clarence-Smith, *The Third Portuguese Empire*.

IMAGE 1.1 *New sugar refinery under construction at Cassequel, 1914.*
SOURCE: JOSÉ DE OLIVEIRA FERREIRA DINIZ, *NEGÓCIOS INDÍGENAS RELATÓRIO DO ANO DE 1914* (LOANDA: IMPRENSA NACIONAL, 1915), 81.

the government guaranteed a protective tariff to the planters of Mozambique and Angola for a period of fifteen years. After the 1911 ban on rum production, Angolan sugar producers increased production of semi-refined sugar and in 1914, for example, exported nearly 5000 tons to Portugal.[116] By 1914, Angola and Mozambique were providing a third of Portugal's sugar imports, and in that same year the government extended the tariff protection until 1933.[117] These beneficial tariffs, which would remain in place throughout the colonial period, created a favorable market for Cassequel sugar. Because of population growth, industrialization, and a growing demand for chocolate and coffee among Portuguese consumers, the demand for sugar continued to expand until the end of the colonial period in 1975.

116 The most comprehensive overview of sugar production in the Portuguese colonies is Henrique Gomes de Amorim Parreira, "História do Açúcar em Portugal," *Anais da Junta das Missões Coloniais* (no. VII, 1952), 210–309. See also Sena Sugar Estates Ltd., *Moçambique e O Problema Açucareiro* (Lisboa: Sena Sugar Estates, 1945). For an overview of sugar production in Africa, see Gervase Clarence-Smith, "O proteccionismo e a produção de açúcar na África Central e Equatorial (Angola, Moçambique, Zaire, Zimbabwe), 1910–1945," *Revista Internacional de Estudos Africanos* (nos. 4 e 5, Janeiro-Dezembro, 1986), 159–189.

117 For Portuguese policy toward sugar beet production in the Açores see Clarence-Smith, "O proteccionismo e a produção de açúcar," 162.

The second factor that explains Cassequel's profitability was access to forced labor. The plantation's rapid growth during its first couple of decades would not have been possible without sufficient numbers of workers. Cassequel's early directors complained about a local labor shortage for *voluntários* and turned to the government to supply them with *contratados* from the more populous central highlands. These workers did the physically grueling work of clearing (and in some cases desalinizing) new fields, planting, and processing biannual sugar crops.

Labor Recruitment for Cassequel

Contratados contracted for Cassequel came primarily from the central highlands to the east of Catumbela (see the regions delineated in Map 1). In 1914, a majority of Cassequel's *contratados* came from Quillengues and Gambos.[118] In Cassequel's early years, founder António da Costa likely made personal contact with individual *chefes de posto* serving in inland districts to request a certain number of *contratados*. The promised salary, length of service, and food allowance were included in the request.[119] How the *chefe de posto* acquired the requisite number of workers varied somewhat, but in most cases, he simply sent an order to the *sobas* [African chiefs] under his jurisdiction to send a certain number of men to the *posto* to fulfill their labor obligation. If a *soba* failed to fulfill the request, he faced disciplinary action, and the *chefe de posto* would then send *cipaios* [African policemen working for the Portuguese colonial state], who rounded up men indiscriminately. By the 1920s, as the Portuguese colonial administration solidified its control in the interior, there really was no choice for an individual but to do his term of service as a *contratado*. The burden fell heavily on younger men because they often did not have sufficient funds to pay their taxes: the hut tax and, from 1920, the *imposto indígena*.

Colonists and Portuguese administrators justified the forced labor system as the only solution to a perennial labor shortage. According to the colonists' newspapers, it was nearly impossible to find sufficient numbers of voluntary workers willing to work for the wages offered at the coastal plantations and fisheries. The headline "*Mão-d'Obra Indígena*" [native labor] is a constant theme of editorials in the 1910s and 1920s. The gist of the editorials is that because of

118 Ibid., 1.

119 For an example of such a request, see "Requisações de serviçães," 26 de Junho de 1921, Districto de Benguela, Folha 136, Caixa 2115, AHA.

a labor shortage, the only way to create a profitable and productive plantation agricultural sector is to use forced labor. The administrator for the Circunscrição Civil [Administrative District] of Bailundo explained how Bailundos viewed working for colonists: "The only native who will work on agricultural plantations is a forced native. The repugnance that they [natives] have for this kind of work is great."[120] It is not difficult to understand repugnance for a forced labor system that required a man to leave his home for up to a year, against his will, for virtually no pay, to perform grueling plantation work. Only deference for authority, backed by the threat of violence against one's self or his family, and the prospect of being sent even farther from home to São Tomé, compelled men to agree to the labor contract.

During Cassequel's first quarter century, at least until the late 1940s, workers walked down the escarpment from Bié, Bailundo, Balombo, and Quillengues, to Catumbela. According to Faustino Alfredo, "they descended on foot from these hills and when they arrived there (at Cassequel) they began to sing 'Tueya tumala volongingi' which [in Umbundu] means 'we came as the children of ants'."[121] Alfredo, who began working at Cassequel in 1946, remembered that walking down the escarpment was a humiliation because of the beautiful roads and the railway that could have, but did not, carry workers.[122]

Work, Wages, and Life on the Plantation

It is tempting when assessing Angolan labor history to make sweeping generalizations about the extent of forced labor without recognizing the variations in labor experiences. At Cassequel, for example, plantation administrators relied on a mixture of *contratados* and *voluntários* from the earliest days of the plantation. And, as Todd Cleveland has shown in his work on labor in the diamond mines of northeast Angola, *contratados* exercised some influence over the conditions of work.[123] At Cassequel in 1914, African workers numbered 1,700 and Europeans totaled about 40. About half of the African workers came as *contratados* from the interior without their wives and families. These men lived in work *guias* [groups] in villages dotting the plantation. They often appointed a

120 Ibid.

121 Author interview with Faustino Alfredo, Catumbela, July 5, 2001.

122 Ibid.

123 Todd Cleveland, "Rock Solid: African Laborers on the Diamond Mines of the Companhia de Diamantes de Angola (Diamang), 1917–1975" (PhD diss., University of Minnesota, 2008).

young member, usually a boy about fourteen or fifteen years old, to cook meals because he would not have been strong enough to perform the heavy labor required in the fields. These men usually constructed their own *cubatas* out of mud and grass. The remaining half, *voluntários*, lived in their own villages dotting the plantation with their families and created village and family life, including music and dance (Image 1.5).[124]

These two categories of workers experienced the work environment in distinct ways. Most importantly, *voluntários*, as their designation implies, worked at Cassequel by choice. Voluntary workers received their wages in monthly installments, which gave them some control over their living conditions. *Voluntários* earned salaries equivalent to workers on the British-owned Benguela Railway—rates that were considered the best in the colony.[125] The minimum salary set by law was *escudos* 1$20 a month,[126] thus *voluntários* at Cassequel earned more than double the legal minimum wage. *Contratados*, on the other hand, had to return to the administrative post in the interior where they were contracted to receive what was owed them after the subtraction of the *imposto indígena*. During the 1910s and 1920s, their in-kind wages consisted of a blanket and a *pano* [a bolt of cloth used as a dressing wrap] at the end of service, a weekly food allowance, including 1 kilo (2.2 pounds) of flour or beans and palm oil, plus a cup of *garapa* [sugarcane juice] with sugar at the end of each work day,[127] and some rudimentary health care during service. Cash wages were always small and paid at the completion of the contract at the home *posto* of the *contratado*. As we will learn in Chapter 3 from oral interviews with former *contratados*, more individuals did not volunteer for contract labor because of the difficulty of the work, the long absence from home, and the miniscule pay.

Cassequel's administration went out of its way to downplay any appearance of coercion. In 1914, for example, António da Costa emphasized to a visiting reporter for *O Commercio de Benguella* that Cassequel profited from an abundance of voluntary labor, with "dozens asking for work."[128] And in a sense, he was being truthful. *Voluntários* did ask for work and were not under compulsion

---

124 "A Fazenda Agricola do Cassequel," *O Commercio de Benguella* (ano III, no. 109, 27 de Março de 1914), 1. For more on Umbundu music see John T. Tucker, *Drums in the Darkness* (New York: Doran Company, 1927), 46–47.

125 "Letter from Consul-General H. Hall to Sir Edward Grey," 2.

126 Portaria Provincial No. 1:455, de 20 de Dezembro de 1912.

127 "Relatorios das Inspeções Feitas as Fazendas Agricolas e Industriaes do Dombe Grande e Egito, pela capitão medico Carlos Da Costa Araujo Chaves, Caixa 5492, Maço 10–72, Processo No. 133, AHA.

128 "A Fazenda Agricola do Cassequel," *O Commercio de Benguella* (ano III, no. 109, 27 de Março de 1914), 1.

and they made up nearly half of Cassequel's workforce. The same year, the British consul visited Cassequel and the Sugar Company of Angola in Dombe Grande. Both visitors described Cassequel as a good employer, representative of the progressive, modern thinking of the First Republic and the administration of Governor Norton de Matos. The reporter visited on payday for *voluntários* (presumably not a coincidence) and described workers receiving cash salaries of between *escudos* 2$50 and 4$50 (roughly £1) a month, with some earning as much as *escudos* 15$00 (roughly £3).[129]

According to the consul, these early voluntary workers enjoyed leeway over the number of days worked.

> Apparently the laborers are perfectly free to absent themselves from work whenever they wish to. The card of one of the men I spoke to had entries somewhat as follows: "4" (i.e., the 4th May) "5,6,8,9,12,14,15,18"—i.e., in thirteen working days he had worked nine; another had still longer intervals of absence. One I saw had No. 1 on his card, the manager called him up for me to see; he had been the first to be put on the register in April 1912 and had been on the plantation, with intervals, ever since.[130]

The flexibility evidently afforded to voluntary workers in 1914 must have reflected a certain modus operandi with African work rhythms during a period when Cassequel's managers wanted to mollify their voluntary workers because they needed their labor to expand the plantation's cultivated acreage and to harvest and process the sugar crop. An English engineer working at Dombe Grande commented that African workers, all men, were "allowed to be exceedingly, almost excessively, independent; that in carrying out a piece of work he [the English engineer] never knew whether the men who had been engaged upon it on one day would be there to go on with it on the next."[131] The engineer's exasperation underlies differing concepts of time and work. As historian Michael Adas has explained, Europeans "'went out' to cultures still closely attuned to the cycles of nature, to societies in which leisure was savored, patience was highly regarded, and everyday life moved at a pace that most Western intruders found enervating if not downright exasperating."[132] The managers sent to run Cassequel confronted their workers' concepts of time and season. European concepts of

129 Ibid.

130 "Letter from Consul-General H. Hall to Sir Edward Grey," 2.

131 "Letter from Consul-General H. Hall to Sir Edward Grey," 3.

132 Adas, *Machines as the Measure of Men*, 243. Also see discussion of Zulu and English concepts of time in Keletso E. Atkin, *The Moon Is Dead! Give Us Our Money! The Cultural*

IMAGE 1.2 *Workers planting sugarcane.*
SOURCE: SUGAR COMPANY OF ANGOLA PHOTO ALBUM, CIRCA 1920 (*IN THE PERSONAL COLLECTION OF THE LATE PROFESSOR JILL DIAS.*)

time would have likewise exasperated Africans. For most of the workers at Cassequel this would have been their first experience working according to a European clock (Images 1.2–1.3). The difference would have been most apparent to those who worked in the refinery, with its heavy machinery and regular, determined work hours. There was no task work in the factory (Image 1.4).

Contratados, who worked almost exclusively in the fields or clearing and maintaining the plantation's extensive irrigation ditches, divided their work by task.[133] In 1914, the consul met a group of four men returning from the fields at 11:00 a.m.:

> The manager informed me that they had probably done a day's work. The cutting of one row of cane, equivalent to the load of the light railway cars, is reckoned on the plantation to be a day's work for two men, and provided it is finished, it is reckoned as such at whatever hour it is finished.[134]

Origins of an African Work Ethic, Natal, South Africa, 1843–1900 (Ann Arbor: University of Michigan Press, 1993), 78–98.

133 A method of work in the fields used into the 1970s.

134 "Letter from Consul-General H. Hall to Sir Edward Grey," 2–3.

IMAGE 1.3 *Workers carrying cane*
SOURCE: SUGAR COMPANY OF ANGOLA PHOTO ALBUM, CIRCA 1920.

IMAGE 1.4 *Factory workers*
SOURCE: SUGAR COMPANY OF ANGOLA PHOTO ALBUM, CIRCA 1920.

IMAGE 1.5 *Family*
SOURCE: SUGAR COMPANY OF ANGOLA PHOTO ALBUM, CIRCA 1920.

Cutting a row of cane was exhausting and dangerous work. Workers had to make a clean cut as close to the ground as possible to preserve the part of the cane with the highest sugar content.[135] The size and sharpness of the scythe used to cut the cane posed a danger to workers as well. Serious lacerations and severed limbs did occur. Task work allowed workers to work during the coolest time of the day: the early morning from about 5:00 a.m. until noon. Others carried the cut cane from the fields to the light railway that carried cane to the factory for processing. For decades cane carriers worked at night to avoid the heat, especially during the hot season from October to the end of May, when daily temperatures crept to about 90°F.

Conclusion

During the 1890s and 1910s successive Portuguese governments—the constitutional monarchy and First Republic—worked to expand Portuguese hegemony in the interior of Angola and to make the colony a more profitable part of the overseas empire. During the same period, Angolan and foreign critics of a

135 Richard Barbosa Casqueiro, *A Cultura da Cana do Açúcar com Especial Referência ao Caso de Angola* (Lisboa: Instituto Superior de Agronomia, 1956), 115.

forced labor system they likened to slavery exerted pressure on the Portuguese to reform their labor policies. It was within this context that new labor legislation in 1899 established the principle of forced labor for both public purposes and private enterprise and enacted a government-regulated system of labor contracts to prevent the abuse of workers. Reformist governor, Norton de Matos (1912–1915) attempted to improve Portuguese administration through the creation of a native affairs department and stricter adherence to the terms of labor contracts; however, he met stiff resistance from colonists who resented efforts by government to limit their access to *contratados*.

The creation of a regulated system of forced labor that delivered *contratados* from the recently conquered central highlands to coastal plantations and fisheries served well the plantation interests in Catumbela. Colonial policy makers understood that the availability of migrant labor would be key to attracting Portuguese businessmen to invest in Angola. The government aimed to see Portuguese investment in the colony as a means of making Angola profitable for Portugal. Protective tariffs and government-supplied forced labor served as inducements for such investment and they explain the foundation of Cassequel in 1913. Cassequel's growth and development during the 1910s and 1920s epitomized what policy makers aimed to achieve through an expanding colonial economy closely tied to the metropole. The export of Cassequel sugar to Portugal contributed to national self-sufficiency in sugar: profits accrued to Portuguese investors (a serious concern in an era of neo-mercantilism); and a thriving agro-industrial enterprise in Catumbela stood for the progress of Portuguese colonialism, provided employment to thousands, and contributed to a growing Angolan market for Portuguese exports.

CHAPTER 2

Cassequel and the Estado Novo, 1921 to World War II

In 1936, Luiz de Sousa Lara, son of a pioneer businessman in Angola and owner of the Angolan Sugar Company, told a conference at Lisbon's Geographical Society:

> We remember and revere those few and unknown heroes who went out to Africa to colonize, created wealth day by day, giving up pleasure and comfort, conquered the land, and sacrificed their health living among savages in an inhospitable climate.[1]

Sousa Lara proceeded to pay homage to the settlers' courage and work "for progress, civilization, and the fatherland."[2] His comments reflected a reinvigorated commitment to Portuguese colonialism in the 1930s. Between 1920 and 1926, colonial high commissioners in Angola had been given considerable financial autonomy. Their heavy borrowing caused a financial crisis, which contributed to the military's overthrow of the democratic First Republic in 1926 and its replacement with a military dictatorship until the installation of the autocratic Estado Novo [New State] in 1932. In 1930 António Salazar, minister of finance and colonies, promulgated the Colonial Act, which ended financial autonomy for Angola and put Angolan administration firmly under the control of the Colonial Ministry in Lisbon. In 1932, Salazar became the leader of the Estado Novo, and he ruled Portugal until 1968, when he suffered a severe stroke. Salazar believed fervently in what he considered the sacred duty of the Portuguese as a colonizing people, and he used his power to provide economic incentives to encourage Portugal's small economic elite to invest in the colonies and support the colonial mission.

Ricardo Espírito Santo, who assumed the directorship of the Espírito Santo Bank in 1932, became an important ally and beneficiary of Salazar's Estado Novo policies. He increased his family's investments in Cassequel, and by the late 1930s, the Espírito Santos emerged as the company's most important

1 Luiz de Sousa Lara, *A Indústria do Açúcar na Economia do Império: Conferência Realisada na Sociedade de Geografia em 6 de Março de 1936* (Lisboa: Sociedade de Industrial de Tipografia, 1936). 16.

2 Ibid.

 | DOI 10.1163/9789004301757_004

shareholders. Espírito Santo investments in the colonies would grow to include sisal, insurance, and banking, as well as sugar. The close working relationship with Salazar and support for the Estado Novo helped the Espírito Santo Group to become one of seven large economic monopolies that controlled Portuguese banking and dominated the economy.[3] The same corporatist system that offered the large monopolies protection at home provided unhindered access in the colonies. In addition to the Espírito Santo family holdings, two other monopolies made major investments in the colonies, including the group of companies established by António Champalimaud and the Companhia União Fabril. These companies, their owners, and senior management developed and maintained a central role at the economic heart of Portuguese imperialism.[4]

Cassequel developed in the interwar years to become one of the largest, most profitable agro-industrial enterprises in Angola. The close relationship between the family and leaders of the Estado Novo helped to ensure profitable contracts and government backing for labor needs. Annual production of semirefined sugar increased fourfold from 5,000 tons in 1915 to 20,000 tons in 1940. Cassequel relied on the government to supply a growing number of *contratados* on nine- to twelve-month contract, ranging from approximately 1,000 in 1921 to 3,000 by the end of World War II. Throughout the 1930s and early 1940s sugar exports remained the fourth most profitable Angola export after diamonds, coffee, and maize.[5] It is not an exaggeration to say that during these years, Cassequel epitomized the highest hopes of Portugal's colonial policy in Angola. As a wholly Portuguese owned enterprise, Cassequel's processing of sugarcane into refined sugar and alcohol and its vertically integrated operation stood out as among the most technically advanced industries in Angola. The dividends it paid shareholders vindicated those leaders who insisted Angola would benefit Portugal.

In 1938, President General Carmona made the first visit of a Portuguese head of state to an African colony. His itinerary included stops at Lobito and an afternoon at Cassequel. His motorcade entered Catumbela through an honor guard of khaki-clad *contratados* waving Portuguese flags. Cassequel's administrators entertained the presidential party with lunch in As Palmeirinhas (the little palms), an old property on the plantation surrounded by lush gardens and oil palms, along

3 M. Anne Pitcher, *Politics in the Portuguese Empire: The State, Industry, and Cotton 1926–1974* (Oxford: Clarendon Press, 1993), 218.

4 Norrie Macqueen, *The Decolonization of Portuguese Africa Metropolitan Revolution and the Dissolution of Empire* (London and New York: Longman, 1997), 51.

5 "'A Obra Administrativa da Ditadura Em Angola' Governo do Senhor Coronel do E.M. Eduardo Ferreira Viana durante o periodo de 1931 a 1934. Elementos fornecidos por diferentes Servicos Publicos da Colonia," Maço 2, Folder 929, AHU.

with Portuguese managers, their wives, and local dignitaries. The visit symbolized Cassequel's prominent place in the New State's colonial policy. The President cited Cassequel to assembled guests as an example of Portugal's work to "transform this important region—that only thirty years ago was practically all just forest—through cultivation and industrialization."[6] He also referenced the state's support of Cassequel through legislation, thus underpinning the close relationship and emphasizing their shared goal to develop Portuguese Angola.

In many respects, the change in government from the democratic First Republic to the authoritarian Estado Novo made little difference to Africans who experienced forced labor under both regimes. In the 1920s the Temporary Slavery Commission of the League of Nations sent American sociology professor Edward Ross to investigate labor conditions in Angola; his report documenting Angolan forced labor contributed to the drafting of the 1930 Forced Labor Convention, which leaders of the Estado Novo refused to sign. Instead the Estado Novo maintained the labor regulations of the First Republic and refused to abandon forced labor. In its efforts to improve efficiency and better regulate and control Angolan administration, the New State formulated the Indigenato, which structured relations between *indígenas* [natives] and *não-indígenas* [non-natives]. An example of this regulation was the requirement that all male *indígenas* fourteen years and older carry a *caderneta indígena* [native booklet], which contained his tax record, work history, and identifying information.[7] An *indígena* had to show his *caderneta* upon request by a white official and could not move from one district to another without permission. Controls such as the *caderneta* combined with draconian press censorship and laws prohibiting political associations in the colonies suppressed the dissemination of ideas critical of the status quo. In order to understand the rise of the Estado Novo, it is necessary to understand the economic and political chaos that characterized the First Republic during the 1920s.

Politics and Legislation: Norton de Matos

After World War I, the First Republic decided to deliver on promises to devolve more power to colonial administrators in the colonies and thus created the

6 *Boletim Geral das Colónias* (no. 162, 1938), 362. Cited in Gonçalo Inocentes, *As Cheias do Rio Catumbela* (Self-Published, 2012), 104–105.

7 Portaria n.° 4950, December 19, 1942. Cited in Cláudia Castelo, *Passagens para África: O Povoamento de Angola e Moçambique com Naturais da Metrópole (1920–1974)* (Porto: Edições Afrontamento, 2007), 285.

new position of high commissioner to replace the old governor-general. The high commissioner controlled the armed forces stationed in Angola, could rule by decree, and exercised an unprecedented financial autonomy.[8] The first high commissioner was José Norton de Matos, who had served previously as governor from 1912 to 1915 (see Chapter 1). In 1921, Norton de Matos returned to Angola and initiated an ambitious development program to spend £13 million on infrastructure projects, financed by borrowing money from English banks and the Belgian-controlled diamond concession company Diamang, the wealthiest and most powerful company in Angola.[9] To pay for his plans, Norton de Matos ordered the Banco Nacional Ultramarino [The Bank of the Colonies] in Luanda to print more paper money, which led to rapid inflation. Norton de Matos resigned at the end of 1923 in response to escalating debts and a spiraling rate of inflation. By the end of 1923, the cost of living in Luanda had risen forty to forty-five times in comparison to 1914.[10] The runaway inflation led to a closure of the ports and restriction on transference of money out of the colony. Nevertheless, Norton de Matos doubled the colony's road network—built primarily by forced labor—to 21,251 miles, founded the new city of Nova Lisboa in the central highlands, and did much to develop Angola's infrastructure.

In addition to implementing a massive infrastructure investment, Norton de Matos attempted to regulate the forced labor system as he had attempted to do during his earlier stint as governor in 1912–15 (see Chapter 1). Almost as soon as he reached Luanda in 1921, he issued Decree 40, outlawing per-head payments from private employers to *chefes de posto*. In the introduction to the legislation, he beseeched colonists to encourage Africans to work for wages without resorting to coercion. He argued that the solution to attracting sufficient voluntary labor included the payment of fair wages, the provision of nutritious food, and the creation of good work conditions.[11] Colonists and

8 Malyn Newitt, *Portugal in Africa The Last Hundred Years* (London: C. Hurst & CO., 1981), 77.

9 The Belgian Société Générale controlled Diamang in association with its French associate, the Banque de l'Union Parisienne, two American groups (Ryan and Guggenheim), and two South African groups (Anglo-American and Barnato Brothers). See Gervase Clarence-Smith, *The Third Portuguese Empire, 1825–1975: A Study in Economic Imperialism* (Manchester: Manchester University Press, 1985), 129. For more on the inner workings of Diamang, see Todd Cleveland, "Rock Solid: African Laborers on the Diamond Mines of the Companhia de Diamantes de Angola (Diamang), 1917–1975" (PhD diss., University of Minnesota, 2008).

10 Armindo Monteiro, "O Problema das Transferências de Angola," *Boletim da Agência Geral das Colónias* (no. 7, ano 7, Julho de 1931), 50.

11 Alto Comissariado da República, "Decreto No. 40," Caixa 2115, AHA. There is an English translation in British Consul-General A.B. Hutcheon, Angola August 12, 1922, Dispatch No. 41, FO 371/7211, PRO.

Angolan business associations responded by criticizing Decree 40 as unworkable.[12] An editorial in the *Jornal de Benguela* argued, "The labor question is the 'eternal question' in all colonies, whether of Portugal or foreign powers...better or worse regulation will not make a difference because at the end of the day no African colony is able to obtain labor without coercion."[13] Decree 40 remained on the books, but as Edward Ross concluded "the decree exists only on paper, not in reality."[14]

Norton de Matos also reorganized the Negócios Indígenas [Native Affairs Department], which he had founded in 1913. It had not produced a report since 1916 and had no investigative capacity. In 1923, Norton de Matos created a special investigatory service consisting of three inspectors in the Department of Native Affairs to inspect conditions of contract labor recruitment and working conditions, but the positions were not funded because of lack of support after the high commissioner's resignation at the end of the year.[15] Whatever his failings as an administrator, the resignation of Norton de Matos ended the most serious attempt to protect African rights until the reforms enacted in reaction to the start of the nationalist war for independence in 1961.[16]

Salazar and the Estado Novo

Cleaning up the Angolan financial crisis was an important part of the agenda of the military officers who overthrew the First Republic in a bloodless coup on May 28, 1926. The instability of the parliamentary system—there were forty-five governments between 1910 and 1926—coupled with high inflation led to widespread dissatisfaction among the Portuguese people. In addition, many in Portuguese society resented particular reforms of the First Republic, such as the separation of church and state. The new military government instituted the Ditadura Nacional [National Dictatorship], which would later be renamed

12 Cláudia Castelo, *Passagens para África*, 333.

13 Editorial, "Mão de Obra," *Jornal de Benguela* (no. 29, 22 July 1921).

14 Edward Alsworth Ross, *Report on the Employment of Native Labor in Portuguese Africa* (New York: The Abbott Press, 1925), 21.

15 Decreto do Alto Comissariado, No. 265, de 16 de Marco de 1923, *Boletim Oficial de Angola* (no. 14, 1st series, 1923).

16 For a more critical view of Norton de Matos's record on African rights than my own, see Douglas L. Wheeler, "Angola and the Republic, 1910–1926" in Douglas L. Wheeler and René Pélissier, *Angola* (New York: Praeger Publishers, 1971), 114–115.; and Douglas L. Wheeler, "José Norton de Matos (1867–1955)," in L.H. Gann and Peter Duignan, eds., *African Proconsuls Europeans Governors in Africa* (New York: The Free Press, 1978), 445–463.

the Estado Novo [New State]. The new government deployed fascist methods of governance and promoted nationalism as a means to unifying the population.[17] The new nationalism exalted the colonial empire as an historic inheritance of the Portuguese nation. Colonial plantation interests represented by the Grémio dos Produtores de Açucar Colonial [Association of Colonial Sugar Producers] favored the overthrow of the democratic First Republic and worked closely with the dictatorship.[18]

The military leaders of the coup wasted no time in addressing the two principal causes of the economic crisis in Angola: the instability of the currency because of runaway inflation and the lack of credit.[19] New legislation in 1926 created the Bank of Angola, which would serve as the sole bank of issuance in the colony.[20] In addition to the new Bank of Angola, the government created a Currency Board of Angola (*Junta da Moeda de Angola*) based in Lisbon to monitor currency circulation in Angola.[21] These reforms led to the creation of a new currency, the *angolar*, which was given a fixed parity of two-thirds the value of a metropolitan *escudo*.[22] The reforms succeeded in controlling inflation and restored stability, but the controls made credit difficult to obtain and gave administrators in Angola little power to raise revenue or invest in infrastructure.

In 1928, the military leaders of the dictatorship asked António Salazar, then a professor of economics at Coimbra, Portugal's oldest and most prestigious university, to lead the Ministry of Finance. Salazar set out to make Angola an economic asset to the metropole. The immediate task was to make Angola conform to the basic economic strategy he had adopted for Portugal. This strategy focused on the reduction of government deficits, the elimination of floating debt, and the payment of all current expenditures from revenue. These measures aimed to reduce interest rates, stabilize the exchange rate and halt inflation. As far as the colonies were concerned, the initial target was to produce balanced budgets and make the colonies self-financing. In a context of tight monetary policy and strict regulation (measures taken to ensure that

17 Pitcher, *Politics in the Portuguese Empire*, 9–10.

18 Douglas Wheeler, *Republican Portugal: A Political History, 1910–1926* (Madison: University of Wisconsin Press, 1978), 210.

19 Alto Comissariado da Província de Angola, *Regime Monetário e Bancário e Bancário da Província de Angola* (Lisboa: Imprensa Nacional, 1926), 4.

20 On the Banco Nacional Ultramarino in Mozambique, see Leroy Vail and Landeg White, *Capitalism and Colonialism in Mozambique* (Minneapolis: University of Minnesota Press, 1980), 202–205.

21 Monteiro, "O Problema das Transferências," 61.

22 Alto Comissariado da Província de Angola, *Regime Monetário e Bancário e Bancário da Província de Angola* (Lisboa: Imprensa Nacional, 1926), 21.

Angola served the economic interests of Portugal), foreign imports became more expensive, taxes ensured advantages for Portuguese imports, and forced labor became an important strategy for extracting wealth from Angola. Leaders of the Estado Novo such as Armindo Monteiro, diplomat and minister, informed colonists that they would have to sacrifice and put Portuguese interests above their own because the necessities of the day required an "intense nationalism."[23] In other words, budgets for infrastructure and services would be reduced, imports and exports closely regulated, and credit tight and expensive. Monteiro did not speak to Africans, who were considered outside the boundaries of the Portuguese nation; ironically, it would be Africans—who made up more than 98 percent of Angola's roughly three million people and bore the brunt of low wages, lack of services, and forced labor—who would make the most sacrifices. In 1920, only 20,700 whites lived in Angola.[24]

In 1930, Salazar promulgated the Colonial Act, which instituted a new type of administration for Angola: centralized, hierarchical, and ultranationalist.[25] Salazar aimed to create a clear hierarchy to subordinate Angola to the interests of Portugal. The act eliminated the position of high commissioner and replaced it with a colonial governor with curtailed powers. The colony's budget was based on a strict balance of payments and needed approval from the colonial minister in Lisbon. Angola could not contract loans on its own, and the government in Lisbon controlled the currency, which meant that exports had to be shipped via Lisbon, which would then absorb foreign currency. In 1931, a pool system for foreign exchange was established with the government issuing import licenses on a basis of political priorities. It was a determined effort to bring the whole commercial economy under state control and, aided as it was by the crisis situation in the colonies, it was largely successful. The shift toward more protectionist trade policies was not unique to Portugal. In fact, as the depression of the 1930s hurt metropolitan economies, all the European colonial powers adopted a similar system of neo-mercantilist policies.[26] Cassequel received an annual quota for its exports of semirefined sugar to Portugal, where refining took place before distribution across the country. Profits were realized in Portugal and in Portuguese currency, with only the necessary funds transferred to Angola for running the company. The reliance on forced labor for

23 Monteiro, "O Problema das Transferências," 61.

24 Castelo, *Passagens para África*, 174.

25 Castelo, *Passagens para África*, 63.

26 Ralph A. Austen, *African Economic History: Internal Development and External Dependency* (London: James Currey, 1987), 203.

much of the plantation's labor needs and the relatively low wages paid to voluntary workers contributed to Cassequel's profitability and to achieving Salazar's goals of national self-sufficiency in semiprocessed foodstuffs such as sugar.

Salazar used the colonies to help construct his nationalist program along the lines of corporativism.[27] Under Salazar, corporativism asserted the state's role as arbiter among the various interest groups of society. Each interest was organized into a collective association, with employers forming *gremios* [societies] and workers *sindicatos* [unions]. The government arbitrated any conflicts.[28] Corporativism provided Salazar's Estado Novo with an ideology, one expressed in sponsored events such as the Exposição Colonial Portuguesa [Portuguese Colonial Exposition] held at Porto in 1934 and the Exposição do Mundo Português [Portuguese World Exposition] in Lisbon in 1940.

The Portuguese World Exposition aimed to boost trade, garner popular support for the colonial empire, and create an imperial mystique.[29] Henrique Galvão, then director of the Portuguese Colonial Exposition, declared the exposition a great success for instructing the Portuguese people about the importance of the colonies in balancing Portugal's chronic budget deficits. Propagandistic images (Image 2.1) reinforced an imperial mythology harking back to the Age of Discovery when Portuguese mariners discovered sea routes to Asia and circumnavigated the globe.[30] The message *Portugal não é pequeno* [Portugal is not small] was reinforced by the superimposition of the Portuguese colonies over a map of Europe and thus celebrated the idea of empire while cultivating support among the Portuguese public for colonialism.

In another attempt to boost nationalistic pride in the colonies, the Estado Novo lionized colonial explorers and settlers, erecting monuments in their honor throughout Angola. Naming became another popular form of commemoration; African place names were replaced throughout Angola by Portuguese names, which often commemorated these same pioneers and

27 Francisco Bethencourt and Kirti Chaudhuri, eds., *História da Expansão Portuguesa: Último Império e Recentramento (1930–1998)*, Vol. 5 (Navarra, Spain: Temas e Debates e Autores, 2000), 12.

28 Perry Anderson, "Portugal and the End of Ultra-Colonialism," *New Left Review* (no. 15, May/June 1962), 88–89. For a comprehensive explanation of corporativism as theorized by the Salazar regime, see Dr. Pedro Teotónio Pereira, *Organização Corporativa* (Lisboa: Edições SPN, 1935).

29 Eugénia Mata e Nuno Valério, *História Económica de Portugal: Uma Perspectiva Global* (Lisboa: Editorial Presença, 1993), 193.

30 Bethencourt and Chaudhuri, Eds., *História da Expansão Portuguesa*, Vol. V, 27.

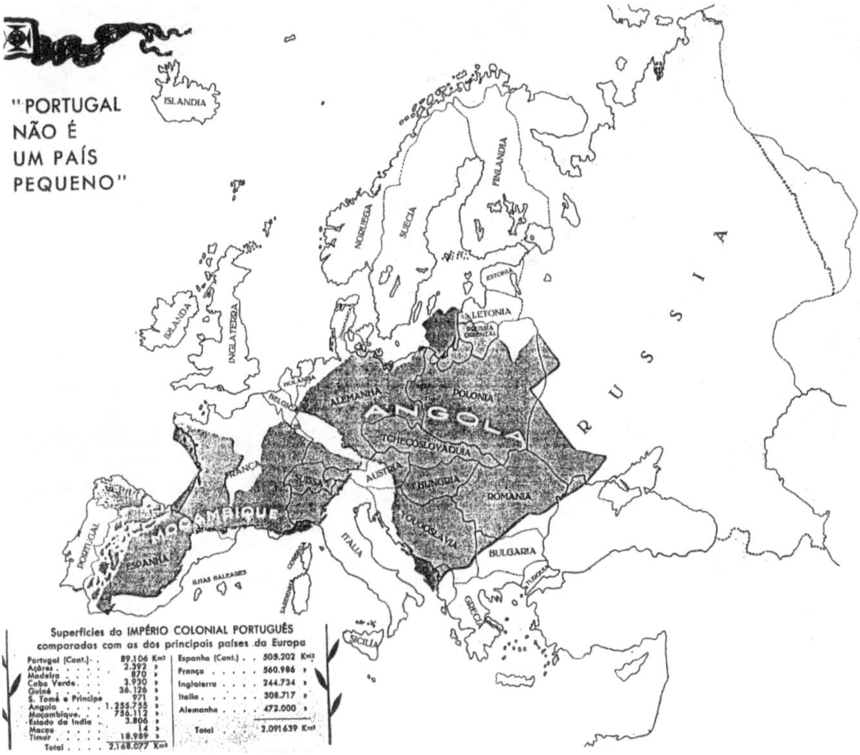

IMAGE 2.1 *Portugal não é pequeno*
SOURCE: HENRIQUE GALVÃO, *ÁLBUM COMEMORATIVO DA PRIMEIRA EXPOSIÇÃO COLONIAL PORTUGUESA* (PORTO: IMPRENSA NACIONAL, 1935), 5.

settlers.[31] The architecture of the monument honoring the nineteenth-century Portuguese explorer Silva Porto, in the city of the same name, is a case in point (Image 2.2). The distinctive *calçada Portuguesa* [Portuguese sidewalk] depicts scenes of African animals and Silva Porto as a hunter and explorer. In the foreground two African men carry what looks to be a dead elk. The statue depicts Silva Porto in motion in a modernist style common among monuments built by the Estado Novo. The words at the foot, "Travessia da Africa 1857," commemorate the explorer's crossing of the continent in 1857.

31 For example, the town of Bocoio became Villa de Sousa Lara, Balombo became Villa de Norton de Matos, and Lubango became Sá de Bandeira, all names of colonial settlers and officials. For an interesting perspective on colonial memory, see the special edition of *Cadernos de Estudos Africanos*, "Memórias Coloniais" (no. 9/10, Julho 2005/Junho 2006).

IMAGE 2.2 *Silva Porto Monument in Silva Porto [Kuito]*
SOURCE: COTA DME/PO/A-*/029, ARQUIVO DE FOTOGRAFIA DE LISBOA, NO DATE.

Cassequel and the Estado Novo

During the financial uncertainty of the 1920s and 1930s, Cassequel's expanding production and profitability earned it a reputation as one of Angola's most important companies.[32] The fact that Portuguese shareholders owned the bulk of company stock made the company an important asset in the eyes of the nationalistic leaders of the Estado Novo. Cassequel's profitability during the international depression of the 1930s resulted from its protected market in Portugal and the granting in 1932 of the Angolan monopoly for the distillation of industrial and absolute alcohol, which was blended with petroleum (one part alcohol to three parts petroleum) to make a biofuel called "Cassecol." Cassecol was sold throughout Angola and aimed to reduce the colony's need for imported oil (see Appendix for Cassequel's dividends and profits for select years between 1916 and 1971). Cassequel built a new distillery in 1935 to meet

32 In 1927, after having been absorbed into the Sociedade Agrícola da Ganda for nine years, the Sociedade Agrícola do Cassequel was reconstituted as a separate company with its own bylaws and board of directors. The reconstituted Cassequel had £300,000 in capital, divided into 300,000 shares valued at £1 each. The statutes for the Sociedade Agricola do Cassequel, Limited, were published in the *Jornal de Benguela*, (April 8, 1927).

the demand. Cooperation between the Espírito Santo family and Salazar dates to 1930 when Cassequel's founder, António da Costa, and another major shareholder named Bernardino Alves Correia used Cassequel as collateral to cover other money-losing investments.

In 1930, Correia and da Costa contracted two loans in the names of companies they controlled: the Companhia Colonial de Navegação[33] [Colonial Shipping Company], the Sociedade Agricola da Ganda, the Sociedade Agricola de Cassequel, and the Companhia do Amboim.[34] The first loan, concluded on April 18, 1930 for 20,000,000$00 *escudos*. The signatories, Correia and Da Costa, used Cassequel's 1930 harvest, with an estimated value of 16,500,00$00 *escudos*, as collateral. The second loan, concluded on June 30, 1930 for 27,000,000$00 *escudos*, used Cassequel's property holdings as collateral.[35] The second loan went to pay off loans made previously by the Banque des Colonies based in Brussels and the Banque Credit Commercial based in Anvers to the Sociedade Agricola da Ganda and the Companhia do Amboim. In other words, Correia and da Costa borrowed using the 1930 harvest and assets of Cassequel as collateral in order to pay off debts accrued by other companies in their portfolios.

When other members of the board of directors, and most notably José Espírito Santo, learned about the loans, they forced Correia to resign.[36] According to an audit ordered by the board of directors following the loan scandal, "the loans [would] lead the Sociedade Agrícola do Cassequel to ruin."[37] The audit concluded that the loans were channeled to bankrupt companies and "sacrificed the life and prosperity of the Sociedade Agrícola do Cassequel."[38] The bankruptcy of one of Angola's largest and most profitable businesses during a period of economic restructuring worried Portuguese leaders and added to the urgency to save Cassequel from bankruptcy. Portuguese leaders feared

---

33 Correia founded the Companhia Colonial de Navegação in 1922 to service his agricultural properties in Angola and even named one of the steam ships *Cassequel*.

34 "Coorespondência sobre as seguintes questões: Companhias coloniais—Sociedade Agricola do Cassequel, 1930–1934; 1940–1941," AOS/CO/UL-8, Arquivo Salazar, ANTT, 452–479.

35 Both loans were contracted from the Caixa Nacional do Credito, the National Credit Bank.

36 "Copia da acta da reunião do Conselho de Administração da Sociedade Agricola do Cassequel realisada no dia 20 de Agosto de 1930," "Coorespondência sobre as seguintes questões: Companhias coloniais—Sociedade Agricola do Cassequel, 1930–1934; 1940–1941," AOS/CO/UL-8, Arquivo Salazar, ANTT, 85.

37 Octavio da Fonseca Brito and J. Mattos Rodrigues, "Memorial," "Coorespondência sobre as seguintes questões: Companhias coloniais—Sociedade Agricola do Cassequel, 1930–1934; 1940–1941," AOS/CO/UL-8, Arquivo Salazar, ANTT, 495.

38 Ibid., 497.

that Correia and da Costa's reckless borrowing would scare off Portuguese investors from investing scarce national capital in the colonies and that bankruptcy would lead to further Belgian inroads and the denationalization of Angola.[39] Salazar, in his dual capacity as minister of finance and colonies, saved Cassequel with an emergency loan from the Caixa Geral dos Depósitos, the state savings bank.[40]

The specter of Cassequel's bankruptcy would have damaged Salazar's efforts to encourage Portuguese capitalists to invest in the colonies. Between 1870 and 1936, more than three-fourths of the private capital invested in Angola came from British and Belgian sources.[41] Salazar aimed to increase the Portuguese share of this investment as part of his campaign to integrate the metropole and colonies, using the colonies to aggrandize how the Portuguese viewed their nation. Cassequel's Portuguese stockholders epitomized Salazar's nationalist agenda for colonial investment. Outside of trade and shipping, Portuguese capitalists had been reluctant to invest in the colonies; hence, Salazar needed Cassequel to serve as a successful model of colonial investment.[42] The corporatist philosophy also emphasized cooperation between the government and Portuguese business, so intervention indicated the sort of working relationship Salazar promoted between government and the business community. The prominence of members of Cassequel's board of directors, especially José Espírito Santo, who also headed one of Portugal's leading banks, must surely have influenced Salazar's decision to intervene.

In spite of his role in the fraudulent loans, António da Costa managed to remain on the board of directors and held on to his large investment in Cassequel stock. Correia resigned his position on the board of directors and his name no longer appeared on the scattered lists of stockholders available after 1930. Cassequel paid off the loans throughout the 1930s and 1940s from its annual profits while still paying dividends to shareholders, and by the 1950s, the payments no longer appeared in company records. In a 1940 letter to Salazar, Ricardo Espírito Santo, who replaced his elder brother as president of

39 Ibid., 499–500. White settlers also resented the presence of foreign capital. On this point, see Clarence-Smith, *The Third Portuguese Empire*, 129–134. For steps taken to support Portuguese capital in Mozambique, see Malyn Newitt, *A History of Mozambique* (London: Hurst & Company, 1995), 458–459.

40 Octavio da Fonseca Brito and J. Mattos Rodrigues, "Memorial," "Coorespondência sobre as seguintes questões: Companhias coloniais—Sociedade Agricola do Cassequel, 1930–1934; 1940–1941," AOS/CO/UL-8, Arquivo Salazar, ANTT, 495.

41 S. Herbert Frankel, *Capital Investment in Africa: Its Course and Effects* (London: Oxford University Press, 1938), 158–159.

42 Clarence-Smith, *The Third Portuguese Empire*, 128.

the Banco Espírito Santo in 1932 and assumed the presidency of Cassequel's board of directors, attributed Cassequel's rapid progress in paying off the loan "to the sacrifices of her shareholders."[43] Ricardo Espírito Santo went on to become one of the most important Portuguese bankers of his era, and he served as president of Cassequel's board of directors for most years between 1932 and his death in 1955.[44]

Moreover, Salazar's protective tariffs—prohibitive taxes levied against sugar from outside the Portuguese empire—made sugar a lucrative business for its owners. In 1927, 90 percent of the Portuguese market, or 77,000 tons, was reserved for colonial sugar, and colonial sugar producers supplied 80,000 tons of refined sugar, with 66,000 tons from Mozambique and 14,000 tons from Angola. In 1928, Minister of Finance Salazar decided that the Mozambican share of the quota was unjust to Angolan producers; the Angola share was increased to 25,000 tons and the Mozambican share was lowered.[45] The move was widely interpreted as indicative of Salazar's policies, which encouraged the Portuguese-owned Angolan sugar industry to succeed while curtailing the primarily foreign-owned Mozambican sugar industry. Angolan sugar production grew dramatically during the 1930s and by the 1940s produced two-thirds as much as Mozambique.[46]

The importance of imperial protection was made clear in 1930, when a glut on the international sugar market led to a sharp decline in world sugar prices. In response, Salazar raised duties to such an extent that foreign sugar cost more than colonial sugar. This legislation ensured profits for Portugal's colonial sugar producers during a period of increasingly low sugar prices on the international market. For example, in 1936, the price for colonial sugar entering the Portuguese market was fixed at 15 pounds sterling per metric ton, whereas the price on the world market was a mere 5 pounds sterling.[47] The sugar quota insured that whatever the international price for sugar, ninety percent of the Portuguese market would be reserved for colonial producers at fixed prices.

43 Ricardo Espírito Santo Silva to Salazar, "Coorespondência sobre as seguintes questões: Companhias coloniais—Sociedade Agricola do Cassequel, 1930–1934; 1940–1941," AOS/CO/UL-8, Arquivo Salazar, ANTT, 698–702.

44 Carlos Alberto Damas and Augusto de Ataíde, *O Banco Espírito Santo uma Dinastia Financeira Portuguesa 1869–1973* (Lisboa: Banco Espírito Santo, Centro de Estudos da História, 2004), 220–227.

45 Gervase Clarence-Smith, "O Proteccionismo e a Produção de Açúcar na África Central e Equatorial (Angola, Moçambique, Zaire, Zimbabwe), 1910–1945," *Revista Internacional de Estudos Africanos* (nos. 4 e 5, Janeiro-Dezembro, 1986), 165.

46 Vail and White, *Capitalism and Colonialism in Mozambique*, 257–260.

47 Clarence-Smith, "O Proteccionismo e a Produção de Açúcar," 166.

Foreign sugar entering the Portuguese market was taxed to such an extent as to make it as costly as colonial sugar. This system resulted in higher sugar prices for Portuguese consumers and substantial profits for colonial sugar producers.[48] By 1936, there were an estimated 770 *contos* invested in the sugar industry in the Portuguese colonies, which made sugar one of the most important colonial industries.[49]

In 1936, Luiz de Sousa Lara, director of the Companhia de Açúcar de Angola, described the importance of the Angolan sugar industry for the Portuguese economy:

> The economic, financial, and political influence that such an important industry exercises in the Colonies and in the Metropole is truly extraordinary, and it would not be impertinent to say that if the country profits from the development of lucrative industries in the Colonies, still greater is the profit when an increment [in the sugar quota] is given to Angola where commerce is overwhelmingly conducted by Portuguese merchants, with Portuguese capital, whose business is almost exclusively with the marketplaces of Lisbon and Porto, hence profits from development obtained in Angola reach the Metropole.[50]

Sousa Lara's comments reflected exactly Salazar's neomercantilist goals for colonial integration with and subordination to the national economy.

Portugal was not alone in protecting its sugar producers from foreign competition. Most European countries, for example, protected their sugar producers, whether colonial cane producers or metropolitan sugar beet producers. This international movement for protection surely influenced Salazar's 1930 sugar policy, which also met a number of political goals important to the Estado Novo.[51] First, self-sufficiency in sugar saved foreign exchange; second, it provided the necessary protection for colonial sugar producers to thrive; third, it contributed to the development of the colonies; and, finally, it led to the

---

48 Alberto Diogo and Jorge Eduardo da Costa Oliveira, "Regime Açucareiro," *Actividade Económica de Angola* (no. 61 a 63, Setembro/Dezembro 1961 e Janeiro/Agosto 1962), 170.

49 Luiz de Sousa Lara, *A Indústria do Açúcar na Economia do Império Conferência Realisada na Sociedade de Geografia em 6 de Março de 1936* (Lisboa: Sociedade Industrial de Tipografia, 1936), 17.

50 Ibid.

51 In 1936, Luiz de Sousa Lara published a pamphlet that argued that protecting colonial sugar producers was necessary because, in essence, everyone else was doing it, and because colonial sugar was a benefit for the colonies and thus the nation. See Sousa Lara, *A Indústria do Açúcar na Economia do Império.*

settlement of hundreds of Portuguese families in the colonies. Colonial sugar producers used these political objectives as leverage when negotiating the price of sugar.[52]

In this context, colonial sugar producers argued that the sugar industry benefited not only the national economy but also the social welfare of thousands of Portuguese and African workers. In 1936, Luiz de Sousa Lara estimated that the colonial sugar industry employed 50,000 Africans, for whom employers annually "purchased tens of kilometers worth of textiles and thousands of blankets" from Portuguese manufacturers.[53] The social mission of the major plantations, according to Sousa Lara, included building Catholic chapels, schools, hospitals, housing, and recreational facilities.[54] Sousa Lara couched the sugar companies' social welfare mission in both the paternalism of colonialism and Portuguese tradition.

Throughout the 1920s and 1930s, sugar remained the fourth most valuable Angolan export, after coffee, diamonds, and maize. Colonial sugar producers understood that their industry depended on the protected Portuguese market. Cassequel's annual report to shareholders for 1941 acknowledged that the expansion during recent years "was possible thanks to the providential politics of protection for colonial sugar established by our government."[55] The value of sugar exports as a percentage of Angolan exports reached a high of nearly 14 percent in 1939, while the domestic Angolan market continued to increase and was almost entirely supplied by Angolan sugar producers. This expansion necessitated increases in Cassequel's labor needs. To meet these requirements, Cassequel's administrators turned to forced labor supplied by the colonial government.

Forced Labor Recruitment at Cassequel

The consolidation of Portuguese administration throughout Angola by 1920 led to the imposition of a new *imposto indígena* [native tax] in 1921, which replaced the old hut tax and required all African men to meet their tax obligation in Portuguese currency. High rates of inflation and a paucity of specie during the

52 See, for example, SAC, "Relatorio da Visita ao Cassequel em Junho de 1954, Presidente do Conselho da Administracao," *Correspondencia diversos do Administrador Exmo. Senhor Eng. Vasco Moneteiro*, AC, 6.

53 Sousa Lara, *A Indústria do Açúcar na Economia do Império*, 18.

54 Ibid., 20.

55 SAC, *Relatório e Contas*, 1941, 2.

1920s in particular made payment of salaries and taxes more difficult. The new tax aimed to raise needed revenue for the Angolan treasury and to serve as an indirect means of pushing African men into contract labor. The tax system, coupled with more effective and extensive colonial administration, created a network of labor extraction funneling *contratados* from the more densely populated central highlands to the coastal fisheries and plantations. In other words, labor recruitment from the 1920s through 1940s operated much like it had in the 1910s, but with more efficiency.

The failed tenure of Norton de Matos as high commissioner, the overthrow of the First Republic, and the implementation of the Estado Novo discredited and silenced free labor advocates in Angola and Portugal. With the exception of the Ross Report in 1924, which colonists and the Portuguese government dismissed as foreign propaganda, Portuguese labor policies did not elicit sustained international concern. Portugal refused to sign the 1930 Forced Labor Convention, and the Estado Novo effectively banned political opposition. Foreign missionaries working in Angola were among the few who documented labor abuses during the inter-war years. In 1944, two Canadian missionaries in Angola described "a definite and concerted attempt…to put all natives, educated and uneducated, into a labor pool in the hands of the officials and make it impossible for anyone to employ labor freely contracted."[56] The missionaries judged that since the establishment of the Estado Novo labor conditions had deteriorated, and "since the year 1940 the degeneration has been catastrophic."[57]

As it had been from the late nineteenth century forward, the "labor problem" was a common subject in editorials and settler delegations to officials. In an address to the Geographical Society in 1936, Luiz de Sousa Lara explained that one of the greatest threats to the colonial sugar industry was "the difficult and always delicate problem of native labor."[58] For many colonists, convinced of their duty to "civilize" Angolans and develop the colony, the labor problem justified legal mechanisms such as forced labor and corporal punishment. White settlers also often lacked capital and had a difficult time paying workers; thus, they fought to retain their right to benefit from forced labor.[59]

---

56 "Letter from Tucker and Scott to Foreign Office," Document 4887, FO 371/39583, PRO, 2. The same letter describes how Ovimbundu call the sugar plantation "Bom Jesus" (Good Jesus) "Ombulutu," from the Portuguese word *bruto* (brutal). The name indicated the brutal treatment workers received at Bom Jesus.

57 Ibid.

58 Sousa Lara, *A Indústria do Açúcar na Economia do Império*, 17.

59 Cláudia Castelo, *Passagens para* África, 332–334.

To meet its labor needs, Cassequel's administration worked with colonial administrators from the governor to local *chefes de posto* in the interior districts. By the 1920s, Cassequel's director sent detailed requests for *contratados* to the provincial governor. The governor then sent labor requests to individual *chefes de posto* in interior districts, who then requested a given number of *contratados* from *sobas* and *seculos* under his jurisdiction. Contracts consisted of entering a worker's personal information in a book called a *Registo de Contractos de Serviçais* [Register of Workers' Contracts]. Personal information included the date of the contract, name, the name of the worker's father and mother, *sobado* [chieftaincy], administrative post, length of the contract, type of work, post where the contract was signed, monthly salary, and employer.[60] Once the requisite number of workers had been "recruited," the *chefe de posto*, working in his capacity as *curador*, verified that workers assented to their "contract" without being forcibly compelled to do so. This arrangement ultimately constituted forced labor because the men were given no choice; they were simply ordered to report to the *chefe de posto* to fulfill their labor obligation. If they failed to comply, the *chefe de posto* sent policemen to bring the men to the *posto* in chains. For example, on April 21, 1927, the *curador* of the administrative post of Sambo contracted 222 men for ten months to Cassequel at 30 *angolares* a month.[61] Although workers did not sign or mark the contracts, the fact that the *curador* entered the names of their parents and *sobado* indicated that the *curador* spoke to each man. Ultimately, these contracts served a dual purpose of providing the appearance of consent and giving the authorities useful information should the *contratado* flee his contract.

Fostering a close working relationship with government officials became one of the strategies employed by Cassequel's administrators to secure the requisite number of *contratados* needed in a given year. In a 1926 letter, Cassequel's director asked his bosses in Lisbon to "maintain a permanent contact with individual authorities" to ease Cassequel's access to forced labor.[62] Indeed, Cassequel's administrators had worked with the colonial administration to supply their labor needs from the company's early years, but the relationship grew closer during the interwar years.[63] During the 1920s, António da Costa relied on

60 Curadoria Geral de Angola, *Registo de Contractos de Serviçães*, Códice n. 10848, Cota 10-4-25, AHA.

61 Ibid.

62 Letter to Directors in Lisbon March 8, 1926, *Copybook marked Confidential, 1926–1935*, AC, 13.

63 "Relatório do Exercício de 1932/1933 apresentado pelo Director em Africa Francisco Regado," Cassequel, Abril de 1933, AC, 46.

colonial authorities in favored recruitment districts to supply *contratados*. Company correspondence does not mention cash payments to colonial officials, but observers argued that kickbacks to colonial administrators kept the labor wheel turning.[64] For example, in 1926, da Costa sent the *chefe de posto* in Quillengues two sacks of refined sugar as a thank you for sending *contratados*.[65] Another method that colonial administrators used to receive payment for *contratados* was deduction of a fee from the wages that were to be distributed to workers at the completion of their contracts.[66] In short, many colonial officials abused the system, and workers had no legal recourse in that Portuguese law did not afford *indígenas* the rights of citizens.

The 1924 Ross Report corroborates the abuses described above in detail.[67] Ross questioned a random selection of people, including chiefs, pastors, and teachers, but also nonprofessional people, including women. Ross's report is one of the few sources we have that provides a space for ordinary Angolans to explain the conditions of forced labor. In the central highlands, Ross met a woman performing forced labor maintaining the roads:

> Sometimes after the men are taken from the village, they take some of the women [to work on road maintenance]. Some men were taken to Catete on the railroad to work in the cotton fields. They may have to stay two or three years as contracted laborers. Some of them have been sent to work on sugar plantations for a six month's term, but under various pretexts the time may be prolonged to seven or eight months. The planter told them that he had "bought" them of the Government, that they were his slaves and that he did not have to pay them anything. They got only their food and a receipt for their head tax.[68]

Withholding pay was a chronic abuse documented in the similar narratives relayed by workers to Ross at several villages: that they worked, received food and a receipt for their tax, but no pay. According to Portuguese colonial labor law, employers were supposed to send approximately three-fourths of a worker's

64 For a comparative case of kickbacks to labor recruiters in Pondoland, South Africa, see Diana Wylie, *Starving on a Full Stomach: Hunger and the Triumph of Cultural Racism in Modern South Africa* (Charlottesville: University Press of Virginia, 2001), 68.

65 Letter from António da Costa to Chefe do Posto, Quillengues, José Julio d'Assessção, 10 de Junho de 1926, *Copybook marked Confidential, 1926–1935*, AC, 25.

66 "Consul Smallbones to Foreign Office," November 26, 1928, FO 371/13480, PRO.

67 Ross, *Report on Employment of Native Labor in Portuguese Africa*, 5.

68 Ibid., 6.

wages to the *chefe de posto* in the worker's home area. When the worker finished his contract, he would collect his wages from that *chefe de posto* in his home area. Workers reported that they rarely were able to collect their wages from the administrators. For example, a worker explained to Ross that:

> The government recruited him in 1920 and "sold" him to the petroleum company. He worked for it seven months, at the end of each three months he got a *pano* worth three *escudos*. At the end of the seven months he was told that he had seventy escudos due him, which would be paid him at the station where he had been recruited. However, he got nothing there but the receipt for his head tax. He asked about his wages but was told there was nothing for him.[69]

Workers expressed the suspicion that employers had paid, but that it was government officials who pocketed the money. Ross summarizes:

> In practice forced labor works out as follows. A laborer works for the coffee planter and at the close of his term of service the planter says, "I can't pay you anything for I have deposited the stipulated wage for you with the Government; go to such and such an office and you will get your pay." The worker applies there and is told to come around in a couple of months. If he has the temerity to do so, he is threatened with the calaboose [jail] and that ends it. It is all a system of bare-faced labor stealing. They think that the planter has really paid for their labor, but that the official does them out of it.[70]

The structural violence depicted in Ross's report was corroborated by former *contratados* interviewed in 2006, who used the Umbundu word *okukwatu* [to abduct] to explain how they were selected for forced labor in the 1940s. There was no choice in whether to accept, or even to where one would be sent for the next year. João Kutakata explains:

> In 1940 when I was abducted, I had no notion of where I would be sent, and I received no explanation, nobody would take the time to explain to you that you will be sent here…what options does a prisoner have?[71]

---

69 Ibid., 8.

70 Ibid., 9.

71 Author interview with João Kutakata, February 21, 2006, Balombo (Province of Benguela).

Most men complied with forced labor because their local *soba* ordered them to do so. If they failed to fulfill their forced labor obligation, the local *chefe de posto* might arrest or beat their *soba* and would certainly send the police to hunt down those who refused to fulfill their labor obligation.

Historically, the highest authority in an Umbundu village was the *sekulu yimbo* [village headman; *seculo* in Portuguese].[72] The *sekulu yimbo* acted as the chief judicial officer and highest authority in the village. In an Umbundu context in which age meant status, young men would have been sent by the headman to fulfill forced labor demands. Over the course of the twentieth century, however, the position of the *sekulu yimbo* declined in importance as cultural norms shifted and age became less significant as a measure of status.[73] It was also common, especially in the early decades of the twentieth century, for *sobas* and *seculos* to send dependents and slaves acquired from farther east to fulfill the labor requirement of the village.[74] Individuals out of favor with the *chefe de posto*, *soba*, or *seculo* made up another category of contract worker.

Among the Ovimbundu of the interior, disease and death were common facts of life. Missionary John T. Tucker described the Angolan disease environment in the 1920s, which remained about the same until the government began expanding the Angolan health services to the African population in the 1950s and 1960s:

> At points along the coast bubonic plague is endemic while in certain regions animals are exterminated and human beings suffer from the dread sleeping sickness caused by the tsetse fly. Hookworm is everywhere prevalent. Malaria, however, is the chief factor in the health situation. This disease…complicates every medical case, especially pulmonary complaints causing the death of hundreds of natives during the cold weather of June and July. Smallpox constantly breaks out in native villages, dysentery is common, whilst lepers wander about at will. Tropical ulcers, filariasis, conjunctivitis, eye diseases, goiter, worms, food deficiency diseases, stomach troubles and other diseases of fearsome nature not classified as yet, scourge the populations and retard the full development of native

72 Gladwyn Murray Childs, *Umbundu Kinship and Character* (London: Oxford University Press, 1949), 36.

73 Adrian C. Edwards, *The Ovimbundu under Two Sovereignties: A Study of Social Control and Social Change among a People of Angola* (London: Oxford University Press, 1962), 46.

74 John T. Tucker, *A Tucker Treasury* (Winfield, BC: Wood Lake Books, 1984), 163.

> physique and ability. Many natives struggle under the burden of half a dozen diseases.[75]

The health condition of *contratados* before forced labor is significant to Cassequel's history because it affected worker health and mortality.

The *contratados* sent to Cassequel were frequently in a state of poor health, as they were often among the weakest members of their societies and subject to the prevalence of malnutrition and disease. Many of the physically strongest and most powerful men would either own sufficient wealth in land and agricultural output to pay the *imposto indígena* and thus bypass forced labor, or they would opt to migrate out of Angola for better-paid work on the farms and in the mines of neighboring colonies.

Workers' poor health concerned Cassequel's administration because sick men made less productive workers. According to company administrators, workers arrived from the interior generally weak and thin. Experience had shown that providing a greater quantity of rations had few benefits in that the worker sold what he did not eat. As a result, malnourished *contratados* were started on a "more moderate work regimen" until they acclimated and built up their strength.[76] In response to a 1942 questionnaire about the health of *contratados* on arrival at the plantation, Cassequel's doctor wrote that he "almost always had to reject a part of the *contratados* who underwent a health inspection."[77] For example, of the 300 *contratados* sent to Cassequel from Bailundo in 1941, fewer than 10 percent failed their medical exam and were sent home (Table 2.1). The majority of those rejected for service did not possess the physical strength to perform heavy labor in the fields. In an effort to improve workers' health and keep them strong for the grueling demands of manual labor, Cassequel's administrators provided *contratados* bananas, papayas, and, when possible, soap and "native tobacco," in addition to *fuba de milho* [maize flour], the workers' preferred staple.

During periods when *contratados* were at a premium because of the competing labor demands of other industries, Cassequel's administrators took a more conciliatory approach. In 1933, for example, Cassequel paid twelve *sobas* and *seculos* from the recruitment areas of Bimbale and Balombo to visit the

75 John T. Tucker, *Drums in the Darkness* (New York: Doran Company), 178–179.

76 SAC, *Copy Book of Letters marked Confidential, 1930s*, June 21, 1943, AC.

77 "Resposta as seguintes alineas, do questionario sobre pessoal indigena, constante da nota confidencial No. 68/1/1942, de 19 de Agosto de 1942, do Exmo. Senhor Administrador do Concelho do Lobito," *Cartas Confidenciães Diversos Desde o Ano de 1942*, Letter to Board of Directors in Lisbon, AC.

plantation. The point of the visit was to win over the *sobas* and *seculos* to ensure their cooperation in labor recruitment.[78] According to Cassequel's director, the visit was a success and "all declared that the accusations made against our Society were unfounded, and they guaranteed us that in their villages they would influence their sons to contract their services with our Society."[79] Clearly, the visit of these authorities demonstrates their integral role in the system of labor recruitment in Angola. *Sobas* and *seculos* often received a cut for providing workers. In 1921, for example, the *curador* for the district of Huambo reported payments of 28 *escudos* and 40 cents "to the sobas of Canjangue, Chirumbo and Quipeio for the furnishment of 100 workers."[80] Some *sobas* also received 1 percent of the *imposto indígena* collected in their area.[81]

Given the relative power relationships, *sobas* and *seculos* faced few options. They either cooperated in labor recruitment or faced penalties. For example, on August 30, 1921, 500 Africans arrived at the office of the *chefe de posto* in the district of Quipeio to be contracted and distributed to employers. Of the 500, 27 fled the post. In response, the *chefe de posto* sent two policemen to capture the *seculos* responsible for the initial recruitment. The *chefe de posto* wrote to the *curador* in Huambo that he thought it appropriate to give the *seculos* responsible thirty days of correctional labor as punishment.[82] "Correctional labor" could have meant either unpaid work for a private employer or unpaid work on public works, such as road maintenance.

African authorities, whether they owed their appointment to the local *chefe de posto* or had roots predating the colonial period were in a difficult position vis-à-vis labor recruitment. They faced, on the one hand, pressure from colonial officials to produce workers and, on the other, expectations for protection and advocacy from their own people. If a *soba* or *seculo* failed to produce the number of workers demanded by the *chefe de posto*, he would be liable for arrest. The intermediary position took a heavy toll on African authorities.[83] For example, sixteen *seculos* committed suicide between 1903 and 1945 as a result

78 Ibid.

79 SAC, *Correspondência Confidencial ate fins do ano de 1934*, June 1, 1933, AC.

80 "Circunscrição Civil do Huambo, Posto Civil do Quipeio," Agência da Curadoria (1922), July 8, 1921, Caixa 466, AHA.

81 Distrito de Benguela, "Posto de Policia Civil do Sambo," February 10, 1922, Caixa 466, AHA.

82 "Letter from the Posto Civil do Quipeio, No. 40/6/1, Quipeio, 30 de Agosto de 1921, to Snr. Agente do Curador, Huambo," Caixa 466, AHA.

83 On this same point see Emmanuel Esteves, "O Caminho de Ferro de Benguela e o Impacto Econômico, Social e Cultural na Sua Zonas de Influência 1902–1952" (PhD diss., Universidade do Porto, 1999), 539.

of the pressure.[84] In 1920, *Soba* Mabongo of Huambo committed suicide because he was unable to send the number of *contratados* ordered by the *chefe de posto* and also faced popular scorn from the people in his *sobado* for collaborating with the Portuguese.[85]

Contratados often did not constitute a compliant work force. For example, in its 1941 annual report, the Negócios Indígenas listed statistics for the number of workers contracted, the number of those workers who completed their contracts, and the reasons for not completing the contract. In the district of Bailundo, for example, during 1941, 3,688 workers were contracted for twenty agricultural and industrial companies situated across Angola.[86] The most accurate available population estimate is the 1926 census of the district of Bailundo, in which colonial officials estimated the adult male population at 25,856.[87] Thus, approximately one in seven men in Bailundo were contracted in 1941. Of the 3,688 *contratatdos*, Cassequel contracted 300 (Table 2.1). Nearly 70 percent completed their contracts, but almost 20 percent fled their contracts, and another 4 percent died on the plantation. Of the eleven largest employers in Angola, Cassequel had the second highest percentage of runaways (17 percent), more than double Angola's other large sugar producer, although its death rate of 4 percent was lower than nine of the eleven employers listed. These statistics provide some insight into how *contratados* experienced Cassequel in 1941. Most labored through their contract, with nearly one in five absconding, a decision that rendered the worker a fugitive for several years; if he returned home, he would face arrest, beatings, or both at the hands of local government officials. One common punishment for apprehended *fugidos* was to be sent on a five-year contract to work on the island of São Tomé. Banishment to São Tomé was viewed as particularly harsh because it was known as the island of no return because a high percentage of *contratados* sent to the island never returned to their home districts.

---

84 Susan Welty, "Slavery Is Not Dead," *Negro Digest* (vol. IV, no. 6, April 1946), 58.

85 *Jornal de Benguela*, April 23, 1920), 4, quoted in Linda Heywood, *Contested Power in Angola, 1840s to the Present* (Rochester: University of Rochester Press, 2000), 49. For an insightful account of scorn for government-appointed chiefs in the Quelimane District of Mozambique based on songs, see Leroy Vail and Landeg White, *Capitalism and Colonialism in Mozambique*, 166–178.

86 Repartição Central dos Negócios Indígenas, *Ano de 1941 Relatório*. "Angola Relatórios Curador e Negócios Indígenas," Maço 1725, Sala 3, AHU, 118.

87 Dr. José de Oliveira Ferreira Diniz, "Contribuição para o Estudo de Demografia Indígena de Angola," *Boletim da Agência Geral das Colónias* (ano VI, no. 58, Abril de 1930), 48.

TABLE 2.1 Contratados *from Bailundo at Cassequel, 1941*

TOTAL	Completed contract	Runaways (fugido)	Failed medical exam	Died
300	208 (69%)	52 (17%)	27 (9%)	13 (4%)

SOURCE: SAC, *RELATÓRIO 1941/42*, CASSEQUEL ARCHIVE, ARQUIVO HISTÓRICO DO BANCO ESPÍRITO SANTO, LISBON.

Flight was perhaps a "weapon of the weak"[88] or, as many former *contratados* interviewed in 2006 attested, *fugidos* simply could not or did not want to perform the physically grueling work at Cassequel (see Chapter 3). The prospect of an untimely death, far from home, may have motivated *contratados* to flee. Periodic epidemics and the very real possibility of dying at Cassequel, led to an increase in *fugidos*. As historian Charles van Onselen has argued for the labor compounds of the mines of Southern Rhodesia, desertion was a rational response to a dangerous work environment.[89] In 1944, the head agricultural agent for the districts of Benguela and Cuanza-Sul reported mass flight of *contratados* from Cassequel.[90] The agent provided an oblique explanation that "the spirit of the *indígenas* is bad."[91]

The Negócios Indígenas reported that proximity to a worker's home district resulted in a larger number of runaways.[92] Other reasons workers deserted included (1) the long initial journey to the place of work, generally on foot with little food; (2) an employer with a bad reputation; (3) deficiency of food; (4) an excess in hours of work; (5) beatings; (6) long periods under contract; and (7) nonpayment of salary.[93] In a system in which *indígenas* had essentially no rights in the colonial court system, flight was an effective way of resisting the conditions listed above.[94] Removing oneself from a particular district or place

88 The term comes from James Scott, *Weapons of the Weak: Everyday Forms of Peasant Resistance* (New Haven, CT: Yale University Press, 1985).

89 Charles van Onselen, *Chibaro African Mine Labour in Southern Rhodesia 1900–1933* (Johannesburg: Ravan Press, 1976), 239.

90 "Jorge Marcal, Regente Agricola, Assistência Técnica as Granjas Administrativas nos Distritos de Benguela e Quanza-Sul pelo Governador da Provincia de Benguela," December 27, 1944, Caixa 2064, AHA.

91 Ibid.

92 Repartição Central dos Negócios Indígenas, *Ano de 1941 Relatório*. "Angola Relatórios Curador e Negócios Indígenas," Maço 1725, Sala 3, AHU, 122.

93 Ibid., 123.

94 On desertion in the mines of Southern Rhodesia, see Van Onselen, *Chibaro*, 229–230.

of employment as a strategy for survival under colonial domination was not unique to Angola.[95] Indeed, colonists had been complaining about Africans' ability to flee as a means to resisting forced labor since the beginning of the century.[96] Some interior districts were known for workers being prone to flee. For example, in 1939, the *chefe de posto* in the district of Bocoio recruited 600 *contratados*. Of these, 400 fled their assigned employers. The following year, two-thirds of 260 contracted workers fled.[97] Bocoio, which is only about 50 miles from Cassequel, became an unpopular recruiting ground and the people of Bocoio were spared the presence of labor recruiters for a number of years. The flight of so many *contratados* from Bocoio demonstrates how flight could be used as a somewhat effective kind of resistance, although in the Angolan case, most *fugidos* had to abandon their homes and permanently relocate.

Working Conditions at Cassequel

In the absence of written or oral accounts by African workers for the interwar years, reports about living conditions—food allotment, work regimen, housing and health care—offer the best criteria for analyzing a worker's lived experience at Cassequel in the 1920s through the 1940s. Yet these sources too are limited: before the end of the 1940s, Africans' work and living conditions received relatively little attention from Company administrators or the colonial government. The confidential correspondence between administrators in Catumbela and the board of directors in Lisbon focused instead on strategies for ensuring that the government supply a sufficient number of *contratados*. This focus demonstrates a clear colonial bias with little understanding of the issues and difficulties facing *contratados* and their families.

The labor performed by *contratados* at Cassequel was strenuous. Almost all *contratados* worked in the fields, where conditions remained much as they had

95 See, for example, Edward A. Alpers, "'To Seek a Better Life:' The Implications of Migration from Mozambique to Tanganyika for Class Formation and Political Behavior," *Canadian Journal of African Studies* (vol. 18, no. 2, 1984), 372–374.

96 Viuva Bastos, *A Escravatura em Mossamedes: Carta Aberta dirigida a S. Ex. O Presidente da Republica por um Grupo de Agricultores, Industriaes e Commerciantes de Mossamedes* (Lisboa: Typographia do Commercio, 1912), 22–23.

97 Ministério das Colónias Relatório Inspecção Ordinária á Provincia de Benguela—Concelho do Lobito e Postos, Maço 1669, AHU, 91. For runaway slaves in Southern Angola see W.G. Clarence-Smith, "Runaway Slaves and Social Bandits in Southern Angola, 1875–1913," in Gad Heuman, ed., *Out of the House of Bondage: Runaways, Resistance and Marronage in Africa and the New World* (London: Frank Cass, 1986).

since the nineteenth century; the adoption of tractors in the 1920s would later reduce the amount of manual labor needed for plowing fields. In existing fields, work began with the preparation of the soil. In a cleared field, after the burning of the leftover stalks, workers plowed the ash and remaining stalks into the ground. The next step was making furrows, a task which was also mechanized in the 1920s, followed by planting the cane. Planting was done by hand until the 1970s.[98] Before planting cuttings in the ground, workers moistened the soil and added animal dung or compost to the hole. Fertilizing the soil with the burned compost of old cane stalks and animal dung was essential given the sandy, nitrogen-poor soil.[99] Once planted, the cane required extensive maintenance. Workers weeded the fields. Cassequel introduced pesticides to control weeds in the 1940s, which reduced labor needs from fifty to sixty men per hectare to thirty to thirty-five men per hectare.[100] In the dry climate at Cassequel the cane required irrigation, which involved inundating fields from an extensive system of irrigation ditches. The miles of ditches required the laborious clearing of sediment and plants by hand. Harvesting the cane entailed cutting the cane with a scythe, and gathering, loading, and unloading the crop on to the plantation's railway network. Former *contratados* cited the hauling of cut cane as among the most physically demanding tasks on the plantation. For this reason, women did not work as *contratados*, although the wives of voluntary workers living on the plantation did sometimes work as salaried workers in the fields and in the community, where they cleaned and cooked in the homes of the Portuguese residents of Catumbela.

Contratados made up roughly half of Cassequel's workforce, which by the 1940s numbered about 5,000. The next largest category of workers consisted of *voluntários*—those who volunteered for wage labor—who lived in Catumbela in worker villages dotting the plantation. These men and a few women received their pay in weekly allotments and bought their food through a company cooperative. Salaried work, however low paying, often provided the best means for supporting a family, as agricultural lands were difficult to attain. *Voluntários* also secured the more desirable jobs available to Africans, including work in the factory, the machine shops, and tending to Cassequel's ancillary areas of production such as harvesting oil palm trees, tending the company's cattle, or staffing the fishery.

---

98 A.G. Wethmar and P.C. Brutel de la Rivière, "The Sugar Industry in Angola and Mozambique" (Holland, 1954), Sala 2, Maço 192, AHU, 16.

99 Ibid., 31.

100 Ibid., 27–28.

The better work experience for *voluntários* begs the question: why did more Africans not volunteer? Plantation work was not popular, and few Africans living in the central highlands would willingly leave their homes and families to work on coastal plantations for meager pay. *Voluntários* were, like *contratados*, classified as *indígenas* under colonial law and thus earned meager salaries and were denied access to more privileged jobs. A small number of Africans—no more than a dozen in the 1940s—were classified as *assimilados* and were thus eligible for more skilled and higher-paying jobs such as nurse or mechanic and therefore earned higher wages.[101]

Portuguese workers dominated the highest echelon of company employees and numbered around 100 by the 1940s. The most skilled of these employees were generally recruited in Portugal to serve as medical doctors, engineers, accountants, and administrators. No European served in a position of manual labor, but some worked in the less remunerative jobs of mechanics, secretaries, and *capatazes* [field foremen]. All European employees experienced a separate salary scale, health-care system, housing, and, for some, a yearly paid furlough in Portugal. Cassequel's well-paid jobs afforded a good quality of life, a close-knit Portuguese community, and the privilege of belonging to a colonial elite.[102]

Bairros indígenas [worker villages] existed in a generally poor state of hygiene. Workers drew water from the same canal system used to irrigate the sugarcane. In addition to the nonpotable water, poor housing and a rudimentary health care system took a toll on workers' health. Before the late 1940s, Cassequel's small hospital (with one doctor and several nurses) focused on the health of Portuguese employees and their families. Indeed, keeping colonists and colonial administrators alive was the primary focus of Western medicine across Angola as late as the 1950s.[103] Colonists faced endemic diseases to Angola, such as malaria and yellow fever. The director of the Angolan Health Service, António Damas Mora, described this interdependence at the Third National Colonial Congress in 1930:

---

101 Author interview with Faustino Alfredo, Catumbela, July 5, 2001. Alfredo worked for forty years as a nurse in Cassequel's São Pedro Hospital.

102 For more on these memories of former settlers who returned to Portugal after independence in 1975, see the special edition of *Cadernos de Estudos Africanos*, "Memórias Coloniais" (no. 9/10, Julho 2005/Junho 2006).

103 Martin F. Shapiro, "Medicine in the Service of Colonialism: Medical Care in Portuguese Africa 1885–1974" (PhD diss., University of California, Los Angeles, 1983), 24. An important exception to the focus on Europeans were the medical posts and hospitals established by Protestant missionaries. See Tucker, *A Tucker Treasury*, 200–201.

> The conquest of territory would not be possible without a health service. The most important coastal towns were often provided with permanent doctors. Their principal objective was assistance to the European in his role as conqueror and occupant.[104]

At Cassequel, European workers received free health care and preventative medicines. The board of directors understood that the successful management of their Cassequel plantation necessitated healthy European managers. Before the 1950s, the health care provided to African workers focused on screening out sick *contratados*, occasionally providing vaccines, and treating only the most severely ill in the hospital's separate wing for *indígena* patients. The relatively high death rate and periodic outbreaks of disease among workers reflected these low standards of sanitation and the poor state of health care generally in Angola.

In 1929, for example, a deadly typhoid epidemic killed hundreds of Cassequel's workers. Typhoid was and is endemic to Angola and is caused by *Salmonella typhi* bacteria, which spreads through contaminated food and water or through close contact with someone who is infected. The first mention of the epidemic in company correspondence came in May 1929: "We are able to consider as debilitating the sickness that rages among the native personnel. As a preventative, we have administered the typhoid fever vaccine and we are hoping that it will produce the desired results."[105] In the first three months of the year, sixty workers had died. The high death toll continued throughout the rest of the year, in spite of the 500 vaccinations administered.[106] By the end of the year, 324 workers, or roughly 7 percent of the workforce, died.[107] In addition to those who died at Cassequel, many more perished en route home after having been discharged because of their incapacity to work.[108] In September, the administration provided the false explanation to the board of directors

104 António Damas Mora, "O estado actual da assistência médica aos indígenas na colónia de Angola e outras colónias do grupo da Africa inter-tropical," in *III Congresso Colonial Nacional, Actas das sessões e teses, 1930* (Lisboa: Sociedade de Geografia de Lisboa, 1934), 5. Cited in Shapiro, "Medicine in the Service of Colonialism," 27.

105 SAC, *Copybook marked Confidential, 1926–1935*, May 8, 1929, AC.

106 Ibid.

107 "Nota confidencial no. 88," August 10, 1942, Correspondência confidencial, Distrito de Benguela, Proc. 19, Caixa 3521, AHA. Quoted in Emmanuel Esteves, "O Caminho de Ferro de Benguela e o impacto econômico, social e Cultural na sua zonas de influência 1902–1952," Ph.D diss., Universidade do Porto, 1999, 585. In 2001 I was unable to find this document in the cited *caixa* in the AHA.

108 *Copybook marked Confidential, 1926–1935*, September 5, 1929, AC.

TABLE 2.2 *Official mortality at Cassequel, 1937–1948*

1937	1938	1939	1940	1941	1942	1943	1944	1945	1946	1947	1948
500	540	560	470	1,650	1,080	350	430	200	130	110	68

SOURCE: CARLOS VERDETE, O CHEFE DOS SERVIÇOS DE SAUDE, SOCIEDADE AGRÍCOLA DO CASSEQUEL, "MORTALIDADE." HOSPITAL S. PEDRO, CATUMBELA, CASSEQUEL ARCHIVE, ARQUIVO HISTÓRICO DO BANCO ESPÍRITO SANTO, LISBON.

TABLE 2.3 *Cassequel's average annual expense per European employee, 1927–1933*

	Workers (yearly average)	Total cost	Cost per employee
1927/28	71	£14,357	£202
1928/29	100	£17,760	£177
1929/30	130	£21,622	£166
1930/31	102	£20,318	£199
1931/32	99	£17,270	£174
1932/33	98	£16,015	£163

SOURCE: SAC, RELATÓRIO DO EXERCICIO DE 1932/1933 APRESENTADO PELO DIRECTOR EM AFRICA FRANCISCO REGADO, CASSEQUEL, ABRIL DE 1933, CASSEQUEL ARCHIVE, ARQUIVO HISTÓRICO DO BANCO ESPÍRITO SANTO, LISBON, 45–47. THE DECREASING COST PER WORKER IN POUNDS STERLING REFLECTED THE DECLINING VALUE OF THE ESCUDO TO THE POUND. FOR THE NUMBER OF ESCUDOS TO THE POUND STERLING BETWEEN 1910 AND 1939, SEE CLARENCE-SMITH, THE THIRD PORTUGUESE EMPIRE, ANNEX 2, 227.

that the heightened death rate of July and August resulted from the lower temperatures of *cacimbo* [the cool period on the Angolan coast between June and September] and to the "practice of the native to eat sugar-cane, which resulted in dysentery."[109] This deliberately inadequate explanation was designed so as not to alarm the board of directors and to deflect responsibility away from the administration and onto the workers themselves.

In 1941/42, a second deadly epidemic—this time pneumonia—swept through Cassequel's African workers and their families. In total, 1,650 people died in 1941, followed by 1,080 more in 1942.[110] Statistics for the 1941/42 epidemic come from Cassequel's São Pedro Hospital and include deaths among workers' families; thus, the percentage of workers who died is not clear. Table 2.2 illustrates total

109 Ibid.

110 Carlos Verdete, O Chefe dos Serviços de Saude, Sociedade Agrícola do Cassequel, "Mortalidade" Hospital S. Pedro, Catumbela, AC.

TABLE 2.4 *Cassequel's average annual expense per African employee, 1927–1933*

	Workers (yearly average)	Total cost	Cost per employee
1927/28	3,275	£48,020	£14
1928/29	5,118	£57,245	£11
1929/30	6,090	£59,338	£9
1930/31	5,005	£46,475	£9
1931/32	4,680	£34,365	£7
1932/33	3,803	£23,025	£6

SOURCE: SAC, RELATÓRIO DO EXERCICIO DE 1932/1933 APRESENTADO PELO DIRECTOR EM AFRICA FRANCISCO REGADO, CASSEQUEL, ABRIL DE 1933, CASSEQUEL ARCHIVE, ARQUIVO HISTÓRICO DO BANCO ESPÍRITO SANTO, LISBON, 45–47.

deaths at the hospital between 1937 and 1948. European deaths for the same years averaged two per year.[111] Investments in preventative vaccinations and potable water after World War II explain the lower mortality rates by the late 1940s.

Costs per employee between 1927 and 1933 varied considerably between Portuguese and African employees (Tables 2.3 and 2.4). The cost differential provides another means with which to measure working conditions at Cassequel. Labor costs included salary, food, health care, and related expenses such as recruitment costs, transportation and recreation. For example, in 1933 Cassequel spent an average of £163 per European employee and £6 per African employee. In other words, Cassequel spent more than twenty-seven times as much on white employees than it did on African employees in 1933. Furthermore, between 1927/28 and 1932/33, the ratio of money spent per European employee increased in comparison spent per African employee, from approximately 14:1 in 1927/28 to approximately 27:1 in 1932/33. As Table 2.4 indicates, costs for African workers, including both including both *contratados* and *voluntários*, declined between 1925 and 1939.

Conclusion

During the period 1921 through World War II, Cassequel underwent tremendous development. Although the Angolan economy floundered through high inflation and budgetary austerity in the 1920s and early 1930s, Cassequel's protected

111 Ibid.

market in Portugal and access to forced labor shielded it from the worst effects of the depression. The 1926 military overthrow of the First Republic resulted in a new relationship between Portugal and the colonies. In Angola, the government jettisoned the ambitious development schemes and labor reforms of Norton de Matos and focused on balancing the budgets in order to exploit Angola's natural and human resources for the benefit of Portugal's ailing economy. António Salazar—who became minister of finance in 1928, colonial minister in 1930, and prime minister in 1933—maintained preferential tariffs for colonial sugar and encouraged Portuguese capitalists to invest in the colonies. When Cassequel faced bankruptcy in 1930, Salazar intervened to protect one of the most important Portuguese owned agro-industrial enterprises in Angola. A couple of years later, he granted the Angolan monopoly for producing industrial-grade alcohol to Cassequel. These ties between Salazar and the Espírito Santo family demonstrated the cohesiveness of Portugal's economic and political elites under the Estado Novo.

In Angola, the colonial state constructed a legal infrastructure to put Africans to work for colonial interests. This infrastructure included forced labor, the *imposto indígena*, and the *caderneta*, and its quotidian effectiveness contributed to the enormous profits made by the Espírito Santo Group and other metropolitan interests during the middle decades of the twentieth century. (See Appendix for Cassequel's dividends and profits during these years.)

Cassequel's profitability in the 1940s resulted in part from the boom in commodity prices during World War II. Cassequel's production doubled and the number of African workers increased from 1,700 to nearly 5,000. The quality of life for Cassequel's African workers, however, did not improve significantly. Workers built their own huts, drank from the irrigation ditches, received extremely low—if any—wages, and suffered two major epidemics in 1929 and 1941. At different points Cassequel developed a reputation in the interior recruitment districts for not paying wages and keeping people past their stipulated contracts. After World War II, the new international human rights discourse, the emerging welfare colonialism in European colonial territories, and the Cold War changed how the international community viewed colonialism. This changing international attitude affected demands for universal labor standards and challenged the status quo of one rule for the West and another for the rest of humanity. Portuguese officials theorized a new ethos of colonialism called *luso-tropicalismo* and pressured prominent employers such as Cassequel to wean itself off forced labor. These changes in policy, aimed to maintain Portuguese colonialism, are discussed in the next chapter, which focuses on the period post-1945 until 1960, the year of African independence, and draws on the memories of former *contratados* to augment the story told by company statistics.

CHAPTER 3

"I Escaped in a Coffin": Remembering Angolan Forced Labor from World War II to 1960

Some of the men sent to Cassequel as *contratados* in the 1940s and 1950s are still alive and remember their experiences. Men such as Mr. Tchimbe Ngucika described his work as a *contratado* at Cassequel in the 1940s:

> The first time I entered Cassequel was in 1943/44, I worked on clearing out the irrigation canals and the planting of sugar cane. The work was by task, and if you did not complete your task for whatever reason you would be whipped (*chicotada*). Each time I went there the system worked the same: carrying cane by hand to the railway cars, cutting cane by hand with your cutlass, without any clothes except a loin cloth (*chilambo*) made of burlap.[1]

The post-World War II era ushered in a period of dramatic change for European colonial powers and their empires, but in Angola reforms of forced labor would not happen until the late 1950s and especially after the outbreak of the nationalist war for independence in 1961. In Article 73 of the United Nation's Charter of 1945, member states committed to moving their colonies toward independence. In 1948, member states of the United Nations adopted the Universal Declaration of Human Rights, which recognized the right to self-determination. The two emerging superpowers—the United States and Soviet Union—committed themselves to anti-colonial platforms, and the emerging Cold War led both nations to look to African nationalist movements as potential allies. Portuguese leaders responded to these changing circumstances in 1951 by reiterating the integral relationship between the metropole and colonies, dropping the terms "Portuguese Colonial Empire"[2] and "colonies" in favor of "overseas provinces" of a pluricontinental Portugal. The Estado Novo promulgated the idea that a unique type of Portuguese assimilation policy known as *luso-tropicalismo* would ward off demands for independence.[3] *Luso-tropicalismo* stemmed from the writings of Brazilian sociologist Gilberto Freyre, who argued that the Portuguese had a

1 Author interview with Tchimbe Ngucika, February 21, 2006, Balombo.

2 Cláudia Castelo, *Passagens para África: O Povoamento de Angola e Moçambique com Naturais da Metrópole (1920–1974)* (Lisboa: Edições Afrontamento, 2007), 107–108.

3 Cláudia Castelo, *"O Modo Português de Estar no Mundo": o Luso-Tropicalismo e a Ideologia Colonial Portuguesa* (Porto: Edições Afrontamento, 1999).

DOI 10.1163/9789004301757_005

special capacity as colonizers because they created multiracial societies and did not practice the strict type of racial segregation characteristic of British colonies. He cited racial mixing in Brazil as a leading example. Leaders of the Estado Novo, who on the political front were making alliances with the white supremacist regimes of South Africa and Rhodesia, touted the relative lack of an absolute color bar in Angola as evidence of assimilation.[4] *Luso-tropicalismo* gave theoretical support to Portugal's efforts to settle more Portuguese in Angola after World War II,[5] and a commodity boom led by high coffee prices and increased government investment attracted tens of thousands of Portuguese to immigrate to Angola to make money.[6] The growing settler population increased the demand for Portuguese exports and thus support among Portuguese manufacturers for the regime's colonial policy.

During this period, the Espírito Santo Group expanded its portfolio beyond Cassequel into an array of colonial manufacturing and agricultural enterprises, including investment in 1944 in *CADA*, the Companhia Angolana de Agricultura (which produced coffee, palm oil, and coconuts), and in 1956 in the new sugar plantation Sociedade Agrícola do Incomati in Xinavane, Mozambique.[7] These investments in colonial enterprises reflected Espírito Santo commitment to the idea of the Portuguese empire and the belief that colonial investment and development would further the interests of Portugal. In Angola, the Estado Novo moved gradually to phase out forced labor by the late 1950s, but essentially the reforms aimed to maintain the colonial status quo without conceding any significant self-determination to Africans.

The details of how Angolan forced labor functioned has been well documented by investigative commissions, missionaries, and Angolan reporters and civil servants. One lacuna, however, is how forced laborers themselves viewed the system. Investigative reports portray forced laborers as victims, but it is not clear whether these men and women resisted the system, and whether the genders experienced forced labor similarly. Fortunately, recent scholarly studies of Angolan labor—specifically Todd Cleveland and Jorge Varanda's work on the workers of Diamang in the northeast, Linda Heywood's work on the Ovimbundu, and

4 For more on Portugal's alliances with Rhodesia and South Africa, see Filipe Ribeiro de Meneses and Robert McNamara, "The Last Throw of the Dice: Portugal, Rhodesia and South Africa, 1970–74" *Portuguese Studies* (vol. 28, no. 2, 2012), 201–215.

5 Castelo, *Passagens para África*, 116.

6 Castelo, *Passagens para África*, 110–111.

7 Carlos Alberto Damas and Augusto de Ataíde, *O Banco Espírito Santo uma dinastia financeira portuguesa 1869–1973* (Lisboa: Banco Espírito Santo Centro de Estudos da História do BES, 2004), 218–219.

Emmanuel Esteves on the Benguela Railway—have provided a much richer understanding of how forced labor functioned. Because forced labor was abolished in 1962, memories are filtered through a half century of life, including war, independence, and the official memory of colonialism. With these caveats, this chapter argues that men and women have distinct memories based on their gendered experience of forced labor. Former *contratados* and women forced to maintain the roads—work done across a huge geographical area—describe the same structural violence. In fact, forced roadwork for women made up a significant part of a family's experience of forced labor. Often while a man fulfilled his *contratado* obligation, his wife, daughters, and sons worked on the roads. In their narratives, women described sexual abuse, lamented suffering, and questioned the work regime, but interviewees attested that women rarely challenged the system directly. Most simply tried to survive, a situation that presented ethical and moral dilemmas—for example, a woman might agree to sleep with a *cipaio* [African policeman] or *capataz* [Portuguese foreman] to get out of grueling road construction. The only clear act of resistance was to flee [*fugir*], a practice well documented in the men's interviews. Indeed, *contratados* commonly exercised this option (see Chapter 2) and often went to great lengths to re-locate to new districts and towns to evade the authorities.

Legislation and Politics

In 1946, the colonial governor of Benguela and the chief of the Negócios Indígenas [Native Affairs Department] visited Cassequel. Writing to his bosses in Lisbon, Cassequel's director reported:

> There is good will [from the colonial administration], but it is impossible to augment the number of native workers. We would like to take the opportunity to call the attention of your excellencies to this subject: the old days of requesting blacks without keeping an account is over in Angola and it is over forever. The excesses of the past put the Colony in its present tragedy...Only with organization and with adjusted methods in relation to the native will we be able to resolve our problem.[8]

The old days of "requesting blacks without keeping an account" referred to Cassequel's annual requests for *contratados* from colonial administrators and

8 Letter to administration in Lisbon, *Copy Book of Letters 1930s and 1940s (Confidential)*, no. 39/46, AC, 278.

the clear expectancy that the government would simply supply the forced laborers without much oversight or expectations from Cassequel. The "present tragedy" referred to a labor shortage for colonial enterprises such as Cassequel. Cassequel's director recommended improving work conditions in order to attract more voluntary workers, as *contratados* were becoming increasingly difficult to obtain through colonial officials. Cassequel's annual report for 1946 reported the same difficulties in attracting both contract and voluntary labor. The old recruitment strategy was being judged a failure: "It is our duty to emphasize our disagreement with the road followed until now, which consisted of the following: to put pressure on the authorities to supply greater numbers of workers."[9] The report concluded that the company could no longer rely on the government to solve its labor shortage: "We can not trust in the ability of the State to resolve a problem so large…the problem has an economic root, which is that the salaries and privileges conceded to the natives…is pathetic."[10] In past decades—indeed, since the end of slavery in the late nineteenth century—colonial administrators sent *contratados* to meet Cassequel's labor demands. There were not sufficient voluntary workers willing to work for the "pathetic" wages on offer to meet Cassequel's labor demands.[11] After World War II, in the context of demands for African independence and a vocal anticolonial movement, forced labor was deemed increasingly unacceptable because it risked stoking anticolonial sentiment and increasing demands for Portugal to decolonize.

In 1947, Henrique Galvão submitted his *Relatório sobre problemas dos nativos nas colónias Portuguesas* [*Report on Native Problems in the Portuguese Colonies*] to an in camera committee of the Portuguese National Assembly.[12] Galvão, a former inspector for the colonies and governor of Huíla Province in southern Angola, concluded that forced labor, lack of payment of salaries, and abusive working conditions were leading to a depopulating of Angola as

9 SAC, *Relatório de 1946*, AC, 72.

10 Ibid., 74.

11 For a comparative cases study of how miserly wages undercut labor reform, see Alexander Keese, "The Constrains of Late Colonial Reform Policy: Forced Labour Scandals in the Portuguese Congo (Angola) and the limits of reform under authoritarian colonial rule, 1955–1961" *Portuguese Study Review* (vol. 28, no. 2, 2012), 186–200.

12 Henrique Galvão, "Exposição do Deputado Henrique Galvão, á Comissão de Colónias da Assembleia Nacional, em Janeiro de 1947." Arquivo Histórico-Parliamentar, Assembleia da República. See also Douglas L. Wheeler, "The Galvão Report on Forced Labor (1947) in Historical Context and Perspective: Trouble-Shooter Who Was 'Trouble'," *Portuguese Studies Review* (vol. 16, no. 1, 2008), 115–152.

African men migrated out of the colony to access better working conditions in neighboring colonies. A worsening of labor conditions under the Estado Novo coupled with increasing demands for African labor as a result of the post-World War II commodity boom explains the push factors. Pull factors included improving labor conditions and higher salaries in Rhodesia and the Belgian Congo.

Galvão did not cite African interviewees and so provides little space for African views of the labor system. His analysis argued for reform to "save" Angola for Portugal. Colonial officials, according to Galvão, had become labor recruiters who forcibly sent workers to employers in return for bribes and then stole salaries from workers whose interests they were supposed to protect. Paternalism characterized Portuguese colonial policy, and thus colonial administrators were supposed to "protect" and "develop" their colonial subjects. These paternalistic ideas informed the policy of assimilation by which Africans would gradually be taught the benefits of Portuguese civilization. According to Galvão, these practices were "required in confidential circulars and official orders."[13] He concluded that the system was crueler than pure slavery because employers had no vested interest in "their" *contratados*, who could easily be replaced.

Salazar's government made no immediate effort to enact reforms as a result of the Galvão Report. Increasingly disillusioned, Galvão decided to make a public condemnation of the corrupt and incompetent colonial administration in Angola. On the floor of the Portuguese National Assembly in 1949, he charged that the discrepancy between law and practice made the colonial administration a "colossal lie":

> This lie, that attempts to deceive the country and hides its own mediocrity and incompetence from our Government...has thrown Angola into a political, economic, and moral crisis without precedent in her troubled history of the last hundred years.[14]

Galvão argued vehemently—based on his two-decade career in Angola—that labor and living conditions for the African population had deteriorated under the Estado Novo. Hence, it is no surprise that Salazar squashed the Galvão

13 Galvão, "Exposição do Deputado Henrique Galvão, á Comissão de Colónias da Assembleia Nacional, em Janeiro de 1947." Arquivo Histórico-Parliamentar, Assembleia da República, 30.

14 Session of February 24, 1949, Caixa 48, n. 10 "Henrique Galvão," Arquivo Histórico-Parliamentar, Assembleia da República.

Report immediately; it was not published until Galvão fled Portugal as a political refugee in 1959.

Recognizing the increasing pressure to reform forced labor, Cassequel's administrators responded to the anticipated labor shortage by advocating for a combination of mechanization, higher salaries, and better amenities for workers on the plantation. In 1948 Vasco Monteiro, Cassequel's director, argued that voluntary workers performed at a higher level than *contratados* and he proposed to construct *senzalas* [worker housing] "equal to those already in existence at Cassequel in the native quarter next to the factory."[15]

As colonial officials and Cassequel's administrators debated how to attract more voluntary workers, the international community put Portuguese leaders on notice that forced labor for private employers was no longer acceptable to member states of the United Nations and international public opinion. In addition to the recognition of self-determination embedded in the U.N. Charter of 1945 and the Universal Declaration of Human Rights in 1948, the International Labor Organization (ILO) revisited the issue of forced labor in the 1950s. In 1953, the ILO's Mudaliar Committee, under the leadership of the Indian diplomat Ramaswami Mudaliar, issued a report highly critical of labor regimes in the Eastern Bloc, South Africa, and the African colonies of Portugal and Belgium.[16] The ILO treated forced labor as a human rights issue and used the findings of the 1953 Mudaliar Committee to draft the 1956 Abolition of Forced Labor Convention. The new document banned forced labor (1) as a means of political coercion and political education and (2) as a method of mobilizing and using labor for purposes of economic development.[17] The adoption of the 1956 Forced Labor Convention demonstrated a significant change in tone from pre-World War II labor debates, which had often treated colonial labor issues as exempt from universal human rights and protections. The war against a totalitarian state, the new United Nations, and burgeoning nationalist movements across the colonized world all contributed to changing the parameters of the discussion. No longer did European colonial powers declare the educative merit of forced labor for their African and Asian subjects. The emerging

---

15 *Cartas Confidenciaes de Diversos Desde o ano de 1942: Correspondência Diversos do Administrador Exmo. Senhor Eng. Vasco Monteiro*, March 7, 1948, AC. Until this time, the vast majority of Cassequel workers constructed their own huts in different villages scattered across the plantation.

16 For more on the context and intent of the Mudaliar Committee, see Daniel Roger Maul, "The International Labour Organization and the Struggle against Forced Labour from 1919 to the Present," *Labor History* (vol. 48, no. 4, November 2007), 485.

17 Ibid., 487.

dialogue emphasized universal rights, including the freedom from forced labor. Portugal's decision in 1959 to adopt the Abolition of Forced Labor Convention signaled a recognition and acceptance of this changing political context and a commitment to finally abolish forced labor. In Angola, the government decreed the shift away from the use of force in labor recruitment, but it would not be until after the outbreak of the nationalist war for independence in 1961 that Salazar banned forced labor definitively.

Remembering Forced Labor

Nearly a half century since the end of forced labor, former *contratados* still have vivid memories of their servitude. From January to June 2006, I worked with Manuel Domingos, in conjunction with the Oral History Project at the Arquivo Histórico de Angola (AHA), to interview people in former labor recruitment districts on the Angolan central plateau: Bocoio (formerly Vila de Sousa Lara), Balombo (formerly Vila de Norton de Matos), Bailundo, Chinguar, and Quilengues (see Map 1). With a letter of introduction from the National Archives in Luanda, we set out in a rented jeep to locate former *contratados*. Our first stop in each province was the provincial administration to request permission to conduct interviews. This process necessitated at least a couple days in each capital to schedule meetings. Authorities were always accommodating and willing to help. Several voiced support for studying Angola's history and thanked us for our efforts. Official letter in hand, we set out for the former recruitment districts.

Interviews generally took place in a local *onjango* [a covered, open-air gathering place]. We recorded the interviews with a tape recorder. In every village we visited, multiple generations gathered to hear their elders "making history in dialogue," which gave this interviewer the sense that the occasion of the interview was truly momentous.[18] Approximately 90 percent of the 56 in-depth interviews we conducted with former *contratados* in recruitment districts (see Introduction) were conducted in Umbundu by my colleague, Manuel Domingos, as I do not speak fluent Umbundu. We always asked for the interviewee's language preference and permission to make the interview publicly available at the AHA. Although the vast majority of interviews were in Umbundu, often interviewees peppered the interview with Portuguese words and expressions. As Manuel made a running translation into Portuguese for my

18 Della Pollock, ed., *Remembering Oral History Performance* (New York: Palgrave MacMillan, 2005), 2.

benefit, I often asked a follow-up question in Portuguese, which an interviewee would answer directly in Portuguese rather than waiting for the translation. Most interviewees, although more comfortable in Umbundu, spoke at least some Portuguese, Angola's lingua franca since the colonial era.

We took a life-history approach to interviews, asking each participant to give his or her name, birthplace, and age.[19] We followed up with general questions about family and profession. We asked about the colonial era generally, and then asked interviewees to talk about their service as a *contratado*. We asked specific questions about recruitment, work conditions, life on the plantation, the kinds of work performed, treatment by the authorities, payment, and impact on their families. Manuel read from a typed list of questions we prepared in advance, then he translated responses into Portuguese for my benefit. The translations meant that each group interview took several hours. After conducting interviews, Manuel and I transcribed all the interviews from Umbundu to Portuguese to English. We deposited copies of all the interviews in the AHA.[20] (See the Introduction, pp. 16–20, for more about the broader methodological considerations of this oral history research.)

The kinds of manual labor described in interviews remained relatively constant from Cassequel's early years until the 1950s, when the Portuguese government decided to phase out forced labor to improve its image as a colonial power and to make a case for its newly adopted theory of *luso-tropicalismo*. Therefore, it is possible to hear the experiences recounted by interviewees as reflective of forced labor not just for the years they worked but for the entire span of forced labor at Cassequel. Likewise, the memories of women forced to perform unpaid roadwork provides a fuller understanding of the systemic violence of Portugal's colonial labor policy.

There was certainly an element of theater involved in the group interviews. In nearly all the villages, we set up chairs and a table, on which sat the tape recorder (Image 3.1). Given such a setting, I often thought about what it means to stage oral histories.[21] Did the performative aspect of the group interview presuppose how interviewees would answer? To begin, we always explained, in both Portuguese and Umbundu, the objective of the group interview: "to learn about migrant labor from the 1940s and 1950s." I explained that we were working with the National Archives in Luanda and that I had written a study

19 For more on the life-history approach to oral history, see Valerie Raleigh Yow, *Recording Oral History A Guide for the Humanities and Social Sciences* (Lanham, MD: AltaMira Press, 2005).

20 A selection of interviews has also been made available on the Aluka Struggles for Freedom in Southern Africa website, http://www.aluka.org/struggles Accessed January 30, 2015.

21 Della Pollock, ed., *Remembering Oral History Performance*, 2–3.

IMAGE 3.1 *Interview, Bocoio, February 16, 2006*
PHOTO: BY THE AUTHOR.

on the subject of labor in colonial Angola. As my manuscript was passed around, I told of my research in the National Archives and pointed out several reproduced photographs of *contratados* taken at Cassequel in 1961 (see Images 4.1–4.3 in Chapter 4). These photos jump-started our conversation. The photos were then usually passed outside the immediate circle of *mais velhos* to younger men and women sitting on the outside the circle, waiting to hear their elders speak of the past.

Memories of how the forced labor system functioned were consistent throughout the region, and they supported the conclusions of investigative reports, though with some variation in mechanisms for control. *Sobas*, who answered to the local Portuguese *chefe de posto*, delivered a specified number of men to serve as *contratados*. If a *soba* failed to fulfill the request, he faced disciplinary action, including being beaten. João Ndamba remembers, for example, a *soba* from Chibungo who received 200 *palmatórias* divided equally between his hands and feet [a *palmatória* is a wooden paddle with holes in the striking surface; it was used for corporal punishment] and as a result spent nine months in bed recuperating.[22] Men from distant areas describe similar

22 Author interview with João Ndamba, February 17, 2006, Monte Belo (Benguela).

consequences for *sobas* who failed to fulfill their labor quota. Augusto Katchilele from Chinguar remembers his *soba* receiving *matapalos*, an Umbundu term for *palmatórias*, because he arrived at the government post with thirty men rather than the fifty demanded by the *chefe de posto* to work on the roads.[23] Katchilele says those beatings explain why *sobas* "abducted men without rest."[24]

Chefes de posto often used labor recruitment to supplement their low salaries.[25] Many of the *chefes de posto* knew little about the cultures and languages of the people they governed. Francisco Fernandes, a *chefe de posto* in Mozambique who authored a manual to assist *chefes de posto* with little idea of how to perform the job, described the isolation of a *chefe de posto* who "the greater part of the time has to act on his own."[26]

In 1952, Vasco Monteiro, director of Cassequel, wrote to Manuel Espírito Santo, president of Cassequel's board of directors, about how not paying bribes to *chefes de posto* made it difficult to receive sufficient numbers of *contratados*: "I believe that the principal reason for our labor shortage is that we have not wanted to buy blacks. I do not want to enter into details here, but I have approached the Governor of the Province (Benguela) and the Governor-General [of Angola]."[27]

When Monteiro spoke of "buying blacks," he was referring to bribes paid to colonial administrators for ensuring the delivery of *contratados*. British Consul S.P. House explained, "The price paid to the administrator in bribes for forced labour has reached extraordinary heights. It goes up to 1500 Angolares a head for men and 1,000 Angolares for little boys of ten or twelve."[28] Cassequel preferred young men ranging in ages from the late teens to early thirties because of their physical stamina and relatively fewer responsibilities in their home villages.

Youth was a common characteristic among *contratados*. For example, in 1947, the Huambo office of the *Curadoria* contracted seventy-nine men to work

---

23 Author interview with Augusto Lopes Katchilele, April 18, 2006, Chinguar (Bié).

24 Ibid.

25 "British Consul General, Luanda," June 28, 1950. FO 371/80769, PRO.

26 Francisco Alfredo Fernandes, *O Posto Administrativo Na Vida Do Indígena* (Lisboa: Publicações Europa-América, 1955), 15. This is an interesting book of advice written by a concientious colonial administrator who graduated from Portugal's Instituto Superior de Estudos Ultramarinos (Institute for Colonial Studies).

27 "Correspondencia trocada entre Vasco Alexandre do Valle Monteiro (Administrador em Africa) e Manuel Espirito Santo acerca de diversos assuntos, 25/11/1951 a 30/09/58," May 25, 1952, AHBES.

28 British Consul S.P. House, Luanda, 16 October 1951, FO 371/90313, PRO.

at Cassequel for one year at the monthly salary of 66 *angolares*.[29] All of the workers came from the administrative post of Quipeio, and at Cassequel they went to work as a *guia* [work group]. Cassequel divided *contratados* into *guias* according to recruitment district and language.[30] A majority of the workers were younger than twenty-five years, and only seven were older than forty years (Table 3.1). The relatively smaller number of men between the ages of twenty-five and thirty-nine suggests that most men in their working prime either met their tax requirements or migrated to more lucrative job markets outside Angola. Contract workers from Balombo who worked at Cassequel in 1948 reflected a similar breakdown by age (Table 3.2).[31] Of the forty-seven *contratados*, thirty were younger than age twenty-five.Interviewees discussed repeatedly how subservience and daily humiliations characterized social relationships. José Inácio explained that "not even *sobas*" had the right to speak to or question the orders of colonists. "If he told you to get naked, you did what he said because if you didn't you would become a target for abuse."[32] In response to whether *contratados* exercised any choice in employer, Félix Alberto Satuala responded: "Not at all, because the term *contratado* signified slave…nobody had the right to stand next to a white to say his name, much less to voice a preference [for employer]."[33] Francisco Segunda explained that the few whites living in

TABLE 3.1 *Age distribution of contract workers from Quipeio at Cassequel, 1947*

Age (years)	Number
15–19	24
20–24	23
25–29	8
30–34	9
35–39	8
40–44	5
45–49	2
TOTAL	79

SOURCE: "AGENCIA DA CURADORIA DO CONCELHHO DO LOBITO," SEPTEMBER 2, 1948, CAIXA 1273, AHA.

29 "Colonia de Angola Agencia da Curadoria de Huambo," Benguela, Caixa 575, AHA.
30 Interview with Daniel Sowende Fiqueiredo, Catembela, 4 July 2001.
31 "Agencia da Curadoria do Concelhho do Lobito," 2 September 1948, Caixa 1273, AHA.
32 Author interview with José Inácio, February 17, 2006, Monte Belo.
33 Author interview with Félix Alberto Satuala, April 18, 2006, Chinguar (Bié).

TABLE 3.2 *Age distribution of contract workers from Balombo at Cassequel, 1948*

Age (years)	Number
15–19 years	8
20–24	22
25–29	7
30–34	6
35–39	4
40–44	0
45–49	0
TOTAL	47

SOURCE: "AGENCIA DA CURADORIA DO CONCELHHO DO LOBITO," SEPTEMBER 2, 1948, CAIXA 1273, AHA.

Bailundo treated him with outright contempt: "Several decades ago here (Bailundo) you would not be able to approach a white because he would treat you like an animal with a horrible smell…the fact that we are still alive to tell this history to a white here in Bailundo, we give thanks to God."[34]In response to a question about whether they missed any aspect of Portuguese colonialism, interviewees disagreed. Benedito Chitumbo's response mirrored the feelings of many: "You never feel nostalgia for one who mistreats you…the black was used like a tool, or better yet a machine…I will say that the Portuguese presence in Angola was very good in respect to development, but their regime killed many Angolans."[35] Cristina Vatchia dismissed the idea that the Portuguese developed Angola and said simply that "it is because of this history that the Portuguese are not welcome in Angola."[36] Most who served at Cassequel said that by the 1950s, corporal punishment was rarely used to discipline *contratados*, but others remembered the impunity with which whites exercised their control. José Inácio recalled interactions on the plantation: "We were humiliated in front of the whites. When you saw a white coming in your direction with a whip, your sides ached because it was for you that the whip was intended."[37] Inácio described his year as a *contratado* at Cassequel as a time when "grown men cried and asked continually 'how much longer?'"[38] João Kutakata cited abuse from a member of

34 Author interview with Francisco Segunda, April 12, 2006, Bailundo.

35 Author interview with Benedito Chitumbo, April 18, 2006, Chinguar.

36 Author interview with Cristina Vatchia, April 12, 2006, Bailundo.

37 Author interview with José Inácio, February 17, 2006, Monte Belo.

38 Ibid.

the Catholic clergy: "We had a bishop of the Catholic Church named Daniel Gomes Nova Lisboa[39] who said that if you wanted to beat a black, don't use a *chicote* [whip], use a hammer, because if you beat him with a *chicote*, it might fall out of your hand."[40] Although it is doubtful that the bishop actually beat people with a hammer, the construction of this memory does indicate how Mr. Kutakata—and presumably others as well—viewed the Catholic Church as capable of using extreme violence against Africans. The image of the hammer-yielding bishop also indicates the perception that the Church, or least some members of the hierarchy, supported the colonial order.

Officially, Cassequel prohibited the infliction of corporal punishment on any African or Cape Verdean worker in 1952: "No [white] employee will be able to fire or apply any punishment to the native or Cape Verdean personnel under their charge."[41] Instead, white employees were instructed to send problematic workers to the administration, which would then decide the appropriate disciplinary action. Rather than inflicting corporal punishment themselves, Cassequel's administrators sent employees to the government post across the river, an option documented by the historian/activist Basil Davidson in his 1955 book about the rise of African nationalism, *The African Awakening*. Davidson reported an interview with Cassequel's director, Vasco Monteiro, in which Davidson asked what happened when a *contratado* refused to work:

> Monteiro: "Oh, but they will work. They do."
> Davidson: "Still, supposing they won't?"
> Monteiro: "Then we send them to the police station."
> Davidson: "And what do the police do with them?"
> Monteiro: "To men who won't work? Put them in prison, of course."[42]

Davidson continues, "Put them in prison: yes, and flog them. Witness after witness (although not Senhor Monteiro) told me this—some nonchalantly, taking the thing for obvious and natural, some with bitter loathing, some with painful memories."[43]

39 The bishop's actual name was Daniel Gomes Junqueira. He was appointed bishop of Nova Lisboa in 1941 and served in that capacity until his death in 1970. Email communication with Angolan historian Maria Conceição Neto, September 10, 2009.

40 Author interview with João Kutakata, February 21, 2006, Balombo.

41 "Ordem de Servico N. 6," February 15, 1952, *Correspondencia trocada entre Fernando de Serpa Pimentel, director do Cassequel em Angola, e Manuel Espirito Santo, assuntos pessoal, producao, 26/9/52 a 20/2/61. Caixa 1, Cota 01/01.2*, AHBES.

42 Basil Davidson, *The African Awakening* (London: Jonathan Cape, 1955), 217.

43 Ibid.

Vasco Monteiro reported this conversation to his board of directors:

> We are going to pass through a difficult and dangerous period for Cassequel. One of the accusations that an important Englishman makes in his book with the title *The African Awakening* is that I send the blacks to the Post where they receive blows when they do not want to work. Unfortunately the case has an element of truth…it was common to send [to the Post], above all the Cape Verdeans who complained about their *empreitada* [daily task] to receive *palmatoadas* [slaps on the hand with a *palmatória*].[44]

Vasco Monteiro admitted that the practice of sending workers who did not want to work to the post continued but assured his board of directors that it was no longer common.[45] Yet, according to Jorge Luíz Chiungue, an African foreman in the fields at the time of Basil Davidson's visit, "Whoever made trouble was hit and it was the white man who ordered us blacks to hit them [the troublemakers] with a stick."[46] Mr. Chiungue explained that many workers ran away from Cassequel because of corporal punishment, "but others endured the beatings in order to provide the essentials to their families."[47] Former *contratados* who began working at Cassequel after the labor reforms of the early 1960s agreed with Faustino Alfredo, a nurse in Cassequel's hospital, who said, "Cassequel did not beat its workers."[48] Thus, sometime between the prohibition of corporal punishment in 1952 and the early 1960s, corporal punishment at Cassequel apparently ended.

Salomão dos Santos recalls that he was abducted for forced labor while coming home from school in 1943. Because of his young age, he did not cut sugarcane at Cassequel like other *contratados*, but served as cook for a work

---

44 "Letter from Vasco Monteiro to Manuel Espírito Santo," May 30, 1955, *Correspondencia trocada entre Fernando de Serpa Pimentel, director do Cassequel em Angola, e Manuel Espirito Santo, assuntos pessoal, producao, 26/9/52 a 20/2/61*, Caixa 1, Cota 01/01.2, AHBES. The *palmatória* was "a sort of mallet carved from one piece of hard wood, with a handle some ten or twelve inches long, the head being a disk some three inches across and an inch and a half thick. On each side of this disk five tapering holes were bored…The way this implement of torture was employed is this. The victim holds one hand out palm up. The operator brings the *palmatória* with a sharp forceful blow on the outstretched palm." Davidson, *The African Awakening*, 218.

45 "Letter from Vasco Monteiro to Manuel Espírito Santo."

46 Author interview with Jorge Luíz Chiungue, Gama, July 16, 2001.

47 Ibid.

48 Author interview with Faustino Alfredo, Catumbela, July 5, 2001, Catumbela.

guia from Balombo.[49] At this point in the interview, Inácio Boboleta interjected a comment about the intensity of the labor: "At Cassequel, there was work that killed men, which I saw with my own eyes. The clearing of irrigation ditches—4–5 meters deep—killed men. Men worked naked, except for wrapping an old sugar sack around their sensitive areas. You can't imagine how it was."[50] He further explained the graduated consequences for not finishing work: "The work was by task, and if you did not finish your task [*empreitada*], the first time you were given a beating; the second time you had no right to food, even a plate of *fuba*; the third time you had to work throughout the night and continue in the morning."[51] *Capatazes* [foremen] enforced such disciplinary actions and upheld the work schedule on the plantation (Image 3.2). Some *capatazes* even lived on the plantation, rather than in Catumbela with the Portuguese community. Their former homes, painted in Cassequel's signature *cor-de-rosa* [pink], still dot the landscape.

IMAGE 3.2 *Capatazes watching workers cut cane, 1954*
SOURCE: A.G. WETHMAR AND P.C. BRUTEL DE LA RIVIÈRE, "THE SUGAR INDUSTRY IN ANGOLA AND MOZAMBIQUE," HOLLAND, 1954, SALA 2, MAÇO 192, AHU, 54.

49 Author interview with Salomão dos Santos, February 21, 2006, Balombo.
50 Author interview with Inácio Boboleta, February 21, 2006, Balombo.
51 Ibid.

Most interviewees described the work at the plantation as hard labor, but not all agreed with Boboleta's claim that the work "killed men." Of course, the different characterizations may have depended on the type of work one performed. In Chinguar, Félix Alberto Satuala described his work at Cassequel in 1942 as consisting of the transporting of cut cane by hand to the plantation's railcars.[52] During his two years of service, he also fertilized the fields with ground fish bones harvested from the plantation's fishery and cow dung from the plantation's cattle ranch. Chemical fertilizers were introduced in the late 1950s in an effort to reduce labor needs and thus shift the plantation away from its reliance on forced labor. Characterizing his work as a *contratado*, Satuala said:

> It was a work of suffering, not only at sugar plantations, but in all the cities where *contratados* worked. Men left the sugar plantations with sores covering their bodies. But I want to tell you one thing; the work of a *contratado* was violent, even though at Cassequel they did not beat workers. It was the work itself that was violent. You started at 6 a.m., you ate lunch at 12, and afterward you worked more, as each one had to finish his task.[53]

Contratados coped with the heavy labor burden—far from their families, and without any real monetary incentive—as best they could. In response to questions about what they did for diversion, or to pass the time, interviewees said that they worked six-day weeks and were thus so exhausted that they had little time for fun. Sunday was the one day they could catch up on sleep, relax, and perhaps play or listen to music. Several interviewees said that nobody thought of music as a form of resistance, but that it did help "us to attempt to forget our suffering."[54] Men from Balombo remember singing about Brandão, a labor agent who collected *contratados* in the interior and, along with a phalanx of guards, escorted them on a days-long journey on foot to Cassequel:[55]

52 Author interview with Félix Alberto Satuala.

53 Ibid.

54 Author interview with Inácio Boboleta. For a case study of workers' music as resistance, see Leroy Vail and Landeg White, *Capitalism and Colonialism in Mozambique A Study of Quelimane District* (Minneapolis: University of Minnesota Press, 1980). For an analysis of songs sung during Angola's war for independence, see Inge Brinkman, ed., *Singing in the Bush: MPLA songs during the war for independence in south-east Angola (1966–1975)* (Koln: Rudiger Koppe Verlag, 2001).

55 Author interview with Tchimbe Ngucika.

Kalunga kakuenje te Brandão Há Há Há veteéé
Kalunga ka kuenje veteéé
Brandão was the death of the young men[56]

Men from Quillengues remembered a song about the loneliness of forced labor:

Kueva alunu kuakola
Kueva alunu kuakola kola (bis)
Kueva akãi kutalálá
Kueva akãi kutakulala (bis)
Men experience physical exhaustion (2x)
While women live with loneliness (2x)[57]

Another song testified to the effects of forced labor:

Omuenho ivakuenje okupeseka ndo vava
Omuenho ivakuenje okupeseka ndo vava
Suffering causes the life of young men to be poured out like water[58]

Across the board, *contratados* remembered their salaries as being virtually nothing. Men talked about working simply to pay their tax, which remained with the government administrators who "recruited" them:

> At Cassequel I received 40$00 per month, and when I arrived here in Quilengues [his home region] I received only 600$00 after 15 months. From this salary they took out 300$00 to pay my taxes, leaving me with only 300$00. In that time, we worked for the *chefe de posto*...who paid us that unjust salary, while the rest of the money remained with him. Hence, one time I asked the administrator why if we worked, the money to be paid to us remains here [with the administrator]? The Administrator thought about it, and said, "When you have a dog...and this dog goes hunting and brings home an animal, do you give the meat or the bone to

56 "Brandão" was the name of a representative of Cassequel responsible for bringing contratados to the plantation. Author interview with Inácio Boboleta.

57 Author interview with Luís Massuna, May 10, 2006, the village of Mussanji, near Quilengues.

58 Ibid.

> the dog?" We said, "I give him the bones." "Hence," the administrator said, "you are like the dog, because you go to work."[59]

The Port of Lobito paid *contratados* wages similar to those at Cassequel. João Ndamba remembers being paid 400$00 after 15 months of service, from which 150$00 was subtracted to pay his tax, leaving him "only with a few crumbs that did not solve any of your problems, much less those of your wife and children."[60] Describing his work as a *contratado* at the Cassequel Sugar Plantation, José Inácio explains: "You were not able to buy cloth for your wife with what we were paid, much less a shirt for your child. It was obligatory work. We did it not because we wanted to, but because they wanted us to, hence it was not good."[61] One interviewee became exasperated when asked if during his service as a *contratado* he had had a small garden to grow food: "My dear son…this is an absurd question because our work was the work of a prisoner, difficult work, a work without equal, hence it would be difficult for a slave to have a vegetable garden, no?"[62]

Men generally fulfilled their period of forced labor (anywhere from six months to several years) because fleeing potentially harmed one's family. Not incidentally, the potential for runaways also explains the importance colonial administrators attached to compiling statistics at the time of "recruitment": age, *sobado* (village), and names of parents. Once a person's absence had been noted, a message would be sent to the *chefe de posto* in the area of recruitment, who would then relay a message to the *soba* of the *fugido* [runaway]. The *soba* was then expected to supply a replacement worker from the family of the *fugido*; thus, fleeing often carried a price for one's family. As José Samuel explained, "If you fled, he [the *soba*] would have the obligation to abduct your father-in-law…because if he did not, he would receive *palmatórias* and still be required to deliver workers."[63]

In Quilengues (see Map 1), an area where most people kept cattle, the *soba* held a man's cattle as collateral to ensure that he fulfilled his period of service. A *contratado* who fled thus risked forfeiting his family's collective wealth.[64] The fact that men from Quilengues rarely fled reflects and helps explain statistical evidence that men of this region generally served out their contract. Still,

59 Ibid.
60 Author interview with João Ndamba.
61 Author interview with José Inácio, February 17, 2006, Monte Belo.
62 Author interview with José Samuel, February 21, 2006, Balombo.
63 Ibid.
64 Author interview with Manuel Seguro, May 9, 2006, Socobal (Quilengues).

even in areas without cattle, the penalties suffered by families served as a major disincentive to flee. For *contratados* who did flee, returning to one's village was out of the question. A *fugido* had to move to a new area and begin a new life. Some went to cities, others to neighboring agricultural zones. According to Alfredo Domingos, himself a *fugido*: "There were men who fled who abandoned their families, wives, children, and parents."[65]

Workers who fled generally walked for great distances on back roads and relied on the generosity of others for sustenance. A few came up with inventive plans for escape. In the 1940s, for example, several *guias* fled the Cassequel Sugar Plantation by claiming to the *capataz* that one of their members had died. Then, eight to ten men gathered to make up the funeral procession, and with two live "corpses" in the coffin went in the direction of the cemetery; they never returned. As Justino Patrício remembers, "I escaped in a coffin." He thinks the trick "worked like magic, and when it was discovered, a good part of some *guias* had already fled."[66] Some *fugidos* carved out a space in one of Angola's growing and relatively anonymous cities. For *fugidos* from the central highlands, the coastal cities of Benguela and Lobito were favorite destinations. Bento Somuvuango fled a coffee *fazenda* [farm] and ended up spending three years as a domestic servant in Benguela. He avoided returning to his home and family in Bailundo because he feared being sent back to the coffee *fazenda* by his *soba*.[67]

The consequences for men caught fleeing their contract obligation were severe. First, the man would be arrested and put in prison, where he was usually beaten. Next, the *fugido* would be contracted to a new employer for a longer period of service. Often, detained *fugidos* were sent to São Tomé in the Gulf of Guinea. São Tomé was the most feared destination for *contratados* because of its great distance and the fact that periods of service lasted years. Many never returned, some as a result of death; others were simply never heard from again. If a *fugido* did not return to his village, colonial officials insisted that a family member fulfill the period of service.

A person questioned by the authorities outside of his home district and without his *caderneta indígena* was also liable to be sent to São Tomé. Africans had to have permission to travel beyond their home district. In the 1940s, for example, a young son of an important Umbundu *soba* was arrested in the

65 Author interview with Alfredo Domingos, February 17, 2006, Monte Belo.

66 Author interview with Soba Justino Patrício, 23 February 23, 2006, village of Cayengue-Mbola Kavulo.

67 Author interview with Bento Somuvuango, April 14, 2006, Bailundo.

coastal town of Lobito far from home without his *caderneta*. Normally *sobas* and their families were exempted from forced labor, but without proof of identity, the young Augusto Kachitiopololo had no right to an exemption. That young man, who would later return home and eventually become King of Bailundo, served nearly nine years on the São Tomé cocoa plantation Boa Entrada. King Augusto Katchitiopololo explains:

> That work on São Tomé was slavery. I did not want to go, but because of the white [government official], I was sent to São Tomé for not having my passbook…[O]n that plantation [Boa Entrada] I planted cocoa, bananas, coconuts, and later harvested each one, with sufficient whippings [*chicotata*] mixed in…I also had to dig holes in which to plant the cocoa trees, this was surely the work of slaves…as were all of those who were sold in Catumbela and sent to São Tomé, and I was one of them. I worked roughly eight years and seven months until an order came down to liberate all of the slaves. All those who had been sold as slaves now had to be returned to their lands of origin. Thus the government sent ships to carry us home.[68]

It is true that the government occasionally put pressure on the plantation owners to return *contratados* to their home districts, which would corroborate the king's description of events. The general practice, of course, was to return *contratados* to their port of embarkation: a *contratado* from Bailundo would be returned to the coastal port of Benguela and then be expected to make his own way home, up the escarpment and across several hundred miles.[69]

A general consensus emerged among interviewees that by the early 1960s, forced contracting by government agents gave way to voluntary recruitment, a time frame that corresponds with the 1962 abolition of forced labor.[70] At Cassequel, administrators lessened their reliance on forced labor during the 1950s. In the early 1950s, Cassequel focused on working with African *sobas*, whom they considered an important link in steering *contratados* to specific employers. A 1952 visit to Cassequel by two *sobas* from the Bundas (Moxico Province, a large, sparsely populated area that bordered the Belgian Congo and

68 Author interview with King Augusto Kachitiopololo, April 12, 2006, Bailundo.

69 "Ano de 1917 Distrito de Benguela Cirunscrição Civil do Bailundo, Autos de Investagação" Bailundo, Caixa 5647, AHA.

70 Maul, "The International Labour Organization and the Struggle against Forced Labour from 1919 to the Present," 487.

Northern Rhodesia) demonstrated that Cassequel's administrators viewed *sobas* as key partners in recruitment. Cassequel and the governor of the province of Bié extended the invitation both to counter rumors in the interior that workers received bad treatment at Cassequel and to impress the *sobas* with the benefits of working with Cassequel.[71] In many ways, the "rumors" of bad treatment are reflected in the memories of former *contratados* cited above. In exchange for their visit and support the *sobas* each received "all of the articles that they desire to carry with them, for themselves and their five wives. Their loads consisted of various pieces of clothing: pants, hats, collars, pots, plates, mugs, etc., and for each a sack of our good white sugar and a sack of salt that in the interior is very expensive."[72] Cassequel also paid each *soba* 500 *angolares* for the journey, in addition to the 200 *angolares* paid to each one by the administrator of the district of Lobito, and a Portuguese flag to hang in their *ombala* [homestead].[73] The payment of 700 *angolares* was equal to six months of wages for a contracted worker.

What the *sobas* thought of the visit is impossible to know in that a Portuguese administrator at Cassequel recorded the only existing account of the visit. The following quote must therefore be read with caution. The administrator's account quoted one soba exclaiming after a visit to the Port of Lobito and the sugar refinery at Cassequel:

> At last the Portuguese have a lot of power, more than the English. It is to here that our children must come. In Rhodesia our children die without returning, others return missing arms and legs, and still others return unable to work. Hence, it is here, where they will be well treated, that our children will come. They earn well, eat well, have a hospital and

---

71 SAC, *Cartas Expedida 1949–1952*, October 17, 1952, AC. Migrant laborers avoiding employers with bad reputations among workers was not unique to Angola. See, for example, Charles Van Onselen, *Chibaro: African Mine Labour in Southern Rhodesia 1900–1933* (Johannesburg: Ravan Press, 1976), 234.

72 Ibid., On the preciousness of salt, see John T. Tucker, *Drums in the Darkness* (New York: Doran Company, 1927), 48: "Housekeeping in Central Africa is complicated by the scarcity of salt…The craving for salt is intense among Central African tribes and the special word (*esase*) used to describe it is pronounced with drawn mouth wringing pity from the passing traveller." For an interesting interpretation of meanings of European clothing in neighboring colonial Namibia, see Hildi Hendrickson, "Bodies and Flags: The Representation of Herero Identity in Colonial Namibia," in Hildi Henrickson, ed., *Clothing and Difference: Embodied Identities in Colonial and Post-Colonial Africa* (Durham: Duke University Press, 1996), 213–244.

73 SAC, *Cartas Expedida 1949–1952*, October 17, 1952, AC.

> medicine, and the whites in this company do not beat [the workers], that we already know.[74]

The *sobas* visited worker housing, the hospital, and the outdoor movie screen; according to the administrator's account, they came away satisfied and said that work conditions were good enough for their "sons," or rather the men under their authority. It is certainly plausible that the *sobas* left impressed with Cassequel's physical plant and some of the recent improvements in health care and worker villages.

In 1955, the board of directors adopted a new policy of voluntary labor. Manuel Espírito Santo, president of the board of directors, summed up the policy shift in a letter to the administration at Cassequel:

> The labor problem is without a doubt of maximum importance for our business...the most desirable solution to the labor problem would be a voluntary work force, not only at present, but principally in the future given the native labor policy that the Governor General of the province plans to follow.
>
> Hence, everything ought to be done to settle native families around our properties...so that the native is convinced of the advantages represented by the assistance that will be supplied to his children and wife and others that will be able to live in an environment of greater resources, free from the contingencies of bad agricultural years that bring hunger, and with a greater guarantee of income. A more intensive missionary action among our workers will result in their Christianization, which accords with our objective.[75]

This policy shift away from force signified a major shift in thinking about labor. The new emphasis on a voluntary workforce entailed improving several aspects of employment, including addressing recruitment practices and salaries, ending corporal punishment, erecting worker housing, and providing health care and other social services to workers and their families. Cassequel's board of directors took more than a decade to implement these reforms because of their reluctance to spend the required financial resources.

---

74 Ibid.

75 "Letter from Manuel Espírito Santo to Administration in Africa," March 10, 1955, *Cartas Recebidas, 1950–1955*, AC. For a comparative case of improving labor conditions to attract workers to the sisal plantations of southern Tanganyika, see Ewdard A Alpers, "'To Seek a Better Life': The Implications of Migration from Mozambique to Tanganyika for Class Formation and Political Behavior," *Canadian Journal of African Studies* (vol. 18, no. 2, 1984), 375.

Women's Memories

Colonial law obligated men and women to perform annual roadwork. The burden fell the heaviest on women and children, who often performed roadwork while their fathers and brothers served their period as a *contratado* far from home. Women also shouldered the burdens of caring for families during men's absence for contract labor. When a man left to spend six months or more on a faraway plantation, his family received no financial compensation. Indeed, Portugal's forced labor system barely covered the costs of a single *contratado*, and certainly did not pay enough to support his family. Jacinta Cahomas explains: "Our husbands never sent anything during forced labor. With luck, when they arrived home they would buy you a *pano* [piece of cloth] and some clothes for the kids, but the rest went towards the tax. Many had to return to forced labor because they were unable to pay the next year's tax."[76] Predictably, Cassequel did not calculate the sacrifices made by the families of *contratados* in its annual financial reports.

Roadwork also meant that a woman had to be away from her crops—the primary source of sustenance for her family. One of the songs women sang during roadwork lamented the time away:

> Teke Ra Teke tuenda kovinde,
> Katulinu Tuenda Rovindele, Katulimi tuende lovindele
> *Each day that we go with the whites, we do not cultivate*
> *All because we go with the whites.*[77]

Another song cited the long working hours from sunrise and sunset:

> *Capataz kakuete ololocho, ololocho yaco ukuvanja ke kumbi* (2x)
> *Oco vakuene vo vatambulela*
> *The* capataz *does not have a watch, his only watch is the sun.*
> *The men and women run from side to side [of the road] until they crumble in exhaustion*[78]

Forced labor without pay on the dirt roads is remembered as one of the most onerous and resented experiences of colonialism. The work was excruciatingly difficult: repairing holes created by rain and landslides by carrying baskets full

---

76 Author interview with Jacinta Cahomas, February 21, 2006, Balombo.

77 Author interview with Juana Golossi, May 9, 2006, Quilengues.

78 Author interviews with Constantina Baca, April 18, 2006, Chinguar, and Francisco Segunda.

of dirt by hand. Selection for roadwork crews mirrored that for *contratados*: the *chefe de posto* sent word to a particular *soba* that a specified number of people would be needed on a particular stretch of road for a given time, usually several weeks. Workers carried their own food and water to the site and built makeshift shelters in which to sleep at night.

The practice of using unpaid, forced labor for public purposes was common among colonial powers. They justified their reliance on this form of labor on the grounds that it served the public good, arguing that coercion existed in precolonial African societies and that without it they (the colonial power) could not develop their colonies and improve the lives of their African subjects.[79] In the 1920s, these powers had ensured that the ILO would adopt a separate Native Labor Code that explicitly exempted the practice of forced labor for public purposes from regulation.[80] Only with the adoption of the 1956 Abolition of Forced Labor Convention was the legality of forced labor for public purposes in colonial possessions overturned.

Roadwork a half century later is universally described as "slavery" and "work beyond the imagination." Verónica Chilomba explains: "There wasn't even food for us. We certainly were not paid. We worked worse than slaves because a slave has a right to a cup of water."[81] Cristina Vatchia shares a similar traumatic memory:

> I went to work on the roads at a very young age, and I saw the suffering. When we arrived, the first thing to do was to construct a shelter. We were like monkeys living in the rocks, running from one side of the road to the other like ants, our heads carrying huge baskets full of dirt…[82]

Women suffered especially as a result of sexual assaults from *capatazes* and *cipaios*. Rape and abuse caused the women to feel helpless and shameful, emotions they still remember a half-century later. As a *mais velha* in Balombo explains "We were humiliated, our suffering as women passed all boundaries because white men had no shame. We did not have the protection of our husbands because they were also under the thumb of the whites…we were easy

79 For a case study from pre-colonial Asante, see Gareth Austin, *Labour, Land and Capital in Ghana: From Slavery to Free Labour in Asante, 1807–1956* (Rochester, NY: University of Rochester Press, 2005), 432–433.

80 Maul, "The International Labour Organization and the Struggle against Forced Labour from 1919 to the Present," 477–500.

81 Author interview with Verónica Chilomba, February 21, 2006, Balombo.

82 Author interview with Cristina Vatchia, April 13, 2006, Bailundo.

targets…it was really incredible how the colonists mistreated us."[83] These experiences of sexual violence distinguish women's collective and individual memories of forced labor from those of men.

In fact, it was not only whites who sexually assaulted women, but also black *cipaios*, who regularly chose women from among roadwork crews for exploitation. This sexual abuse is documented as far back as 1924 in Edward Ross's *Report on Employment of Native Labor in Portuguese Africa*: "In the village where the *cipaio* sleeps for the night, he takes whatever woman he fancies and no one dares say him nay."[84] Similar practices continued up through the end of forced labor in the late 1950s. Even married women were not immune to sexual abuse. Justina Kalumbo remembers: "The women considered beautiful to the eyes of men served the *cipaios*, and some of exceptional beauty were reserved for the *capatazes*…it was not important if she was married or not."[85] When asked if women ever initiated sex in exchange for exemption from hard labor, all but one of the interviewees said no. They insisted that women were chosen and that they could not say no because it would mean severe reprisals, even though it caused them great shame. As one interviewee explained: "If you did not consent, you would be beaten as if you were an animal…The women were used with tears and with pain [on their faces], with violence, it was an act without equal, when you arrived home, you looked at your husband with tears and sobs, ashamed at the same time."[86] The one interviewee who said she knew of women offering sex in exchange for exemption from forced labor explained that women who did so also ran the risk of receiving a beating: "[I]f the *cipaio* was not interested, you ran the risk of receiving *chicotadas* [whippings], because each one of us was so dirty to be unrecognizable."[87]

Women forced into sex generally received support from their communities, including their husbands, because, as Bernarda Kabyndo explains:

> …though she [a woman raped during roadwork] arrived [back in the village] timid with her husband, and full of shame, she was not discriminated against by the community because in that time it was not only women who were violated, but also our husbands. When the whites said

83 Author interview with Joaquina, February 21, 2006, Balombo. Some interviewees declined to give a second name.

84 Edward Alsworth Ross, *Report on Employment of Native Labor in Portuguese Africa* (New York: The Abbott Press, 1925), 31.

85 Author interview with Justina Kalumbo, April 13, 2006, Bailundo.

86 Author interview with Cipriana Nduva, April 13, 2006, Bailundo.

87 Author interview with Bernarda Kabyndo, April 18, 2006, Chinguar (Bié).

> to do something, even if it was to parade around naked in a public street, you did it. It was not only women who had to comply.[88]

In response to a question about whether they missed any aspect of colonial rule, not one woman said yes, though several said they respected how the Portuguese developed the country. Juana Golossi's comments reflected those of others interviewed in several different centers of recruitment:

> Of course I do not have any nostalgia (*saudade*) for any aspect of the white…The whites here in Quilengues mistreated us, beat us, rounded us up in the street for work made for machines, hence I feel no nostalgia.[89]

Conclusion

Between the end of World War II and 1961, leaders of the Estado Novo went to great lengths to buck the move toward independence across the colonized world. The "colonies" became "overseas provinces" of Portugal in 1951. The government initiated colonial development plans and facilitated the emigration of tens of thousands of Portuguese to Angola during the 1950s in an effort to make Angola more Portuguese. Portugal's economic elites, including the Espírito Santo family, made substantial investments in colonial businesses. At Cassequel, management understood by the early 1950s that the colonial administration would start to phase out forced labor; thus, Cassequel began to mechanize some operations and invest in infrastructure to attract more voluntary workers. The underlying goal of these reforms was, of course, to maintain Portuguese colonial hegemony. The fundamental structure of society did not change.

Interviewees—men and women both—who worked as forced labor experienced little change during the 1940s and 1950s. Interviewees remembered the brutality of the work regimen and the humiliation of colonial race and power relations. It is clear from men and women's memories that Angola's forced labor regime affected men and women in distinct ways. Although exempt from forced contract labor, women carried the burden of maintaining the family while their husbands fulfilled their labor obligation away from home. Women also faced the added humiliation and violence of sexual exploitation at the hands of authorities. As a result of their responsibilities to children and elders,

88 Ibid.

89 Author interview with Juana Golossi.

women had even fewer options for resistance than men. Men, on the other hand, experienced the suffering of long absences from home and performed physically grueling and often dangerous work; death was not uncommon. Men returned home after a nine- or twelve-month term of service with little to show their families. This reality weighed heavily on former *contratados*.

CHAPTER 4

African Nationalism, War, and Labor Reform, 1961–1973

In May 1961, in the midst of an armed revolt against Portuguese colonialism in the north of Angola, Cassequel's administrators hosted a party for *contratados* who had finished their contracts. Portuguese *capatazes* made banners proclaiming the loyalty of the *contratados* and praising the good working conditions at Cassequel. The caption on the banner of the Bailundo *Guia* (Image 4.1) reads: "We are all working of our own free will; God watch over us; Viva Cassequel; Viva Boss Alexandrino; Viva Portugal." To understand this propagandistic show of support by Cassequel's management for continued Portuguese colonialism, it is necessary to go back a few months: to January–March 1961 and the outbreak of the *guerrilla* war for independence.

Armed resistance to the Estado Novo regime first began in a cotton-growing region of Malange Province known as the Baixa de Cassange. The local population was forced to grow cotton and had to sell their crop at a fixed price. In November–December 1960, cotton producers in this region stopped work and refused to pay taxes. In January 1961, the Portuguese military carried out intimidating maneuvers in the area to send a message to the local population to return to work. In defiance, workers attacked several shops, an administrative post, and a Catholic mission. The Portuguese army used force to end the attacks and to compel people back to work by mid-March. Estimates of those killed in the reprisals ranged from Portuguese sources citing several dozen killed to nationalist sources stating as many as 10,000 killed.[1]

Because of press censorship and its remote location, the uprising in the Baixa de Cassange did not receive much coverage in the local or international press. The next uprising made international headlines because on January 22, 1961 Henrique Galvão, author of the infamous 1947 report and former colonial administrator in Angola, hijacked the Portuguese cruise ship *Santa Maria* in the Caribbean. For many weeks, the cruise ship zigzagged across the Atlantic, and many thought Galvão would steer it toward Luanda to jump-start a revolution against Salazar's Estado Novo. The ship never made it to Luanda, but the possibility of its arrival explained the presence of a contingent of the international press in Luanda on February 4, 1961, when, at dawn about 200 people who were aligned with the Popular Movement for the Liberation of Angola

1 Douglas L. Wheeler and René Pélissier, *Angola* (New York: Praeger Publishers, 1971), 174.

 | DOI 10.1163/9789004301757_006

GUIA 58 BAILUNDO

BANDEIRA DE PORTUGAL

Estamos todos

Trabalhamos com vontade

DEUS guardou-nos

VIVA O CASSEQUEL

VIVA o patrão ALEXANDRINO

VIVA PORTUGAL

O capataz HORÁCIO C.

IMAGE 4.1 *Bailundo guia*

SOURCE: SOCIEDADE AGRÍCOLA DO CASSEQUEL COLLECTION, ARQUIVO HISTÓRICO DO BANCO ESPÍRITO SANTO (AHBES), LISBON.

(MPLA: Movimento Popular de Libertação de Angola) attacked the São Paulo de Luanda prison, which housed political prisoners.

The MPLA had its roots in the Angolan Communist Party (PCA: Partido Comunista Angolano), which had begun in 1948 as a cell of the Portuguese party. The PCA and other less organized groups formed the MPLA in 1956. From its start, the MPLA drew most of its support from urbanized Africans, *mestiços*, and among the Luanda region's 1.3 million Mbundu.[2] The attack on February 4 failed and led to severe repression by the PIDE (Polícia Internacional e de Defesa do Estado: International and State Defense Police). The PIDE acted as the secret police of the Estado Novo; in 1957, they established offices in Angola and built up a network of informers.

On March 14–15, 1961, a much more serious challenge to Portuguese colonialism erupted in the coffee-growing areas of northern Angola. A second nationalist movement called the Union of the Peoples of Angola (UPA) orchestrated the revolt. The UPA formed in the mid-1950s under the leadership of the Léopoldville-based Holden Roberto, who, although Angolan by nationality, had spent most of his life in the Belgian Congo. The rebellion killed between 300 and 500 whites and perhaps as many as 1,500 Africans. The major bloodshed, however, occurred after the uprising in a series of brutal reprisals. The Portuguese military instigated extensive military operations, and estimates of African dead over the next several months range between 30,000 and 50,000. Many tens of thousands of Bakongo—the primary ethnic group of the region—fled over the border into the new Congo Republic. The Portuguese military increased from about 3,000 soldiers in Angola at the beginning of 1961 to nearly 50,000 by the end of the year.[3] In 1962, the UPA changed its name to the National Front for the Liberation of Angola (FNLA: Frente Nacional de Libertação de Angola).

In 1966, Jonas Savimbi founded a third nationalist movement: National Union for the Total Independence of Angola (UNITA: União Nacional para a Independência Total de Angola). UNITA's support came primarily from Angola's largest ethnic group, the Ovimbundu of the country's central highlands, which was also the home region for most of Cassequel's *contratados*. The establishment of UNITA completed the tripartite structure of Angolan nationalism that was to remain in place until the overthrow of the Estado Novo in 1974.

International pressure and nationalist demands for independence necessarily increased the pace of labor reform and mechanization. The government cut off Cassequel's forced labor in 1962 and the company's inability to recruit

2 Norrie MacQueen, *The Decolonization of Portuguese Africa Metropolitan Revolution and the Dissolution of Empire* (London and New York: Longman, 1997), 18–19.

3 MacQueen, *The Decolonization of Portuguese Africa*, 24.

sufficient numbers of voluntary workers led to labor shortages. To overcome these challenges, Cassequel invested in improved facilities, social services, and wages to attract *voluntários*. The company began a process of mechanization to reduce its labor needs. In 1968–1969, for example, Cassequel invested 12.500.000$00 *escudos* to attain 25 percent of the cutting and carrying of cane by machine.[4] In 1973 the Grupo Espírito Santo bought Angola's other large sugar plantation, A Companhia do Açúcar de Angola, as well as Portugal's major sugar refinery at Matosinhos. These investments demonstrated Espírito Santo commitment to Portuguese colonialism. For Cassequel's workforce, this period witnessed significant improvement in working and living conditions, an end to forced labor, and heightened political consciousness.

Political and Economic Context

During the 1960s, Salazar opened Angola to foreign investment in an effort to hasten development and defeat the nationalist guerrilla war. Leaders of the Estado Novo hoped that economic development and an improving standard of living would appease domestic and international critics of continued colonialism. The opening up of the economy to foreign investment, the discovery of oil, and the arrival of tens of thousands of Portuguese troops jump-started the economy. Angola's industrial production increased an average of 15 percent annually from 1961 to 1966;[5] the colony's gross internal product increased more than threefold from $850 million in 1963 to nearly $3 billion in 1973, because of a combination of foreign and domestic investment; high prices for commodity exports, such as coffee, diamonds, and oil; and the liberalization of exchange controls between the colonies and the metropole.[6] Customs tariffs and duties were reduced gradually over a ten-year period beginning in 1961 to create an *escudo* zone that incorporated metropolitan Portugal and the colonies.[7] The *escudo* became the single currency for the empire in 1963.

---

4 Gonçalo Inocentes, *As Cheias do Rio Catumbela* (self-published monograph, 2012), 163.

5 Hudson Institute, *Angola: Some Views of Development Prospects*, Vol. 1 (New York: Hudson Institute, 1969), 3.

6 Ana Maria Neto, *Industrialização de Angola Relexão sobre a Experiência da Administração Portuguesa (1961–1975)* (Lisboa: Escher, 1991), 9; and United Nations A/9623, V Report of Special Committee on the Granting of Independence to Colonial Countries and Peoples (1974), October 8, 1974, 6, cited in Lawrence W. Henderson, *The Church in Angola: A River of Many Currents* (Cleveland, Ohio: The Pilgrim Press, 1990), 324–325.

7 Anne M. Pitcher, *Politics in the Portuguese Empire: The State, Industry, and Cotton, 1926–1974* (Oxford: Clarendon Press, 1993), 255.

Almost all groups in Portugal in 1961, including the Communist Party, envisioned a continuing Portuguese presence in Africa, possibly in a commonwealth-type organization.[8] On the political front Salazar argued that the people of Angola were not yet ready for independence, and he cited the violence following Congolese independence in 1960 to argue that the maintenance of Portuguese rule contributed to the peace and stability of southern Africa.[9] In 1968, Salazar suffered a massive stroke and was replaced as prime minister by Marcello Caetano. Caetano shared Salazar's view that independence for the African colonies would lead to prolonged depression in Portugal brought about by the loss of the protected colonial market for her exports and a loss of prestige for Portugal.[10] As late as 1972, the government argued that integration with Europe and unity with the colonies was both possible and beneficial.[11]

The growing numbers of Portuguese settlers in Angola—numbering roughly a quarter million by 1970 out of a total population of 5.5 million—overwhelmingly supported the strong-arm tactics of the Portuguese military to repress the nationalist revolts. Most Portuguese settlers shared the regime's belief in the unity of the empire. A banner below (Image 4.2) welcoming the Portuguese governor general to Benguela in the late 1960s reflects this sentiment: "This is, and will continue to be, Portugal."

The small number of financial-industrial conglomerates that had dominated the Portuguese economy and benefited from monopolies and protectionist economic policies of the Estado Novo remained steadfast allies of Salazar throughout the 1960s. Of the three conglomerates operating in the colonies, the Grupo Espírito Santo was probably the most important and had the largest amount invested, with more than two million *contos* worth of investments in various industrial and agricultural enterprises.[12] In Africa, in addition to a controlling interest in Cassequel, the GES owned a dominant stake in the Angola Agricultural Company (CADA), which operated extensive coffee plantations;

---

8 See speeches by Cunha Leal, Homem de Mello, and Henrique Galvão in Ronald H. Chicote, *Emerging Nationalism in Portuguese Africa: Documents* (Stanford: Hoover Institution Press, 1972), 28–42.

9 Ibid., 278.

10 George Ball, *The Past Has Another Pattern* (New York: W.W. Norton & Company, 1973). 277.

11 Pitcher, *Politics in the Portuguese Empire*, 215.

12 Eugénia Mata e Nuno Valério, *História Económica de Portugal Uma Perspectiva Global* (Lisboa: Editorial Presença, 1993), 217; Pitcher, *Politics in the Portuguese Empire*, 211; Gervase Clarence-Smith, *The Third Portuguese Empire 1825–1975* (Manchester: Manchester University Press, 1985), 168–169; and Fernando Rosas, *Portugal entre a Paz e a Guerra 1939–1945* (Lisboa: Editorial Estampa, 1995), 270–271.

IMAGE 4.2 *Visit of Angolan Governor General Rebocho Vaz (1966–1972) to the district of Benguela.*
SOURCE: "DIÁRIO DA MANHÃ/ÉPOCA," NO DATE, ENVELOPE ANGOLA 4, ARQUIVO DE FOTOGRAFIA DE LISBOA.

large holdings in Angola's other two large sugar companies and the Sociedade Agrícola do Incomati in Mozambique; as well as a role in the Mozambique Company.[13] In Portugal, the interests of the GES centered on the Espírito Santo Bank and included insurance, petroleum, paper, cement, beer, and tires.[14] By the early 1970s, the Espírito Santo Bank held the largest deposits of all the Portuguese banks, with 32 million *contos*. Members of the Espírito Santo family served on the boards of directors of twenty major companies, including Cassequel.[15]

Miles Kahler's concept of political exposure is useful for analyzing the response of the GES to the increasingly inevitable collapse of Portuguese colonialism. According to Kahler, two dimensions of political exposure are necessary to measure a firm's likely response to changes in its political environment: "dependence upon state policy for the firm's viability" and "an estimate of the

13 Carlos Damas, "Carteira de títulas em algumas companhias africanas (1920–1974)," AHBES; Clarence-Smith, *Third Portuguese Empire*, 168.

14 Pitcher, *Politics in the Portuguese Empire*, 218.

15 Ibid.

probability of political change."[16] The GES determined that its dependence on state-granted monopolies, protected markets, and privileged access to political decision making outweighed the possibility of political change; this explains their decision not to negotiate with Angola's nationalist movements. The close personal ties between leaders of the Estado Novo and the Espírito Santo family cemented these loyalties.[17] It is worth noting that when Portuguese presidents visited Angola, they generally included a stop and lunch at Cassequel (the first of these was made by President Carmona in 1938 and the last by President Tomaz in 1963), where they toured the plantation and dined with Cassequel's administrators and local dignitaries.

Cassequel's stockholder reports during the 1960s and early 1970s praised the Portuguese armed forces and the government of Portugal for their resiliency in resisting nationalist attacks and what allies of the regime viewed as a hostile and deflamatory campaign against Portugal in the United Nations. In 1962, Cassequel's board of directors lauded "those who, in fulfillment of their sacred duty, are defending national integrity in the Empire."[18] That same year Manuel Espírito Santo, head of Cassequel's board of directors, reflected on the previous year to shareholders: "For all of us Portuguese 1961 was a year of suffering and sacrifice that will be engraved in the memories of those who lived through it, and remembered in our history as a year of great trial, which we confronted with serenity and a firm determination to defend the principles of western civilization."[19]

In 1962, Cassequel paid 5,222,892$00 *escudos* ($23,212.00) toward a newly implemented special tax for the defense of Angola.[20] Throughout the 1960s, the Portuguese armed forces succeeded in thwarting any serious challenge to Portuguese authority by the nationalist movements, which by 1970 had been largely confined to the eastern and northern fringes of Angola, far from population centers, as well as rich mineral deposits, and agricultural zones. Furthermore, divisions among the nationalist movements weakened their effectiveness, further evidence that must have factored into Espírito Santo calculations.

Portuguese companies with interests in the colonies, including Cassequel, also took the offensive in the propaganda war. In June 1963, the Association of

16 Miles Kahler, "Political Regime and Economic Actors: The Response of Firms to the End of Colonial Rule," *World Politics* (vol. 33, no. 3, April 1981), 384.

17 Pedro Jorge Castro, *Salazar e os Milionários* (Lisboa: Quetzal Editores, 2009).

18 SAC, *Relatório e Contas*, December 31, 1962, AHBES, 1.

19 "Discurso de Manuel Ribeiro Espírito Santo e Silva na AG. De 25 de Janeiro de 1962," *Jornal do Comércio* (26 Janeiro de 1962).

20 SAC, "Letter to Board of Directors," November 17, 1962, *Cartas Expedidas 1961, 1962, 1963*, AC.

Portuguese Companies in the Empire (Associação Portuguesa das Empresas do Ultramar) wrote to its members that "in the next meeting of the General Assembly of the United Nations, to begin in September 1962, would commence a new campaign against Portugal's Empire...an attack that all members should fight by all possible methods."[21] In the United Nations General Assembly, the emerging Afro-Asiatic bloc of nations repeatedly denounced Portugal's unwillingness to decolonize. Throughout this period, Portugal was in breach of General Assembly Resolution 1514 (XV) of December 14, 1960, which committed all members to work toward independence for all non-self-governing territories.[22]

Two other Portuguese conglomerates with extensive investments in the colonies—the Companhia União Fabril (CUF) and the Champalimaud Group—may have been more open to a neocolonial relationship with the colonies along the lines of the relationships established between most of the former British and French colonies and their respective metropoles.[23] In 1969, the CUF hired the American-based Hudson Institute to assess Angola's development prospects. Hudson advised a meeting of CUF executives and leading members of the Estado Novo at a conference in the Portuguese Algarve to pursue a go-for-broke strategy of massive investment as a means of improving the quality of life for average Angolans, which they hoped would potentially undermine the appeal of the nationalist movements.[24] Hudson's advice may have influenced the member of the GES board in attendance because the GES made substantial investments in Angola in the early 1970s, including the founding of the Banco Inter-Unido and the purchase of the Sugar Company of Angola, both in 1973.

The intransigence of the Estado Novo and its allies among Portugal's economic elite helps to explain why all three of Angola's nationalist movements, and the MPLA in particular, rallied against colonial capitalism.[25] In addition, the western powers refused to condemn Portuguese colonialism publicly and

---

21 SAC, "Letter from Associação Portuguesa das Empresas do Ultramar," June 3, 1963, *Cartas Recebidas 1962/3*, AC.

22 MacQueen, *The Decolonization of Portuguese Africa*, 63.

23 Clarence-Smith, *Third Portuguese Empire*, 168–169; and MacQueen, *The Decolonization of Portuguese Africa*, 52.

24 Hudson Institute, *Angola: Some Views of Development Prospects*, Vol. 1, 133.

25 It is worth noting that the MPLA would, after independence, exempt the US-owned Gulf Oil from its wholesale nationalization of private enterprise in Angola, indicating a practical side to the movement. For more on the oil industry before and after Angolan independence, see Ricardo Soares de Oliveira, "Business success, Angola-style: postcolonial politics and the rise and rise of Sonangol" *Journal of African Studies* (vol. 45, no. 4, 2007), 595–619.

thus undermine a North Atlantic Treaty Organization ally. As historian Norrie MacQueen has noted, "Marxism was part of the very zeitgeist" of the period.[26] Communist countries such as the Soviet Union and Cuba offered aid and political support to the cause of independence, and their economic models offered an alternative to the neocolonial relationships being established between newly independent African states and their former colonial powers.

Cassequel in the 1960s

Within two weeks of the MPLA's February 4 attack on the Luanda prison, Cassequel's director imported and distributed 102 pistols and 84 rifles to white employees, who made nightly patrols of the plantation's perimeter.[27] Cassequel's administration worked closely with the PIDE to identify and arrest politically active workers.[28] Across Angola, *assimilados* and any Angolan recognized as *calcinhas* [westernized; educated] came under suspicion by the authorities and colonists. Cassequel's director, Serpa Pimental, explained: "In the first place I discreetly collected information, especially about our most evolved [educated; politically minded] native personnel. In the second place, I have maintained a direct and personal contact with the PIDE and the administration."[29] The PIDE employed a network of informers to identify individuals with nationalist political views. PIDE surveillance in the area aimed to stop the spread of information and revolutionary propaganda spreading from sailors at the Port of Lobito to local Umbundu workers. In March, following the revolt in northern Angola, Pimental decided to repatriate Cape Verdean workers: "There have already been cases [of political organization] among Cape Verdeans in Benguela, none of whom worked at Cassequel, but I know that some of ours will be indoctrinated. As I have no confidence in them, especially the most *calcinhas*, I judged it best to repatriate them to Cape Verde."[30]

---

26 MacQueen, *The Decolonization of Portuguese Africa*, 56.

27 For the revolt in the north, see Wheeler and Pelissier, *Angola*. For the revolt in Baixa de Caassanje, see Aida Freudenthal, "A Baixa de Cassanje: algodão e revolta," *Revista Internacional de Estudos Africanos* (no. 18–22, 1995–1999), 245–283.

28 "Acontecimentos em Angola," April 22, 1961, *Cartas Expedidas 1961, 1962 e 1963*, AC.

29 Letter to Board of Directors, February 16, 1961, "Correspondencia trocada entre Fernando de Serpa Pimentel, director do Cassequel em Angola, e Manuel Espirito Santo, assuntos pessoal, produção, 26/9/52 a 20/2/61," Cota 01/01.2, Caixa 1, AC.

30 Ibid.

According to Soba Justino Patrício, "The colonists played the drums with our heads"; in other words, "We had many massacres here in our region in 1961. The Portuguese panicked and went after the blacks."[31] Munhango Katuvale of Bocoio, who was thirty years old in 1961, remembered the consequences for those active in politics: "Those blacks who had a certain level of learning were either massacred or sent to São Nicolau [a prison for political prisoners located on Angola's southern coast]."[32] It was around this time that interviewees remembered beginning to listen clandestinely to the radio to hear news reports prepared by the MPLA and broadcast from Tanzania, Congo-Brazzaville, Zaire, Zambia, and Ghana.[33] Interviewees said that it was through these broadcasts that they learned about the goals of the revolution and the ascendancy and murder of Congolese nationalist Patrice Lumumba in 1961.

The earliest complaint to the International Labor Organization (ILO) about Portuguese labor practices in Angola came from the Anti-Slavery Society in February 1952. The reports of abuse in the Anti-Slavery Society memorandum mirrored reports made by Ross and Galvão. The memorandum states:

> [A]lmost every day one sees groups of Africans waiting outside the Government offices in Angola, Portuguese West Africa, each with a bag containing his effects. Then Europeans come out and call the Africans, and bind the bargain by presenting to each African a shirt and a pair of shorts. This is contract labor, a system of compulsory labor imposed on the Africans of Angola. It is preceded by a request, addressed to each chief, to furnish a specified number of contract laborers. The chief presses men into this service by persuasion, threats or trickery, and they set out for a year in some place remote from their homes.[34]

In 1952, the ILO had no mandate to investigate labor conditions in Angola because the government of Portugal had not ratified the Forced Labor Convention (1930). In 1955, after a brief visit to Angola and Mozambique,

---

31 Author interview with *Soba* Justino Patrício, February 23, 2006, Cayengue-Mbola Kavulo.

32 Author interview with Munhango Katuvale, February 16, 2006, Bocoio.

33 For an overview of the history of radio in Angola, see Marissa J. Moorman, *Intonations: A Social History of Music and Nation in Luanda, Angola, from 1945 to Recent Times* (Athens: Ohio University Press, 2008), 143–159. On revolutionary songs composed by the MPLA, see Inge Brinkman, ed., *Singing in the Bush:* MPLA *Songs during the War for Independence in South-east Angola (1966–1975)* (Koln: Rudiger Koppe Verlag), 2001.

34 Memorandum of February 22, 1952, printed in International Labor Office, *Report of the Ad Hoc Committee on Forced Labor*, Supplement No. 36, New Series of the International Labor Office (Geneva: ILO, 1953), 229.

the British activist-historian Basil Davidson published *The African Awakening*,[35] in which he concluded that recruitment in Angola still constituted a high degree of force.[36] In November 1959, Portugal ratified the 1930 Abolition of Forced Labor Convention, which came into effect twelve months later. Within a few months, on February 25, 1961, Ghana filed a complaint against the government of Portugal for alleged violations of the Forced Labor Convention. According to the convention, "Each Member of the International Labor Organization which ratifies this Convention undertakes to suppress the use of forced or compulsory labor in all its forms within the shortest possible period."[37] To investigate the alleged abuses, the governing body of the ILO appointed a Commission of Inquiry under article 26 of the ILO constitution to examine the observance of the convention by Portugal. In its final report, the commission made clear that it would not address colonialism and would focus specifically on whether Portugal had, since November 23, 1960, adhered to its obligations under the Abolition of Forced Labor Convention.

Perhaps having heard that its labor policies were mentioned in the complaint Ghana filed against Portugal in the ILO, Cassequel's administration decided to host a party celebrating the completion of contracts by various *guias* [work groups] in May 1961. *Guias* consisted of men recruited together from particular areas in the interior, and at Cassequel, members of *guias* lived and worked together. According to company administrators, this organization contributed to *guia* productivity.[38] Cassequel's administrators hired a photographer to document the supposedly model working conditions at the plantation.

Each contract worker, dressed in newly issued uniforms, shared a meal and posed for photographs with their *guia* banner. The archival sources do not indicate who wrote the captions on the banners, but given the propagandistic messages and the fact that most *contratados* did not write Portuguese, it is most likely that the *capataz* of each *guia* made the banner.[39] For example, the caption on the banner of the Balombo *guia* (Image 4.3) proclaims: "We are happy to have completed our time at the SA Cassequel; good food; [we] receive everything…oil…fish, bananas…."

35 Basil Davidson, *The African Awakening* (London: Jonathan Cape, 1955).

36 For a Portuguese-sponsored rebuttal of Davidson's analysis, see F.C.C. Egerton, *Angola in Perspective* (Lisbon: Agency General for the Overseas Territories, 1955).

37 International Labor Organization, *Conventions and Recommendations, 1919–1981* (Geneva: International Labor Organization, 1982), 29.

38 Author interview with Jorge Luíz Chingue, July 16, 2001, Gama.

39 International Labor Office, *Official Bulletin* (vol. XLV, no. 2, suppl. II, April 1962), 186.

IMAGE 4.3 *Balombo* guia
SOURCE: SOCIEDADE AGRÍCOLA DO CASSEQUEL COLLECTION, ARQUIVO HISTÓRICO DO BANCO ESPÍRITO SANTO (AHBES), LISBON.

The caption on the Chinguar *guia* (Image 4.4) banner exclaimed: "Viva St. Peter Hospital" and then affirmed its members' loyalty to Portugal: "My homeland is Angola; Angola is a part of Portugal, hence I am from Portugal. My fatherland is Portugal."

It is of course impossible to know how these *contratados* actually felt about their work experiences at Cassequel, but interviews with former *contratados* in 2006 give us an idea. The celebration was a carefully choreographed show of purported African support for colonialism during a period of intense military repression of the northern revolt. Portugal was under increasing pressure from Angolans and the international community to decolonize.[40] Memories of former *contratados* cited in Chapter 3 emphasized the inherent humiliation of colonial power relations and the difficult, even brutal, work regimen for *contratados* at Cassequel. As Félix Alberto Satuala said:

40 Photographs are an important source for African history. See Andrew Roberts, ed., *Photographs as Sources for African History* (London: SOAS, 1988).

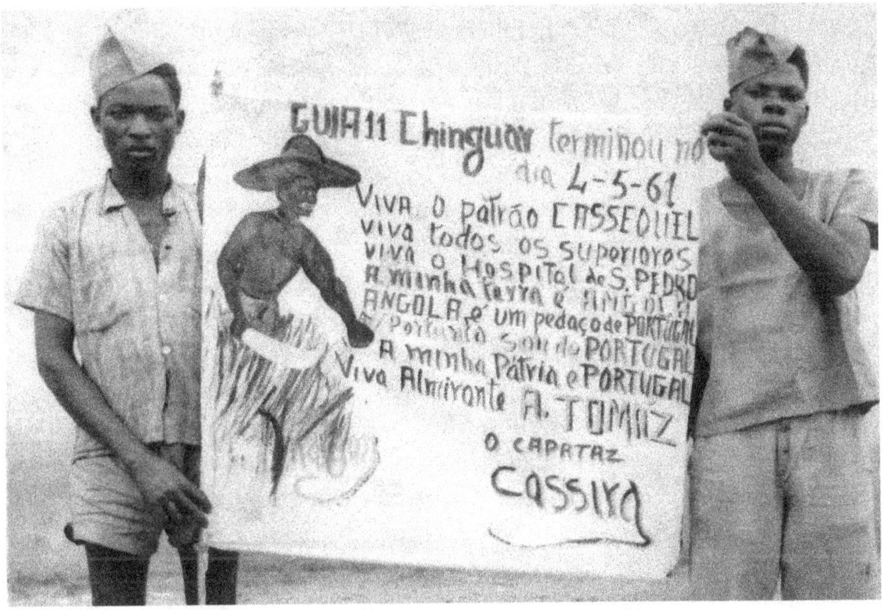

IMAGE 4.4 *Chinguar* guia
SOURCE: SOCIEDADE AGRÍCOLA DO CASSEQUEL COLLECTION, ARQUIVO HISTÓRICO DO BANCO ESPÍRITO SANTO (AHBES), LISBON.

"It was a work of suffering, not only at sugar plantations, but in all the sites where *contratados* worked."[41] Given these memories, there is something obscene about this celebration—with its exploitation of *contratados* to voice support for Portuguese colonialismo—that brings to mind Galvão's memorable phrase *the colossal lie*.

The ILO's Commission of Inquiry consisted of two rounds. The first, held in Geneva September 18–30, 1961, heard from thirty-one witnesses who testified about labor conditions. The government of Ghana called one Angolan student, the historian-activist Basil Davidson, and four Baptist ministers to testify. The government of Portugal called government representatives, including the heads of the Native Affairs Department, the Public Works Department, and the Department of Mines and Industry; a representative of the Bank of Angola; an official of the Benguela Railway; a representative of the trade union of the workers on the Benguela Railway; and representatives from the Diamond Company of Angola, CADA, and Cassequel.[42]

41 Author interview with Félix Alberto Satuala, April 18, 2006, Chinguar.

42 International Labor Office, *Official Bulletin*, 11.

After the hearings, a three-member mission of inquiry spent a week in Angola, December 4–11, 1961, visiting cities and interviewing colonial officials and African workers. The three-member mission included Paul Ruegger, a Swiss ambassador and chairman of the ILO Committee on Forced Labor (1956–1959); Enrique Armand-Ugón of Uruguay, a judge; and Isaac Forster of Senegal, also a judge.[43] In its final report, the commission stated that one of its main aims was "to speak directly to African workers."[44] The commission also spoke to government authorities and representatives of the business community.

Two members of the commission, Armand-Ugón and Forster, spent an afternoon visiting Cassequel. The inspectors' conversations with workers in the fields and in one worker village indicated the fine line between forced and voluntary labor. The "workers questioned by the commission stated that they had come there because they had wanted to do so, but none of them indicated clearly how he had been engaged."[45] In response to a question about how they learned that work was available at Cassequel, "some of them stated that they had learnt this from the *chefe de posto*. Some stated that they had come to the workplace and concluded verbal contracts."[46] What is not clear in the testimony is the larger web of power relationships between, for example, the worker and his local *soba* [chief]. About their visit, the commissioners concluded:

> The unskilled workers at the Cassequel Company...were more backward than any whom the Commission saw elsewhere and gave the impression of being intimidated. They certainly did not speak freely to the Commission and, after the Commission and the representatives of the company had moved on, some of them speaking only an African language attempted to make contact with the Commission through its staff.[47]

Company representatives insisted that they employed no forced labor and had observed the provisions of the Abolition of Forced Labor Convention, both before and after the entry into force of the convention. The commissioners, Armand-Ugón and Forster, were not satisfied with their experience at Cassequel,

43 According Vail and White, there was a widespread rumor that Enrique Armand-Ugón was a PIDE agent. Leroy Vail and Landeg White, *Capitalism and Colonialism in Mozambique A Study of Quelimane District* (Minneapolis: University of Minnesota Press, 1980), 382.

44 International Labor Office, *Official Bulletin*, 29.

45 Ibid., 185–186.

46 Ibid., 185–186.

47 Ibid., 186.

where they had the impression that management was "more concerned to display their technical processes and take credit for their social services than to enable the Commission to form any valid judgment on whether or not their recruiting operations involved any element of compulsion."[48] The commissioners recommended that the government investigate recruitment methods at Cassequel. Cassequel's board of directors reported to shareholders that ILO investigators saw "both the voluntary nature of the Company's workforce, as well as the medical, religious, and social services provided to all workers."[49]

The Commission of Inquiry's final report reflected both the narrow mandate of its investigation—to see if Portugal complied with the Forced Labor Convention—and changes in free labor ideology. In a year following the independence of twenty African countries, the absence of force was no longer sufficient to mollify critics of Portuguese colonialism. The commission recognized government's positive duty to ensure its citizens with choices:

> [T]he policy of abolishing forced labor to which the Government is so completely committed, and in the implementation of which it has already made such substantial progress, cannot be made fully effective in a context of social and cultural backwardness in which for many people freedom and compulsion are equally impalpable and it is very difficult for the Government to know much of what happens in the minds of those most directly affected by the measures which it takes.
>
> Freedom is not a purely negative concept; it does not consist only of, and does not necessarily exist by reason of, the absence of compulsion and constraint; it includes an element of choice, which represents its positive aspect. It is no accident that the Declaration of Philadelphia links together freedom and dignity, and seeks the fulfillment of both in economic security and equality of opportunity. This fundamental consideration has a direct bearing on the question whether labor performed in certain circumstances should be regarded as forced labor or free labor.[50]

In other words, the commission found that Africans in Angola exercised little control over the terms of their existence and had been oppressed to such an extent that their lives were "a series of conditioned reflexes which are less than

48 Ibid., 240.

49 SAC, *Relatório e Contas*, December 31, 1961, AHBES, 2.

50 International Labor Office, *Official Bulletin*, 245. In 1944, the International Labour Conference met in Philadelphia and adopted the Declaration of Philadelphia, which redefined the aims and purpose of the ILO.

human." In this context, "it becomes at times impossible to say whether their labor is the result of a compulsion which makes it technically forced labor because they are so incapable of any choice or of the exercise of any independent judgment that compulsion is unnecessary."[51] The commission concluded that at Cassequel "The bulk of the working force is at so backward a stage of development that freedom and economic opportunity belong to a world so wholly beyond their grasp that the question whether the labor exacted from them is forced labor becomes virtually meaningless."[52]

The ILO commission ultimately voiced optimism about the Portuguese government's commitment to end forced labor.[53] The commission identified recruitment practices as an area for improvement and encouraged the government of Portugal to adopt the 1936 Recruiting of Indigenous Workers Convention and the 1939 Contracts of Employment (Indigenous Workers) Convention, neither of which Portugal had signed. In their report, the commissioners refer to the two treaties because their provisions deal with matters raised in Angola. For example, the Recruiting of Indigenous Workers Convention provided that "public officers shall not recruit for private undertakings except for certain work of public utility" (Article 9), and that "chiefs or other indigenous authorities shall not act as recruiting agents, exercise pressure upon possible recruits, or receive from any source whatsoever any special remuneration or other special inducement for assistance in recruiting" (Article 10). The commission concluded that because of the part played in recruitment by colonial officials and chiefs, the employment of recruited labor in the African colonies had "been alleged to constitute, and has in the view of the commission in certain cases constituted, forced labor."[54]

The commission had no power to punish offenders. It did make formal recommendations indicating the steps to be taken to give effect to obligations in the Forced Labor Convention. The commission advised the government of Portugal to ratify both treaties, and in the meantime it admonished the Portuguese to establish an independent inspection service with the ability to punish abuses.[55] In its final lines, the commission affirmed the principle

51 Ibid., 245.

52 Ibid.

53 In 1970, the ILO conducted a follow-up investigation in Angola and concluded that contract labor no longer involved coercion. "Report by Pierre Juvigny, Representative of the Director-General of the International Labor Office, on Direct Contacts with the Government of Portugal Regarding the Implementation of the Abolition of Forced Labor Convention, 1957 (No. 105)" in ILO, *International Labor Conference* (vol. 56, 1971, 7).

54 International Labor Office, *Official Bulletin*, 245.

55 Ibid.

that "freedom of expression and of association are essential to sustained progress."[56]

By 1961, labor costs for *contratados* escalated as a result of the declining reliance on coercion and implementation of reforms undertaken to attract voluntary workers. Part of these costs included requisite investments in infrastructure, such as worker housing. Before the mid-1950s, Cassequel housed *contratados* in *bairros indígenas* [native neighborhoods] dotting the plantation. Workers constructed their own mud and thatch *cubatas* [huts]. Faustino Alfredo explained that a contract worker arrived from the interior and "improvised huts out of tree branches to serve as his residence and the following day he had to work."[57] There were no toilets, showers, or kitchen facilities beyond rudimentary fire pits. The absence of potable water and toilets helps to explain the high incidence of disease among workers. In 1953, Cassequel's administration commissioned an extensive report to assess the water supply and sanitary installations in each of the plantation's twenty-three *bairros indígenas*.[58] The report recommended the installation of water filtration systems. The cost of the improvements and skepticism about supplying *contratados* with amenities such as potable water led Cassequel's board of directors to postpone a decision until 1956, in spite of annual profits exceeding $500,000 throughout the first half of the 1950s.[59] In 1956, the board of directors did allocate the requisite funds to build potable water stations, kitchens, permanent housing, recreation facilities, and toilets in worker villages.[60]

In 1963, Cassequel and its sisal plantation inland at Ganda contained thirty-eight worker villages housing 5,820 workers and their families.[61] A member of a team assessing Angola's development prospects for the American-based Hudson Institute in 1969 described one of these *bairros indígenas* as "clumps of huts on rises behind the plantation…they are painted pink with brown thatch roofs. They really look like little storybook towns."[62] In Image 4.5, note the sanitary post at bottom left and the covered kitchen bottom center. These new

56 Ibid.

57 Author interview with Faustino Alfredo, July 5, 2001, Catumbela.

58 SAC, "Abastecimento de Água e Instalações Sanitárias dos Bairros Indigenas," June 1, 1953, AC.

59 For annual profits see APPENDIX.

60 "Letter to Associação Portuguesa das Empresas do Ultramar from Telmo Pelouro dos Santos, O Chefe dos Servicos de Pessoal, June 18, 1963, *Cartas Expedidas 1961, 1962, 1963*, AC.

61 "Reposta ao Questionario Sobre Regime de Trabalho Indígena que Acompanhou a Carta Confidencial de 8 de Agosto de 1961," August 9, 1961, *Cartas Expedidas, 1961, 1962, 1963*, AC.

62 Hudson Institute, *Angola: Some Views of Development Prospects*, Vol. 1, 133.

IMAGE 4.5 *Bairro indígena*
SOURCE: CASSEQUEL ARCHIVE, NO DATE, ARQUIVO HISTÓRICO DO BANCO ESPÍRITO SANTO, LISBON.

worker villages represented the late reforms of Cassequel and Portuguese colonialism. They translated into a substantive improvement in workers' health and work conditions.

In 1961, Cassequel's director complained about rising labor costs.[63] More generous housing, health care, clothing, and the cost of recruitment and repatriation made each *contratado* more expensive to employ than a voluntary worker. The problem for Cassequel was that insufficient numbers of workers volunteered for the still low-paid fieldwork performed by *contratados*. The company estimated that the average monthly cost for a contract worker at 501$60 *escudos* (roughly $17). The added expense of having to attract *contratados* with better amenities and pay convinced Cassequel's management to encourage more workers to settle in and around Catumbela with their families.[64]

63 "Reposta ao Questionario Sobre Regime de Trabalho Indígena que Acompanhou a Carta Confidencial de 8 de Agosto de 1961," August 9, 1961, *Cartas Expedidas, 1961, 1962, 1963*, AC.

64 SAC, "Letter to the Board of Directors," March 10, 1955, Cartas Recebidas, 1950–1955, AC.

The End of Forced Labor

The outbreak of the nationalist war for independence and the ILO report increased the pace of labor reform underway since the late 1950s. Within six months of the March revolt, in September 1961, the new colonial minister, Adriano Moreira, revoked the Statute of Natives (*Estatuto dos Indígenas*, Decreto-Lei 39.666, May 20, 1954), thus abolishing legally the distinction between civilized and noncivilized, or *indígena*. This reform made available to all Angolans the identity card that had formerly been the sign of citizenship and therefore restricted to whites and assimilated blacks.[65] Moreira had served as the director of the Escola Superior Colonial, the main training center for colonial administrators. In April 1962, Moreira enacted a comprehensive labor reform, the Rural Labor Code (*Código do Trabalho Rural*), for the African colonies and East Timor. The law abolished forced labor and ended compulsory cultivation for crops such as cotton.[66] The following paragraph summed up the changes in the law:

> [T]he present law corresponds to an evolution characterized by the following: any distinction between ethnic or cultural groups is ended...; no form of compelled work is legal; no penal sanctions for not completing the terms of the labor contract are allowed; there does not exist any paternalistic tutelage of workers; no recruitment of workers by the authorities is permitted; there is not any involvement in the formation of work contracts by the authorities; different treatment for men and women is not allowed...It is hoped that guaranteeing the freedom of work and its just remuneration will ensure better work conditions and social security, labor will go [to the market] spontaneously, the economy will prosper, national production increase, and there will be confidence and harmony between bosses and workers.[67]

The Rural Labor Code abolished the *imposto indígena*, which applied to adult male *indígenas* only. It was replaced as of January 1962 with the minimum general tax. The new tax extended to all male inhabitants aged 18–60 and to

---

65 Lawrence W. Henderson, *The Church in Angola*, 296.

66 For an early statement of this objective, see Dr José de Penha Garcia, "A assistência e a protecção aos indígenas na moderna política colonial,"Ano 6, No. 48, Junho de 1929, *Boletim da Agência Geral das Colónias* (ano 6, no. 48, Junho de 1929), 21.

67 Decreto No. 44,309, "O Código do Trabalho Rural," *Diário do Governo* [Portugal] (I Série, Número 95), 580.

women in the same age group employed by the government.[68] The law also required a phased-in increase in the salaries of agricultural workers—a change opposed by Cassequel's administration—from a base of 200 *escudos* ($7) per month to 600 *escudos* ($21) per month, a 200 percent increase.[69] The opposition of Cassequel's administrators to raise salaries may explain why salaries at Cassequel only reached 300 *escudos* ($12) by 1974, twelve years after the adoption into law of the 1962 Rural Labor Code. Low salaries remained a perennial complaint among Cassequel's workers.

The reforms of 1961–1962 aimed to shield Portugal from growing international condemnation in the wake of Angola's nationalist revolution. For the majority of Angolans the labor reforms, coupled with an expanding economy, improved the standard of living and ended legal racial discrimination. Although the nationalist guerrilla war in Angola never seriously challenged Portuguese hegemony throughout most of the territory, the demise of Salazar's regime after his debilitating stroke and subsequent death signified the waning power of the Estado Novo.

The ILO's Follow-Up Investigation in 1970

By 1965, the government of Portugal had ratified neither the Recruiting of Indigenous Workers Convention nor the Contracts of Employment Convention. As a result, the ILO, meeting in its forty-nineth session in June 1965, passed a "Resolution Condemning the Government of Portugal on the Grounds of the Forced Labor Policy Practiced by the Said Government in Territories under its Administration."[70] The resolution called on the government of Portugal to pass the aforementioned conventions and to put an end to forced labor.

In 1970, the ILO sent a team to investigate the implementation of its 1962 recommendations. One issue that concerned the ILO was that the recruiting of workers might involve improper pressures by traditional chiefs. The ILO also wanted further information concerning the manpower situation and the policy and methods in regard to the engagement of labor for major Angolan employers, including Cassequel. The investigators, Pierre Juvigny and K.T. Samson, spent

68 Carlos G. Nensala, "The Role of Fiscal Policy in the Economic Development of Angola" (PhD diss. The Catholic University of America May 1973), 55.

69 SAC, "Regulamento do Codigo do Trabalho Rural Estatuto do Trabalho em Angola," September 20, 1962, *Cartas Expedidas 1961, 1962, e 1963*, AC.

70 A copy of the resolution exists in the Arquivo Salazar, AOS/CO/UL-20, Pasta 5, ANTT.

eight days (October 9–17, 1970), in Angola. In areas of recruitment in the central highlands, such as Bié and Huambo, they interviewed professional recruiters, their agents, and recruited workers.[71]

The investigators spoke to two workers at a government transit camp in Bié. One worker said that he signed up to be a *contratado* near his home and had received 600 *escudos* as a signing bonus (equal to seven weeks of salary for an agricultural worker at Cassequel). At the plantation, he would receive 100 *escudos* a month, and he would receive the remainder from the *chefe de posto*, about 4,000 *escudos*, upon his return. Another worker said that he was going to work to earn money to buy things.[72] These interviews indicated how increased financial compensation and the absence of force cast migrant labor in a more positive light among workers.

At a second location at Chinguar in Bié, the investigators interviewed two professional recruiters. One of the recruiters held a license to recruit up to 10,000 workers. In 1970, he recruited 250 workers for Cassequel.[73] One worker, who had worked on contract at Cassequel in 1967, 1968, and 1969, said that he had gone to work voluntarily and under no compulsion. The *somas* did not force him to go, and he would not have listened to such an order.[74] In their final analysis the investigators concluded that contract labor in Angola no longer involved coercion. This assessment is confirmed in the oral histories conducted in 2006, which refer to the declining level of coercion for contract labor after 1961. As the interviews iterate, the government no longer forced African men to perform forced labor.

Mechanization and Workers' Experiences

The end of forced labor and the subsequent decline in numbers of *contratados* lent urgency to Cassequel's mechanization efforts. The area most affected by the labor shortage was some of the toughest, least popular work on the plantation—the cutting and carrying of cane—historically performed by *contratados*. Cutting

71 "Report by Pierre Juvigny, Representative of the Director-General of the International Labor Office, on Direct Contacts with the Government of Portugal Regarding the Implementation of the Abolition of Forced Labor Convention, 1957 (No. 105)" in ILO, *International Labor Conference* (vol. 56, 1971), 7.

72 Ibid., 14–15.

73 Ibid., 18.

74 Ibid.

towering cane stalks with a machete and then carrying them to waiting railway cars or tractors was exhausting, dangerous work. The nature of the work partly explains why Cassequel had such difficulty recruiting voluntary workers. Indeed, one of the benefits of being a voluntary worker at Cassequel was exemption from this work. In 1968 the company invested 12.500.000$00 *escudos* to attain 25 percent of the cutting and carrying of cane by machine (Image 4.6). Mechanization of manual labor was not a smooth process. In 1968, Cassequel's purchase of three cane cutters, a harvester, and several cane-carrying trailers curtailed production, and the machines necessitated massive inputs of time and money to maintain.[75]

Alhough Cassequel's workers experienced improved working conditions during the 1960s and 1970s, they also faced continued political repression. Manual laborers saw a marked improvement in social services, including housing and health care. The end of corporal punishment and forced labor improved worker morale. On the other hand, as the political situation evolved, including an ongoing nationalist war for independence, Cassequel's workers feared to

IMAGE 4.6 *Semimechanized sugarcane harvest Cassequel, 1973*
SOURCE: ARQUIVO NACIONAL TORRE DO TOMBO, ENVELOPE "ANGOLA VÁRIOS 1," N°031, PT/TT/AGU/001/023121A.

75 Inocentes, "As Cheias do Rio Catumbela," 65–67.

speak freely about politics or to question the colonial status quo. PIDE agents reported "evolved" employees, who faced interrogation, dismissal or, in the case of Cape Verdean workers, repatriation.[76] By the late 1960s, some Cassequel workers knew about the UNITA cell in Lobito, but given the climate of repression few made contact or discussed politics.[77]

Conclusion

The outbreak of the nationalist war for independence in Angola in 1961 made a profound impact on all aspects of Portuguese colonialism. The Salazar regime, in a defensive effort to undermine nationalist critiques of abusive colonial practices, made all Angolans equal citizens and abolished forced labor. These reforms, coupled with an opening of the Angolan economy and substantive investment in infrastructure, improved the quality of life for most Angolans. However, the reforms came at least a generation too late to win the regime many allies. Angolan nationalists cited the severe repression following the outbreak of war in 1961, the authoritarian nature of the Estado Novo, and the aspirations of Angolans to govern themselves as ample justification for continued guerrilla warfare.

The deep and extensive connections between the regime and the GES and other large financial conglomerates with extensive investments in the colonies explains why the leaders of these powerful economic interests did not make overtures to the nationalist movements to prepare for neocolonial arrangements, as had happened in most other newly independent African states. The increasingly Marxist orientation of the nationalist movements over the course of the 1960s and early 1970s further convinced the leaders of the GES to remain steadfast in their loyalty and support for the regime.

Changes at Cassequel after 1961 reflected the broader changes at work that resulted from Angolan nationalism and increased international scrutiny. The administration responded to the outbreak of revolution in 1961 with increased security measures and the arrest of politically active employees. After this initial response, Cassequel's administration continued policies implemented during the 1950s to ameliorate living and working conditions for workers and completed the transition to a wholly voluntary workforce. In spite of improved conditions, however, the reforms of the 1950s and 1960s failed to win significant support among African workers for Portuguese colonial rule. The photographed

76 E-mail exchange between the author and Victor Ribeiro, August 3, 2012.

77 Ibid.

celebration of the completion of labor contracts in May 1961 reflected the ILO's observation that workers at Cassequel appeared intimidated and unable to speak freely, which in turn reflected the power relationships at Cassequel. The resentment bred by this daily humiliation contributed to support for the nationalist movements and ultimately destroyed Espírito Santo and Portuguese objectives to remain in Angola.

CHAPTER 5

Independence and the Nationalization of Cassequel, 1974–1977

After more than thirteen years of war, during which time the Portuguese armed forces maintained control over most of Angola, events in Lisbon finally brought Portuguese officials and Angolan nationalists to the negotiating table. On April 25, 1974, a group of army officers known as the Movement of the Armed Forces (MFA)—who opposed Portugal's ongoing wars to suppress liberation movements in Angola, Mozambique, and Guinea Bissau—overthrew the dictatorial Estado Novo that had ruled Portugal and its colonies for forty-eight years. These officers instigated talks with Angolan nationalists, and within a year and a half (on November 11, 1975) Angola became independent. Tragically, divisions among Angola's three nationalist parties led to internecine warfare, even before the official handover of independence. In the ideologically charged context of the Cold War, each movement appealed to foreign sponsors for increased military aid. The Popular Movement for the Liberation of Angola (MPLA) turned to the Soviet Union and Cuba, the National Front for the Liberation of Angola (FNLA) to the United States and Zaire, and the National Union for the Independence of Angola (UNITA) to South Africa and the United States. The MPLA, after an airlift of Cuban troops, would ultimately succeed in defeating the other two parties and took power at independence.

The MPLA's postindependence economic plan nationalized nearly all of the country's private industry, including Cassequel. Interestingly, the MPLA exempted the U.S.-owned Gulf Oil from nationalization because Gulf's royalties provided most of the government's revenue.[1] Cassequel's Portuguese administrators left Angola as part of the massive airlift that carried nearly a quarter million people, mostly Portuguese settlers, out of Angola in late 1974 and 1975. After their departure, Angolan workers, aided by Cuban *cooperantes* [friends, comrades], moved into positions of leadership at the newly nationalized Cassequel, which the government renamed Açucareira Primeiro de Maio [Sugar Plantation First of May] in honor of International Workers' Day. The MPLA appointed Victor Ribeiro, an agronomist and party member, to become the plantation's new director.

1 Ricardo Soares de Oliveira, "Business Success, Angola-Style: Postcolonial Politics and the Rise and Rise of Sonangol," *Journal of African Studies* (vol. 45, no. 4, 2007), 595–619.

 | DOI 10.1163/9789004301757_007

One reason that Angola's transition to independence deteriorated into a fratricidal war among nationalist movements was that the Portuguese forces that overthrew the Estado Novo desired a quick exit from Angola. As the U.S. National Security Council noted, "The major Portuguese Government objective in Angola is to get out…with honor if possible, but in any case to get out."[2] Among Angola's three nationalist movements, personal and ideological rivalries, as well as distinct and often antagonistic histories, contributed to a breakdown in a peaceful transition to independence, a process fueled by Cold War foes willing to fight proxy wars.

Caught somewhere in the midst of this chaotic and deteriorating situation were the Espírito Santo family and the Angolan and Portuguese employees of the Sociedade Agrícola do Cassequel. This chapter explains how the events of the years 1974–1976 transformed Cassequel and the people whose lives revolved around it. In spite of its rhetorical demand for a more just workers' state, the MPLA's economic policies and rigid orthodoxy led to a deterioration of workers' conditions at Cassequel/Primeiro de Maio, demonstrating that independence and the nationalization of property did not necessarily equal better working and living conditions. The MPLA's one-party state, with its unquestioning organs—the so-called mass organizations (youth, women, workers)—rewarded loyalty and orthodoxy over competence and independent thought. At Cassequel, many of the highly trained technicians and mechanics necessary for the smooth operation of the plantation left Angola in the run up to independence. Among those who remained, disillusion set in over time with the top-down bureaucracy of the new state-run sugar conglomerate renamed Osuka [the Umbundu word for sugar], which took over Cassequel/Primeiro de Maio, and the Companhia de Açúcar de Angola (renamed 4 de Fevreiro) in nearby Dombe Grande. The combination of low morale among employees, the departure of so many technical staff, the disappearance of contract workers, and a general breakdown in discipline among workers, who often went unpaid for months at a time, led to declining sugar harvests and deteriorating equipment (Image 5.1).[3]

2 National Security Council Interdepartmental Group for Africa, "Response to NSSM 224: United States Policy toward Angola," June 13, 1975, p. 20, enclosed in Nathaniel Davis to the Assistant to the President for National Security Affairs, June 16, 1975, NSA. Quoted in Piero Gleijeses, *Conflicting Missions: Havana, Washington and Africa, 1959–1976* (Chapel Hill: University of North Carolina Press, 2002), 258.

3 Author interview with Victor Ribeiro *via* email, August 3, 2012.

IMAGE 5.1 *Cassequel, circa 1970*
SOURCE: PHOTOGRAPHS, AC.

Political Confusion: April 25, 1974 to November 11, 1975

Soon after the MFA coup on April 25, 1974, it became clear that the officers in charge planned to negotiate an immediate independence for Angola. In general, members of the coup shared with Angola's nationalist movements, and especially the MPLA, a socialist critique of the status quo. As one officer told journalist Jean Daniel of *Le Nouvel Observateur*, "We have no desire to construct a neocolonial community, we are interested more in the formation of a socialist interdependence, and that only to the extent that our brothers in Guiné, Mozambique, and Angola accept, desire, and demand."[4] By June 1974, Portugal's socialist foreign minister, Mário Soares, began talks with Organization of African Unity Secretary-General Nzo Ekangaki, leading to a July 28 pronouncement by the Portuguese president, General Spínola, that offered independence to all African colonies.[5] As he would later come to realize, the most

4 Jean Daniel, "L'armée portugaise face à l'anticommunisme," *Le Nouvel Observateur* (August 11, 1975), 16–18. Quoted in Kenneth Maxwell, *The Making of Portuguese Democracy* (Cambridge: Cambridge University Press, 1995), 97–98.

5 "Historic Move by Portugal Speeds Up Decolonization and Assures Africans' Right to Full Independence," *London Times* (July 29, 1974). Reprinted in *Facts and Reports* (vol. 4, no. 15/16,

difficult challenge in achieving an independent Angola would be negotiating a Portuguese withdrawal and a peace agreement among nationalist movements. During the nine months that elapsed between the revolution in Portugal on April 25, 1974 and the beginning of the multiparty peace talks in January 1975 (known as the Alvor Accords), the nationalist movements showed increasing intolerance of one another. Skirmishes between the FNLA and the MPLA in northern Angola escalated, and the divisive rhetoric sharpened, with distrust characterizing the relationship among all three movements.

In July 1974, clashes between FNLA and MPLA supporters broke out in Luanda, killing forty-three (according to Portuguese government reports) or at least one hundred (according to the MPLA). In response, Lisbon put Angola under immediate military rule. During the following months, as Guinea-Bissau achieved independence and a transitional government took over in Mozambique, Angola remained under siege. Throughout October and November, the Portuguese administration attempted to negotiate with each of the three liberation movements. On October 22, 1974, the MPLA became the last party to sign a ceasefire agreement with Portugal; however, disagreement among the liberation movements hampered assembly of a transitional government. At a press conference on November 26, Admiral Rosa Coutinho, the governor of Angola, announced that all three movements would be represented equally in a transitional government to be headed by Portugal. In his speech, he voiced optimism for a multiracial, economically prosperous Angola as a means of reassuring Angola's white settlers and securing their stake in the Angolan economy.[6] This tone was evident in a further statement by the Portuguese prime minister, Vasco Conçalves, issued in a Paris newspaper:

> [W]e want to decolonize with the agreement of the white population. Nothing will be done without the agreement of the white population there...If the future of Angola is to be based on agreement between blacks and whites, it will be a brilliant one. If we can build there an anti-racialist nation, the economic possibilities are enormous.[7]

August 3, 1974). For views of the colonial question among Portuguese democrats, see Mário Soares, *Portugal's Struggle for Liberty* (London: George Allen, 1975), 168–199.

6 "Angola Independence Nearer," *Financial Times* (November 27, 1974). Reprinted in *Facts and Reports* (vol. 4, no. 25, December 7, 1974).

7 "Whites have Last Say on Angola Future," *Times of Zambia* (October 7, 1974). Reprinted in *Facts and Reports* (vol. 4, no. 22, October 26, 1974).

In December, the MPLA signed an accord with UNITA promising to end hostility. They signed a similar accord with the FNLA in early January.[8] The Alvor Accords formally began January 11, 1975, with the Angolan delegations headed by the leaders of the three movements: Agostinho Neto of the MPLA, Holden Roberto of the FNLA, and Jonas Savimbi of UNITA. The Portuguese delegation was represented by Rosa Coutinho, provisional governor in Angola, and three ministers most involved in the decolonization policy: Mário Soares, the foreign minister; Almeida Santos, minister for the overseas territories; and Melo Antunes, minister without portfolio, unofficially minister for decolonization. During the negotiations, the parties set the date for independence as November 11, 1975. The talks resulted in a plan to establish a framework for a national unity government to oversee matters in the interim and then for the subsequent election of a constituent assembly, which would select a president to receive the transfer of power from the Portuguese.

The transitional government officially took office January 31, 1975, but instability lay on the horizon. By March, heavy fighting between FNLA and MPLA broke out over which movement would control Luanda, with more than two hundred people killed in the ensuing violence.[9] The situation continued to deteriorate to such an extent that on May 15, Portugal declared martial law in an attempt to end the violence and avert an escalation in what was threatening to become a civil war. The transitional government ordered the disarming of civilians, banned heavy weapons, called for an end to "private justice," demanded "the immediate expulsion of all foreigners in the service of the three liberation movements," and declared that offenses by "any of the movements" could be punished by *ad hoc* military courts. To subdue the population, Portuguese officials also established a curfew in major cities from midnight to 6:00 a.m.[10]

Ultimately, however, the Portuguese did not intervene with sufficient enough force to stem the escalating violence. Likewise, the transitional government, which had been rife with distrust from the beginning, became effectively moribund. The escalating violence caused an exodus from the cities as people fled to the rural areas to escape the killing and leaders of the the FNLA and MPLA took advantage of the growing power vacuum to take control of Angola.

---

8 "Text of Accord Signed by the MPLA and UNITA," *Daily News* (Tanzania) (December 21, 1974). Reprinted in *Facts and Reports* (vol. 5, no. 1, January 11, 1975).

9 "Uneasy Calm as Angola Counts its Dead," *Guardian* (May 5, 1975). Reprinted in *Facts and Reports* (vol. 5, no. 10, May 17, 1975).

10 "Portuguese Troops are Ordered to Put End to Fighting among Rival Factions in Angola," *London Times* (May 16, 1975). Reprinted in *Facts and Reports* (vol. 5, no. 11, May 31, 1975).

This violence spread to Catumbela and Cassequel in May 1975 as fighting broke out between the MPLA and UNITA, but in this case, Portuguese troops intervened and successfully stopped the fighting. Peace was only temporary, however, and by early June, the FNLA advocated that "only a real all-out war will once and for all finish the continual attacks by the MPLA, which do serious damage to the country's economy."[11] Fighting increased, and by mid-July, war broke out between MPLA and FNLA in Luanda. On July 3, Vasco de Almeida, minister of economics in Angola's transitional government, blamed the breakdown of peace on the "incompetence and powerlessness of the government which is simply a mirror reflecting the deeper political strife within the country and which does not function at all as an organized body."[12] Portugal's unofficial minister for decolonization, Melo Antunes, flew to Luanda a few days later, explaining:

> I am going to Angola once again in an attempt which, it appears, cannot be repeated much more to bring reality, commonsense and a sense of responsibility to the leaders of the liberation movements, so that once and for all they will put an end to mutual aggressions and show themselves capable of governing a territory which must be independent and which must have the responsibility for being so…I think the blame can be spread among the various political forces in Angola.[13]

Antunes's attitude demonstrated a clear preference for the MPLA and an unwillingness to use Portuguese forces to guarantee the peace.

Operation Repatriation

As the political situation deteriorated and violence escalated in the months preceding the November 11 handover of independence, Angola's white settlers increasingly opted to leave the country. The departure of so many of Angola's technicians, business owners, and managers left a tremendous skills vacuum that affected Cassequel and the rest of the Angolan economy. In his 1972 book,

11 "FNLA Advocates All-Out War," *O Século* (June 9, 1975). Reprinted in *Facts and Reports* (vol. 5, no. 14/14, July 12, 1975).

12 "'Angola on Brink of Collapse' Says Minister," *Financial Times* (July 4, 1975). Reprinted in *Facts and Reports* (vol. 5, no. 15/16, August 9, 1975).

13 "Now Lisbon Warns of Military Action in Angola," *Times of Zambia* (July 15, 1975). Reprinted in *Facts and Reports* (vol. 5, no. 15/16, August 9, 1975).

Portugal's Struggle for Liberty, Mário Soares, who would go on to negotiate with Angola's nationalist movements, wrote about the shared interests of Portuguese and Angolan "brothers":

> [T]he concerns of the Portuguese and African peoples are basically the same. Therefore the colonial problem must be solved by discussion in a spirit of brotherhood, it being admitted that the independent states of the future will be governed by black majorities who will respect the legitimate interests of the white inhabitants. Politics apart, the main battle is really against under-development. Both Portugal and the colonies must be released from the strangle-hold of big, exploitative, multi-national companies.[14]

It was probably unrealistic to expect majorities of Angola's white settlers, who had lived as a racially privileged elite and by and large supported Portugal's military effort to defeat the independence movements, to identify with a new Angolan nationalism. The chaotic transition, with its violence and heightened rhetoric, convinced tens of thousands that there was no future for them in an independent Angola. Thus, on May 13, 1975, the Portuguese government implemented Operation Repatriation to evacuate its citizens from Angola—an estimated total of 250,000—by air.[15] Portugal requested help from foreign governments, and as a result, the airlift became the largest in history.[16]

A number of factors contributed to the panicked departure: (1) the fighting between the nationalist movements in the main population centers of Luanda and Nova Lisboa scared many, (2) the Angolan nationalist struggle caused white settlers to feel caught in the middle of a nationalist struggle they did not support, and, (3) the escalation of anticapitalist, antiwhite rhetoric further alienated settlers and business owners. According to the transitional governor of Benguela Province:

> Without a doubt some members of the MPLA, with their extreme, and at times racist attitudes, also contributed to the exodus of Portuguese settlers, many of whom were already unsure in the face of threatened nationalizations without compensation. The airlift itself caused panic and many who had not made plans to leave decided to use the ticket to Lisbon.[17]

---

14 Soares, *Portugal's Struggle for Liberty*, 198.

15 For a firsthand account of the final weeks of Portuguese rule see Ryszard Kapuscinkski, *Another Day of Life* (New York: Penguin Books, 1987).

16 Clara Viana, "Uma Ponte Aéreo," *O Público* (no. 277, July 2, 1995), 20–31.

17 Sócrates Dáskalos, *Um Testemunho para a História de Angola do Huambo ao Huambo* (Lisboa: Vega, 2000), 179.

Whites who left took with them skills and capital crictical to the economy, thus further undermining the prospects for an independent Angola. MPLA leader Agostinho Neto accused white reactionaries of provoking the mass exodus.[18] Sócrates Dáskalos, the provincial governor of Benguela, singled out the MPLA's trade union movement (UNTA) for aggravating the situation in that they had called for across-the-board nationalizations.[19]

On the Ground at Cassequel

The administration and workers, Portuguese and Angolan, at Cassequel found themselves caught in the cross-fire of the revolutionary situation unfolding in Angola in 1975–1976. The archival record for events at Cassequel in the tumult of 1975–1976 are nonexistent; thus, I turned to oral history methods to bridge the historical gap. To better grasp how events affected individuals, I conducted interviews with eight people who worked at Cassequel in 1974–1977 and a member of the Espírito Santo family, whose family owned Cassequel during these years. Of the eight workers, two had been employed at the highest level of Cassequel's administration as director. Both of these men are white, and although they now live in Portugal, they consider themselves Angolans. I also interviewed a white Portuguese secretary who returned to Portugal. In addition, I interviewed three *mestiço* Angolans who worked in middle management and continue to live near Cassequel. Finally, I interviewed two black Angolans: one of whom worked in Cassequel's hospital and the other who worked as a mechanic. Some of these interviews tooks place in 2000, when I conducted dissertation research; others took place in 2006, when I returned to conduct oral history interviews with former *contratados*. Interviews took place either in Catumbela or in Lisbon. None of the former *contratados* interviewed in the Angolan interior were present at Cassequel in 1974–1976, so the interviews conducted in Catumbela and Lisbon generally reflect a more critical view of Angolan independence (and the MPLA in particular) than I heard in interviews with former *contratados*. The Catumbela/Lisbon interviews are importante because they provide a perspective on the war and Cassequel that is ignored in official Angolan narratives.

18 "Soviet Ambassador to the People's Republic of Angola E.I. Afanasenko, Memorandum of Conversation with President of the Movement for the Popular Liberation of Angola Agostinho Neto, July 4, 1975," Cold War International History Project, http://www.wilsoncenter.org/program/cold-war-international-history-project. [Accessed February 9, 2015].

19 Dáskalos, *Um Testemunho*, 185.

I conducted interviews in Portuguese, then transcribed them into English. The individuals interviewed were referred by word of mouth. It was difficult to locate former Cassequel employees because they have scattered all over the world, many have died, and others do not wish to speak, especially on the record, about events that are painful. I did my best to locate and interview as many people as possible. I think the interviews provide valuable anecdotal evidence about what occurred and how those events are remembered thirty-plus years later.

Among unskilled workers before Angolan independence, the almost unanimous grievance against colonialism, and Cassequel in particular, was low wages. Between 1965 and 1974, for example, a nonskilled worker at Cassequel—representing 5,715 out of 5,983 workers in 1965—earned a monthly salary of between 225 and 400 *escudos* (approximately \$8–\$14) plus a food allowance and housing.[20] Skilled employees, such as Faustino Alfredo, who worked as a nurse at Cassequel's St Peter Hospital, earned more than 1,000 *escudos* (approximately \$35) per month. But skilled African employees represented a small minority, roughly 4 percent of the workforce. Before 1974, Cassequel workers had no union, and because repression and the migratory nature of the majority of the work force, the company had no history of labor unrest.

Low wages and deflated postrevolutionary expectations led to Cassequel's first labor strike between June and August 1974, just two months after the revolution in Portugal. A newly formed workers' committee at Cassequel collaborated with the Lobito Employees Union of Commerce and Industry [Sindicato dos Empregados do Comércio e da Industria do Lobito] to organize workers. Before 1974, Cassequel did not allow union activity, even among its white employees. Now, the vast majority of Cassequel workers walked off their jobs and demanded higher salaries. Cassequel's administration refused the request, arguing that without a raise in the fixed government price paid for Cassequel sugar, the company could not afford to raise salaries. The workers maintained solidarity and flexed their power in a rapidly changing situation while the company lobbied the new government in Lisbon for a raise in the price of sugar.

Union literature of the period reflected a fundamentally anticapitalist, anti-imperialist sentiment. This sentiment contributed to tensions at Cassequel and throughout Angola. For example, in a public statement dated June 22, 1974, the Lobito Union of Employees of Commerce and Industry called on Cassequel workers to maintain unity and wait for instructions "to prosecute our fight and

20 SAC, *Relatório 1965*, AC, 22.

defeat one of the principal methods of Capitalist repression: hunger."[21] In the context of the overthrow of the Estado Novo, Cassequel's administrators agreed in principle to raise base monthly salaries to 3,500 *escudos* ($26).[22] This jump in salaries, added to weeks of lost production, translated into substantial financial losses in 1974, even with a rise in the price of sugar.[23] Thus, the August strike won substantial wage increases for workers and caused a deficit of 19 million *escudos* ($140,000) for the company.[24] Perhaps as a result of these concessions, Cassequel's workers did not participate en masse in the wave of strikes across Angola in May 1975.

Cassequel's 1974 strike, in conjunction with strikes across Angola, invigorated the burgeoning union movement. Initially workers demanded modest gains, such as the right to strike, a forty-hour work week, and a minimum wage.[25] The anticapitalist/anti-imperialist rhetoric escalated in direct proportion to the deterioration of the political situation. By May 1975, the workers' movement interpreted the end of colonial rule and imperialist domination as harbingers of a more just workers' state.[26] The MPLA in particular encouraged workers to discuss their problems, to know their rights, and not to tolerate "criminal exploitation" at the hands of the capitalists and imperialists in Angola.

Meanwhile, António Espírito Santo, head of Cassequel's board of directors and a resident of Lobito (bordering Cassequel's northern boundary), fled Angola in March 1975 as a result of events in Lisbon. On March 11, 1975, the government of Portugal arrested powerful allies of the Estado Novo, such as members of the Espírito Santo family, who spent the next five months in prison. António Espírito Santo, who was to be arrested the following day in Luanda, evaded Portuguese authorities by flying to South Africa with the help of UNITA leader Jonas Savimbi.[27] This working relationship with Savimbi in March 1975 indicates Espírito Santo links with both UNITA and the South Africans well before the transitional government broke down into factional fighting. The arrest of the once powerful Espírito Santos reflected the revolutionary nature of the change in power in Lisbon. During this period, Cassequel's management in Angola "tried everything to avoid the nationalization of

21 Sindicato dos Empregados do Comércio e da Industria do Lobito, "Intersindical Comunicado n 12," A-t/S, I-13, CIDAC.

22 SAC, *Relatório do Conselho de Administração*, 1974, AC.

23 Ibid.

24 Ibid.

25 UNTA, "Camaradas Vigilancia contra as Manobras Reaccionárias," May 1975, A-T/S I-24, CIDAC.

26 Ibid.

27 Author interview with José Manuel Pinheiro Espírito Santo, Lisbon, August 30, 2002.

Cassequel," according to José Manuel Pinheiro Espírito Santo.[28] The Espírito Santos cooperated with UNITA because they felt that a UNITA victory offered the best chance to retain the family's Angolan assets. As Pinheiro Espírito Santo notes, "UNITA was the most noncommunist party in Angola, and our hope was that they would allow the private companies to continue."[29] In Angola, the Espírito Santo Group (GES) owned a controlling interest in Cassequel, and a majority of GES stock in Cassequel was owned personally by members of the family. In addition, the GES owned a controlling interest in the colony's other major sugar-producing company, the Angolan Sugar Company at Dombe Grande, and 50 percent of the Banco Inter-Unido, which it owned as an equal partner with the National City Bank of New York.[30]

At Cassequel, workers continued to demand higher salaries, management threatened closures because of increasing labor costs, and the MPLA labeled the threats "reactionary manipulation."[31] As the political pact holding the three nationalist movements together dissolved, the colony-wide exodus of Portuguese settlers increased, contract workers abandoned Cassequel to return to interior districts, and Portuguese employees joined the air bridge out of Angola. Catarina Rodrigues, who worked as a secretary at Cassequel, left Catumbela in August 1975 as a result of the rapidly deteriorating situation. According to Rodrigues, things were "really bad, really bad," the repetition underscoring her desperation.[32] The Portuguese armed forces did not control the streets, and armed UNITA and MPLA soldiers stopped cars and demanded to know the party affiliation of drivers. In a region with roughly equal numbers of UNITA and MPLA supporters, these roadblocks led many to carry multiple membership cards. Robberies were common, and a general state of chaos prevailed.[33]

From these interviews, it is clear that a majority of Portuguese who worked at Cassequel feared both nationalist movements, but some supported the more cosmopolitan, socialist outlook of the MPLA and others viewed UNITA as providing the most protection for private property and whites' economic interestes.[34] Cassequel's *mestiço* employees tended to support the MPLA, whereas most African workers—the vast majority of whom came from the

28 Ibid.

29 Ibid.

30 Carlos Damas, "Memórias: O Banco Inter Unido," *BES Actual: Revista Interna do Grupo Banco Espírito Santo* (n. 12, April 1999), 30.

31 Ibid., 4.

32 Author interview with Catarina Rodrigues, Lisbon, August 29, 2002.

33 Ibid.

34 Ibid.

Umbundu-speaking *planalto*—probably supported UNITA.[35] In our interview, Rodrigues repeatedly described the fluid situation in 1975 as "confusão" [chaos].

Between August and November 1975, the situation in Angola deteriorated as fighting and foreign intervention escalated. In August, the revolutionary council running Portugal recognized that the political situation in Angola had deteriorated to such a point that the legitimacy of the transitional government was undermined; moreover, the government that did exist was marked by "ineffectiveness, incompetence, and corruption."[36] The council decided to concentrate the resources of the Portuguese armed forces in eight cities declared neutral zones, where the army would "guarantee the security of all the population."[37] Thus, the rest of Angola became a battlefield as the three nationalist movements fought for control.

Cassequel and its employees lived through this violence and uncertainity. In August, the MPLA took effective control of the Lobito-Catumbela-Benguela corridor, including Cassequel. Farther south, South African troops moved 30 miles inside Angola to occupy the Calueque and Ruacana dams; the Portuguese government offered only a feeble protest.[38] By late August, UNITA was fighting the MPLA for control of the Lobito-Benguela cooridor. Armed contingents of both parties patroled the streets and controled different areas of the corridor. In Catumbela, UNITA controlled the streets, and Rodrigues remembered carrying membership cards for both parties in case she had to show identification.[39] She also talked about UNITA soldiers searching door to door for MPLA supporters and sympathizers, and the fear this generated among the population because the soldiers could act with near impunity. The fighting shut down most services, such as electricity and water.[40]

In October 1975, a column of South African Defense Force (SADF) troops entered Angola from the south, thus changing the power dynamic within the country and giving UNITA an opportunity to win the civil war in the run up to independence on November 11. Within three weeks, the SADF passed through the Benguela-Lobito corrdior. It was during this period that South African troops used the facilities of the Sugar Company of Angola at Dombe Grande

35 For more about nationalism among the Ovimbundu, see Linda Heywood, *Contested Power in Angola, 1840s to the Present*. (Rochester, NY: University of Rochester Press, 2000).

36 Conselho da Revolução, "Reunião Extraordinária," August 5, 1975, 2975.031/im.2-im.4, AMS.

37 Ibid.

38 Gleijeses, *Conflicting Missions*, 259.

39 Author interview with Catarina Rodrigues.

40 Ibid.

(a recently acquired property of the GES), south of Benguela, as a refueling post. The Lisbon paper *Diário de Notícias* also reported that António Espírito Santo, head of Cassequel's board of directors, was meeting with officials in South Africa.[41] According to F.J. du Toit Spies, a government-sanctioned South African historian of the 1975–1976 war in Angola, Portuguese settlers in Angola facilitated contact between UNITA's Savimbi and South African officials as early as June 1974.[42] Espírito Santo contacts with South African leaders early in 1975 support charges of treason made by the MPLA in its nationalization of Cassequel and other Espírito Santo assets in 1976.[43]

An airlift of Cuban soldiers helped the MPLA stop the South African advance on Luanda.[44] Cuban forces were also instrumental in stopping an FNLA advance on the capital on November 10, 1975 (the day before Angola's official independence), at the Battle of Kifangondo.[45] The same day, the Portuguese high commissioner, Admiral Leonel Cardoso, left Angola without having transferred power to a nationalist administration, as had been planned.[46] The victorious MPLA proclaimed a people's republic in Luanda and was immediately recognized by eastern bloc and socialist countries, but not by Portugal. FNLA and UNITA subsequently announced the formation of a national revolutionary council based in Nova Lisboa (Huambo) in the central highlands. In December, the US Congress, in spite of Ford administration protestations, cut off covert aid for the FNLA/UNITA alliance, essentially isolating South Africa. The decision to cut off aid reflected a difference in opinion between the Democrats in power in Congress and the Ford administration.

---

41 "A conspiração contra o povo angolana revelada por um comandante das FAPLA" *Diário de Notícias*, 17 (November 1975), 4.

42 F.J. du Toit Spies, *Operasie Savannah: Angola 1975–1976* (Pretoria: S.A. Weermag, 1989), 60–65. Quoted in Gleijeses, *Conflicting Missions*, 276.

43 Manuel Ribeiro do Espírito Santo e Silva, *Discursos nas Assembleias Gerais, 1955–1973*. Banco Espírito Santo Centro de Investigaçã e Documentação da História do BES, 2002; and Maxwell, *The Making of Portuguese Democracy*, 28.

44 On Soviet policy in Angola see Odd Arne Westad, "Moscow and the Angolan Crisis, 1974–1976: A New Pattern of Intervention," *Cold War International History Project Bulletin* (nos. 8–9, Winter 1996/97), 21–37.

45 Miguel Júnior, ed., *A Batalha de Kifangondo 1975 Factos e Documentos* (Luanda: Mayamba Editora, 2013).

46 For Cuban policy in Angola, see Gleijeses, *Conflicting Missions*. For various US State Department analyses of the Cuban role in Angola, see "Soviet Union, Cuban and South African Intervention in Angola, 1974 to 1987," Case No. 198700589. Available in the State Department Annex.

Meanwhile, at Cassequel, in the contested Benguela-Lobito corridor, battles between warring nationalists continued. By early February, the SADF had fallen back to the extreme south of Angola.[47] UNITA returned on February 4, 1976, to Catumbela and fought in the streets with the MPLA's army until February 10, when the MPLA took control. Cassequel officials, including Director Octávio Rocha, who had been supporting the UNITA/South African offensive, fled Angola. Rocha fled Catumebla on a fishing trawler.[48] As South African troops left Angola, the MPLA took effective control over most of the country.[49] According to Rodrigues, Cassequel's new director, Victor Ribeiro, "arrived on an MPLA tank" in early 1976 to take charge of Cassequel.[50] This memory—Ribeiro on a tank—serves as a metaphor for how many of the Portuguese who left Angola felt about the MPLA's victory and subsequent reordering of society. Rodrigues had left Angola several months earlier, so her vision of Ribeiro on a tank must have to do with Ribeiro's political support for the MPLA. Ribeiro worked as an agronomist at Cassequel and joined the MPLA like many educated Angolans. For many loyal to the Espírito Santo family, his support for the new government must have felt like a betrayal.

The "True Cause" and a Centrally Planned Economy

The MPLA victory in February 1976 cleared the way for the remaking of Angolan society. Angolan specialist Christine Messiant describes the MPLA in this period as "authoritarian Marxist-Leninist" in its structure and political philosophy.[51] On Independence Day—November 11, 1975—Agostinho Neto declared that "the organs of the state will be under the supreme guidance of the MPLA and the primacy of the movement's structures over those of the state will be ensured."[52] The MPLA declared itself the only legal representative of the Angolan people and guaranteed "democracy" through popular participation in

47 Gleijeses, *Conflicting Missions*, p. 341.

48 Author interview with Octávio Rocha, Lisbon, June 11, 2001. See also Gonçalo Inocentes, *As Cheias do Rio Catumbela* (self-published, 2012), 168.

49 Gleijeses, *Conflicting Missions*, 345.

50 Author interview with Catarina Rodrigues.

51 Christine Messiant, "The Mutation of Hegemonic Domination: Multiparty Politics without Democracy" in Patrick Chabal and Nuno Vidal, eds., *Angola the Weight of History* (New York: Columbia University Press, 2008), 95.

52 Quoted on Lisbon radio, November 11, 1975. Tony Hodges, *Angola from Afro-Stalinism to Petro-Diamond Capitalism* (Oxford: James Currey, 2001), 45.

the MPLA's *poder popular* ["peoples' power"] movement.[53] In fact, the institutions of the MPLA and the government became one and the same; according to Article 31 of the MPLA's 1975 Constitution for Angola, "The President of the Popular Republic of Angola is the President of the MPLA."[54] The president governed in conjunction with the Council of the Revolution, comprising members from the political bureau of the MPLA, the command of FAPLA (The People's Armed Forces for the Liberation of Angola), and the MPLA-designated government.[55] The negotiated framework of the power-sharing, transitional government was discarded, and supporters of the FNLA and UNITA were officially declared traitors of the Angolan people and enemies of the "True Cause."[56] As a result, leaders of the FNLA and UNITA fled into exile or regrouped in the remote savannas of southeastern Angola.

The MPLA justified its domination of the state as necessary to guard against imperialism. MPLA leaders denigrated UNITA and the FNLA as "proxies of imperialism" and cast the MPLA as both the only legitimate liberation movement and the founder of Angolan nationalism. Amílcar Cabral, a Guinean nationalist leader and ally of the MPLA, cast the struggle for independence from Portuguese colonialism in decidedly anti-imperialist terms. He explained that three forces would ultimately dismantle imperialism: (1) the socialist state, exemplified by the Soviet Union; (2) the workers' movement in industrialized countries; and (3) the national liberation movement, including the MPLA, in the third world.[57] By casting itself as a player in the larger battle against capitalism and imperialism, the MPLA earned itself legitimacy among socialist states. The MPLA benefited as well from Agostinho Neto's positive reputation as an educated liberation leader; he had a medical degree, wrote poetry, and had been imprisoned and persecuted by the Portuguese.[58]

---

53 Articles 2 and 3 "Lei Constitucional da República Popular de Angola," *Diário da República* (I Série, n. 1, November 11, 1975). Reprinted in Adérito Correia and Bornito de Sousa, *Angola História Constitucional* (Coimbra: Livraria Almedina, 1996).

54 Article 31, "Lei Constitucional da República Popular de Angola," *Diário da República* (I Série, no. 1, 11 November 1975).

55 Article 36, "Lei Constitucional da República Popular de Angola," *Diário da República*, I Série, n. 1, 11 November 1975.

56 Frederick Cooper, *Decolonization and African Society: The labor question in French and British Africa* (Cambridge: Cambridge University Press, 1996), 7.

57 Amílcar Cabral, "As três grandes forças anti-imperialistas," *Nô Pintcha*, 17 July 1976.

58 Neto was, for example, well liked by Castro. See "Fidel Castro's 1977 Southern Africa Tour: A Report to Honecker," National Security Archive, http://www.nsarchive.org. For Neto's poetry see Agostinho Neto, *Sacred Hope* (Luanda, 1986). Translated into English by Marga Holness.

In May 1976, the MPLA adopted a plan to create an "economy of resistance" that worked with the "national anti-imperialist forces and responds definitively to the economic block and to the systematic destruction of the country's productive capacity."[59] Law 3/76, known as the Law of Nationalization and Confiscation, called for cooperatives and the development of state companies to control large and strategic industries.[60] According to the legislation, the chaos surrounding the civil war—which the legislation labeled an "imperialist war"—and the mass exodus of Portuguese settlers necessitated that the state nationalize companies abandoned by their owners or belonging to traitors.[61]

Cassequel fit into the second category because of Espírito Santo support for the Estado Novo, UNITA, and the South African invasion. Law 3/76 stipulated that "indemnities...for nationalized property" would be "negotiated between the State and interested parties, with the objective of protecting the owners' interests with the general interest of the Angolan people."[62] On the other hand, "saboteurs" of the national economy and "traitors" to the liberation struggle would have no right to indemnities, "the confiscation of their property being the Angolan peoples' just response to the traitors' crimes."[63] Articles 3 and 4 of Law 3/76 list fifteen specific justifications for confiscating property, including the owners' absence of more than forty-five days; collaboration with fascist organizations, such as the Portuguese secret police (PIDE); and voluntary collaboration with "anti-nationalist" organizations such as UNITA or FNLA. The overwhelming majority of enterprises transferred to the state were confiscated (457 out of 499 transfers) and no indemnities were paid.[64] According to MPLA sources documented by Maria Coelho, 99 percent of the confiscated enterprises resulted from either abandonment or an interruption of activity and referred almost exclusively to Portuguese owners.[65]

In the vacuum left by war, foreign invasion, and the mass exodus of Portuguese settlers, calls for confiscating property abounded. As Sócrates Dáskalos, the provisional governor of Benguela Province (home to Cassequel), explained, the MPLA victory emboldened the most radical *empelistas* [MPLA activists] to demand the confiscation of anything that "smelled of profit or privilege."[66]

---

59 Law n. 3/76, March 3, 1976, *Diário da República* (1 Série, No. 52).

60 Ibid.

61 Ibid.

62 Ibid.

63 Ibid.

64 Maria Antonieta Coelho, "Rupture and Continuity: The State, Law and the Economy in Angola, 1975–1989" (PhD diss., University of Warwick School of Law, 1994), 162.

65 Ibid.

66 Dáskalos, *Um Testemunho*, 186.

The MPLA confiscated Cassequel in May 1976, with Law 11/76 providing four justifications for the confiscation: (1) sugar production was strategic for the national economy, (2) the company employed more than 5,000 workers, (3) the administration of the company abandoned the country and cooperated with the "reactionary conspiracy" led by FNLA and UNITA, and (4) the company had a monopoly of the nation's sugar production.[67] In interviews, former Cassequel employees insisted that Cassequel was never abandoned, although they conceded that the Espírito Santo family supported UNITA and the South African invasion.

There are two historical interpretations of the MPLA's program of nationalizations and confiscations, both of which are reflected in the oral history record for Cassequel. The first, often described as a defensive explanation, argues that the MPLA responded to the sabotage and abandonment of the economy by Portuguese settlers/business owners through state intervention aimed at keeping the economy afloat and thousands of workers employed.[68] The second, an offensive explanation, emphasizes the MPLA's aversion to the market and plans to build a state-directed socialism.[69]

In their interviews, former Angolan workers and Portuguese administrators used the terms "confiscation" or "nationalization," and their language indicates the orientation of an individual's interpretation of the events. Two former administrators interviewed in Lisbon explicitly corrected my use of "nationalization"[70] and described Cassequel's *confisco* ["confiscation"] as arbitrary and unjustified. Most of the Portuguese workers I interviewed who worked at Cassequel in the run up to independence derided the MPLA's communism and pointed to Angola's postindependence economic deterioration as evidence of the MPLA's failed economic policies. On the other hand, most Angolans interviewed answered in the affirmative to the question, "Was the nationalization of Cassequel justified?" The response of Mário Santos represented the consensus: "Yes, it was good because the monopolies that ran the company abandoned it, and the government had to take over in order to employ the workers of these companies, because if the government did not

67 Law n. 3/76, March 3, 1976, *Diário da República*.

68 Coelho, "Rupture and Continuity," 165.

69 Manuel Ennes Ferreira, "Angola: A Indústria Transformadora numa Economia de Direcção Central e Planificada e em Situação de Guerra (1975–1991)" (Dissertação, Doutor em Economia, Universidade Técnica de Lisboa Instituto Superior de Economia e Gestão, 1997), 408–11.

70 Author interviews with Carlos Moita, former Cassequel head accountant, February 5, 2001, Lisbon, and Octávio Rocha, former engineer and company director in 1975, June 11, 2001, Lisbon.

confiscate, the companies would be abandoned and there would be unemployment among the Angolan people."[71] This response reflected the MPLA's argument that it intervened only after company owners abandoned Angola, the version of events promoted by the MPLA in the early days of independence and since taught as Angolan history. In many cases, the MPLA's assertions were true. Many Portuguese business owners sabotaged their businesses and equipment before leaving the country, with bitterness for the end of colonialism, war, and the victory of the MPLA fueling destruction of property.

In the case of Cassequel, however, it is not fair to simply say that management abandoned Angola. Octávio Rocha, Cassequel's last director under private ownership, denied that the administration abandoned Angola. He emphasized his own presence on the ground until 1976 when, because of military combat between the MPLA and UNITA for control of the Lobito-Benguela region, he fled Catumebla.[72] Rocha said he supported a rapprochement with the MPLA and hoped to return to Angola after the fighting abated. Of course, it is also true that many Portuguese who fled Angola in the early months of independence hoped that American and South African intervention would defeat the MPLA-led government and usher in a regime more protective of their economic interests.

The legal basis for a centralized, planned economy began with the MPLA's Angolan Constitution of November 11, 1975. Article 8 established a "state-directed and -planned national economy."[73] The MPLA blamed blocks of capital, such as the one controlled by the GES, as well as all "capitalists and imperialists" for "criminal exploitation" of workers.[74] Before independence, the MPLA-aligned workers' movement called for "a workers' fight against imperialism" and admonished workers to unite, organize, and strike.[75] After independence, the MPLA expropriated the holdings of large companies such as the GES with close ties to the Estado Novo. The new government did not, however, nationalize the holding of large multinational companies such as Gulf Oil. President Agostinho Neto explained that these multinational firms would only be nationalized at some unspecified future date. In the meantime, according to Neto, their presence would ensure a better deal for the Angolan people.[76] Clearly, the MPLA needed

71 Author interview with Mário Santos and João Areias, July 13, 2001, Catumbela.

72 Author interview with Octávio Rocha, Lisbon, June 11, 2001. See also Inocentes, *As Cheias do Rio Catumbela* (Self published, 2012), 168.

73 Article 8, "Lei Constitucional da República Popular de Angola," *Diário da República.*

74 "A Luta dos Trabalhadores contra o Imperialismo," *Vitória Certa* (July 12, 1975), 4.

75 Ibid.

76 Agostinho Neto, "We have Chosen Socialism," speech published in *Vitória Certa* (23 October 1976) and reprinted in *People's Power in Mozambique, Angola and Guinea Bissau* (no. 5, November–Deccember 1976), 8.

the royalties paid by Gulf Oil to sustain itself in power in the context of a collapsing economy and a military threat from UNITA and its supporters. As economic output declined, the MPLA would depend increasingly on revenues earned from Sonangol, the foreign-managed national oil company.[77]

To direct and control Angolan industry, the MPLA created the Ministry for Industry and Energy the day after independence.[78] The new ministry exercised control over "abandoned" companies. Following the confiscation of Cassequel on May 8, 1976, the government changed Cassequel's name to Primeiro de Maio in honor of International Workers' Day. The MPLA also set up a National Commission for Restructuring of the Sugar Industry [Comissão Nacional de Reestruturação da Indústria Açúcareira]. The commission reorganized the administration of Cassequel and the GES's second sugar plantation at Dombe Grande under one management. The combined sugar enterprise became known as Osuku, the word for sugar in Umbundu, the first language of most of the plantations' workers. In 1976, as a result of the civil war and the mass departure of skilled technicians, Cassequel/Primeiro de Maio produced 44 percent of its 1973 production.[79] Indeed, production would never again reach colonial-era levels. The new administration, led by Director Victor Ribeiro lacked the money to purchase spare parts and pay salaries, which further undermined efficiency and net production.[80]

During a visit to 4 de Fevreiro, the former Compahnia do Açúcar de Angola in Dombe Grande, MPLA leader Lopo do Nascimento urged workers to produce for the good of the nation and praised Cuban comrades for supplying decisive aid in the Angolan sugar industry. Cuban *cooperantes* with experience in the sugar industry provided some of the expertise lost after independence. According to Victor Ribeiro, "the first Cuban *cooperantes* [taken from among Cuban military forces] were fundamental to the first few postindependence sugar harvests."[81] A joint 1977 visit to Cassequel/Primeiro de Maio by Agostinho Neto and Fidel Castro underscored the significance of Cuban assistance in the sugar industry [Image 5.2]. According to Christine Hatzky, between the start of

77 Heywood, *Contested Power in Angola*, 205. Ricardo Soares de Oliveira, "Business success, Angola-style: postcolonial politics and the rise and rise of Sonangol," *Journal of African Studies* (vol. 45, 4, 2007), 595–619.

78 Manuel Ennes Ferreira, *A indústria em tempo de guerra (Angola, 1975–91)* (Lisboa: Edições Cosmos Instituto da Defesa Nacional, 1999), 398.

79 "Lembrou o Cda. Lopo do Nascimento aos trabalhadores já conscientes da Açúcareira '4 de Fevereiro' (Dombe)," *Jornal de Angola* (January 27, 1977). I thank Manuel Ennes Ferreira for sharing this article.

80 Author interview with Victor Ribeiro.

81 Ibid.

IMAGE 5.2 *Fidel Castro visit to Cassequel, 1977.*
Fidel Castro escorted by Cassequel/Primeiro de Maio Director Victor Ribeiro. Angola President Agostinho Neto is behind Ribeiro.
SOURCE: PERSONAL COLLECTION OF VICTOR RIBEIRO.

Cuban assistance to the MPLA in late 1975 and the withdrawal of Cuban troops from Angola in 1991, 400,000 Cuban soldiers would serve in Angola, while 50,000 Cuban civilians, the so-called internationalists, would provide civil aid to support Angolan nation-building.[82]

A counterhistory of Cuban assistance at Cassequel/Primeiro de Maio promoted by Cassequel's former Portuguese employees is that the MPLA dismantled and shipped much of Cassequel's machinery to Cuba *via* the nearby Port of Lobito in payment for the help of technicians and engineers.[83] Victor Ribeiro insists that such "payments" never happened.[84] Indeed, such shipments seem unlikely given the scale of Cuban aid to Angola,[85] but like so much of Angola's modern history, the facts about the machinery are contested.

82 Christine Hatzky, *Cubans in Angola South-South Cooperation and Transfer of Knowledge, 1976–1991* (Madison: University of Wisconsin Press, 2015), 4.

83 Inocentes, *As Cheias do Rio Fagulha*, 168.

84 Author interview with Victor Ribeiro.

85 For a comprehensive study of Cuban assistance in Angola, see Hatzky, *Cubans in Angola.*

The MPLA declared 1976 "the year of national reconstruction."[86] The declaration of the Second National Conference of Angolan Workers, held in December 1976, celebrated the Angolan peoples' victory over "American imperialism," "Maoists," "racist South Africans," and "certain African governments who have sold out to imperialism." The document proclaimed that an alliance with the socialist world would "assure Angola a full independence, social progress, happiness, and well-being for all."[87] In early October, Angola and the Soviet Union signed a Treaty of Friendship and Cooperation.[88] The Soviet Union and Cuba encouraged MPLA leaders to look to other communist states rather than the West as a model and for economic and military assistance.[89] The United States refused to recognize the MPLA government.

The MPLA-aligned workers' movement, UNTA, called on Angolans to produce: "In the new situation, the word of the day is to produce: to heal the wounds of war, to get industry on its feet, for agriculture, the transportation system, construction, schools, hospitals..."[90] In spite of the rhetoric and good intentions, the Angolan economy contracted significantly, and production at Cassequel/Primeiro de Maio continued a steady decline from 1976 until the government shut the plantation down completely in 1991. The plantation's demise resulted from the combination of the MPLA's hard-line ideology of economic transformation and the loss of skilled technicians. Most of the technical staff who remained at Cassequel/Primeiro de Maio after independence decided to leave during the first two years of independence. This absence added to a lack of money to buy parts to maintain machinery and the nonpayment of salaries to workers because of the central government's inability or unwillingness to pay cash for processed sugar, leading to a further decline in production.

The MPLA's plan for independent Angola called for mass participation in all decisions. The vehicle to achieve this mass participation was called *poder popular* [people's power]. The theory was that a network of *poder popular* assemblies at the village, district, province, and central government levels would discuss and eventually make policy. In theory it would operate as a form of

86 UNTA, "Declaração da II Confereência Nacional dos Trabalhadores Angolanos" (Luanda: Dezembro 1976). "MPLA" file, A-T/S, I-33, CIDAC, 3.

87 Ibid., 3.

88 K. Uralov, *A Justa Causa de Angola* (Moscovo: Edições da Agência de Imprensa Nóvosti, 1976), 2–3.

89 Confidential State Department Memo, October 1, 1976, 198704129, State Department Annex.

90 UNTA, "Declaração da II Confereência," 6.

indigenous African democracy. Thus, in Catumbela, *poder popular* groups at Cassequel/Primeiro de Maio met to discuss management issues and politics. Victor Ribeiro, the plantation's new director, worked with these groups to discuss policy- and work-related issues. Basil Davidson, a sympathetic observer who visited Angola in 1977, concluded that the action groups functioned as democratic structures and were essential to overcome "the colonial heritage of administrative dictatorship, bureaucratic irresponsibility, and political oppression."[91] A more critical perspective recorded in 2006 argued that "*poder popular* stole everything"[92] because it emboldened employees to claim ownership of the plantation and thus justify theft of company property. Pita Gros, who worked in management for Osuka, said that *poder popular* undermined worker discipline and productivity because it encouraged workers to challenge management on even mundane decisions.[93] According to Christine Messiant, the so-called mass organizations [such as *poder popular* committees] functioned as transmission belts from the central party and provided none of the benefits or process of grassroots democracy. The system bred corruption, double standards, widespread injustice, and discrimination.[94]

After independence, UNTA, the MPLA's union and the only legal union in the country, published "Workers in Power: The Life of the Worker," a pamphlet designed to educate Angolans about the evils of imperialism and the need for worker solidarity. "Workers," the pamphlet admonished, "have the duty to always be organized: in the factories, in the fields, and in all locations of work, so that they form a solid and cohesive block."[95] The pamphlet aimed to teach Angolans that their struggle was not an isolated one: that they were taking part in the larger fight of all the oppressed workers of the world.[96] To educate readers about the international workers' movement, the pamphlet created a dialogue between a salaried worker and an omniscient narrator. The narrator begins by asking the worker about his past. We learn, for example, that the worker was born "in a *cubata* full of mosquitos, always hot, without water, without electricity, and without hygiene." He works for a "powerful capitalist" who tells him it "is a sin and a crime not to work." The capitalist himself does not work "because he has a lot of money." The narrator asks if the worker

91 Basil Davidson, "Towards a New Angola," *People's Power in Mozambique, Angola and Guinea Bissau* (no. 9, July–September 1977), 10.

92 Author interview with Pita Gros, Dombe Grande, February 6, 2006.

93 Ibid.

94 Messiant, "The Mutation of Hegemonic Domination," 95.

95 UNTA, "Trabalhadores no Poder: A Vida do Trabalhador" (Luanda, Abril 1978), 2, CIDAC.

96 Ibid., 3.

eats well. The worker replies, "I always eat the same thing. I always eat *funge* [Angolan staple porridge made from either maize or cassava]."[97]

The conversation then turns to action. The narrator asks if the worker accepts his exploitation. The worker replies that he never accepted his exploitation:

> My grandfather fought against the theft of his fields. My father participated in the great coffee strike of 1956 and in the great cotton strike of 1961. I have already been in strikes, one in July 1974 against the massacres and in the general strike of May 1975 against fascism and the agents of imperialism.[98]

The worker says that in the past he worked to enrich the capitalists, but now it is different. "I ought to work for Angola, for our People. Now we are independent." The narrator asks, "Why do you think the struggle ought to continue?" The worker responds: "The struggle ought to continue against the exploiters." The narrator: "And who are these exploiters?" The worker: "They are the imperialists and their lackeys, they are the capitalists and the bourgeoisie and their agents, they are all in the same pot."[99]

The pamphlet warns: "Our struggle will only be victorious if all the people are organized by their Revolutionary Vanguard, the MPLA," which will create a popular democracy based on peoples' power. The people will elect their representatives in each factory and on each farm, and the peoples' representatives will not only defend the struggle, but will "fight for the improvement of our conditions of life, of work, medical assistance, etc."[100] The pamphlet ends by admonishing workers to produce in order to "defeat reactionary forces, who destroyed the machines, lorries, tractors and fields, because they knew that if the people and the MPLA were not able to increase production, there would be a shortage of food…the people would be hungry and angry and would revolt against their Political Vanguard."[101]

---

97 Ibid., 4.

98 Ibid., 5. The only one of these revolts that has been analyzed by historians is the 1961 revolt against forced cotton production. See Aida Freudenthal, "A Baixa de Cassanje. Algodão e revolta," *Revista Internacional de Estudos Africanos* (nos. 18–22, 1995–1999), 245–278; John A. Marcum, *The Angolan Revolution, Volume 1 The Anatomy of an Explosion (1950–1962)* (Cambridge, Massachusetts: The MIT Press, 1969), 124–126; and Douglas Wheeler and René Pélissier, *Angola* (London: Pall Mall Press, 1971), 174–175.

99 UNTA, "Trabalhadores no Poder: A Vida do Trabalhador," 5.

100 Ibid., 8.

101 Ibid., 10.

As the pamphlet predicted, widespread destruction and hunger did occur across Angola in 1976–1977, but the causes were complex and included the economic policies of the "Political Vanguard." A potential challenge to the political vanguard from populists within the MPLA was brutally put down in May 1977.[102]

Daily life in Catumbela became more difficult throughout 1976 and 1977 as a consequence of diminishing stocks of staple foods. Food shortages resulted from the deterioration of food distribution networks and the absence of a reliable currency. Food became increasingly expensive and negated the wage gains that workers experienced in 1974. Workers at Cassequel/Primeiro de Maio increasingly went unpaid for long periods, and the results were practically catastrophic. Cassequel/Primeiro de Maio workers and their families struggled to obtain consumer goods formerly bought in Portuguese-owned stores in Catumbela or received as part of their pay package from Cassequel.

Facing these challenges in the context of a countrywide economic meltdown, the MPLA declared 1976 a period of national reconstruction. Those Cassequel/Primeiro de Maio workers who remained welcomed the structural changes because they hoped for a better future as promised by the MPLA; they contributed their labor in spite of the erratic payment of salaries. In this context, even as they supported the government, more workers stole sugarcane and company equipment, and others converted parts of the plantation into subsistence garden plots.[103] In an unsigned report about this era, a Cuban *cooperante* recalled "the difficult conditions facing workers, who lacked food, and who went for months without being paid their salaries, which made it impossible to increase production."[104] The decline in production, nonpayment of workers' salaries, and deteriorating equipment at Cassequel/Primeiro de Maio in 1976 reflected structural problems across the Angolan economy resulting from the MPLA's nationalization campaign, the departure of so many of the country's skilled technicians and managers, and the centralization of power. In fact, food shortages affected most Angolans in 1975–1976, including those serving in the FAPLA (the MPLA's military).[105]

---

102 Lara Pawson, *In the Name of the People Angola's Forgotten Massacre* (New York: IB, Tauris, 2014).

103 Author interview with Germano Adelino Castrioto, Catumbela, July 11, 2000.

104 "Assuntos com Cooperação Cubana, 1987," 3. Arquivo do Osuka, Catumbela.

105 Pawson, *In the Name of the* People, 162.

Conclusion

Intervention in Angola by Cold War foes inflated a domestic dispute between rival nationalist movements into a full-scale war. Rather than supporting the forces of moderation and compromise, the United States, the Soviet Union, Cuba, and South Africa empowered the ideologues of each movement and destroyed the chances for a negotiated settlement. At Cassequel/Primeiro de Maio, the socialist rhetoric and policies produced a few early benefits for workers, such as higher wages, but as early as 1975, the vilification of the former owners, skilled technicians, and top-down centralized management resulted in lower production and worsening working conditions. The government finally shuttered the plantation in 1991.

The workers at Cassequel/Primeiro de Maio, including management, but especially the thousands who worked in the fields, paid the highest price for Angola's fractured independence and the MPLA's economic policies. The seizure of private businesses and the repression of those who supported the colonial regime or rival nationalist movements alienated so many whose economic, material, and intellectual assets the country needed desperately to harness for economic growth and political stability.

Looking back from the perspective of nearly thirty years, José Espírito Santo said that members of his family felt great affection for Angola and pride in their investments; he insisted that the family "always reinvested the profits... in order to improve the social conditions, to improve the productivity of the companies."[106] Espírito Santo put the blame for Cassequel's postindependence demise on the disasterous economic policies of the MPLA. Whereas the Espírito Santo family and other investors lost a valuable asset with the demise of Cassequel, it was the employees—Angolan and Portuguese—who lost their livelihoods and, for some, their hopes for a socialist Angola.

Deteriorating conditions at Cassequel challenged those workers at Cassequel/ Primeiro de Maio who believed that socialism would bring higher wages and a better quality of life.[107] In the first couple of years after Independence, workers at Cassequel did their best to cope with shortages in equipment and delayed payment of salaries because by and large they supported the MPLA's stated objective to create a new, independent Angola committed to worker's rights. They believed in a future in which workers ran Cassequel/Primeiro de Maio alongside management, in which their children received universal education

106 Author interview with José Manuel Pinheiro Espírito Santo.

107 Author interview with *Soba* Francisco Sowende Figueiredo, Fabrica Velha, July 4, 2001.

and access to health care. It was a heady time, full of revolutionary promise and pride for the defeat of Portuguese fascism and colonialism. Soba Francisco Sowende Figueiredo summed up the expectations among plantation workers for postcolonial Angola: "Each one had his own thoughts, but all anticipated a different and better way of life, nobody thought of war, or politics, because the objective was to save the people from colonialism."[108]

---

108 Ibid.

Conclusion

Since its sixteenth-century arrival along the coast of the Kingdom of Kongo, Portugal's primary interest in Angola was driven by financial gain, and for centuries, the primary export was African people. With the demise of the Atlantic slave trade in the second half of the nineteenth century, colonial efforts focused on profiting from Africans' labor in Angola. The problem from the colonial perspective was Africans' unwillingness to work in agricultural enterprises, and forced labor provided an answer—albeit one with political and moral consequences. As Portuguese hegemony over the Angolan interior expanded in the early 1900s, more Africans became subjects of the colonial state, which required policy makers to justify the practice as a necessary means to the larger good. They declared its supposed moral benefits in a civilizing rhetoric that emphasized the westernization of Angolans while deflecting criticisms about the perpetuation of a labor system akin to slavery. That this labor system persisted until the mid-twentieth century speaks to the tenacity of the propaganda created by successive Portuguese governments and their supporters.

Another reason forced labor survived for so long is that it benefited from powerful interests within colonial Angolan society, including business and settler organizations. The government used forced labor to build infrastructure and to attract capital investment from Portugal and beyond. Agro-industrial enterprises like Cassequel depended on cheap and readily available labor. As a result, Cassequel—like other Angolan businesses—maintained its headquarters in Lisbon, where the powerful members of its board of directors lobbied government for protective tariffs and sympathetic labor laws. With Portugal's commitment to mercantilist policies, especially after the 1926 coup d'état that ended the republic and ushered in the Estado Novo, the voices of the banking-industrialist Espírito Santo family carried tremendous weight. Government deliverance of *contratados*, a tariff-protected market, the monopoly on biofuel production, and vertical control over sugar production (from field to refinery to distribution) made Cassequel extremely profitable. And yet, this profit was realized on the backs of thousands of forced laborers whose individual stories have been ignored or obfuscated within the historiographical process.

This book thus makes two original contributions to the historiography of labor and business in colonial Angola. First, it helps the reader to understand how forced labor functioned as a system within the context of Cassequel. Through the examination of company records and in interviews with former *contratados*, I explain the purported economic value of forced labor to Cassequel and the methods employed to secure its necessary workforce.

 | DOI 10.1163/9789004301757_008

Company records indicate a reliance on *contratados* dating to the earliest days of the plantation. Although by the 1950s company correspondence indicated government pressure to phase out forced labor—a shift that became law after the outbreak of the nationalist war for liberation/independence—the system of requesting workers from colonial administrators persisted until 1961. Forced labor relied on a web of repression that delivered workers on nine- to twelve-month contracts for minimal pay. The threat of arrest, beatings, or even harsher forced labor on faraway São Tomé island convinced most to cooperate with the system. Moreover, company records about living and working conditions indicate that until the 1950s, the company took only limited measures to ensure the health and wellbeing of its employees.

Second, this study invites the participation and voices of former *contratados* into the telling of Cassequel's history of forced labor via the use of oral history. Archives are largely silent on the feelings and experiences of *contratados*, and the interviews conducted as part of this study provide a means to uncovering and preserving memories that would otherwise be lost. The narratives provided by former *contratados* lend insight into the heavy labor performed at Cassequel and humanize the trauma suffered under the system. Interviewees made clear their lack of choice in whether to serve out their contract and spoke movingly about their loneliness, isolation, and suffering under the system. Throughout the course of their servitude, forced laborers suffered quotidian humiliations by a colonial enterprise in which they had little to no power. Expanding our understanding of forced labor through methodologies such as oral history and archival analysis is therefore key to understanding Angola's modern history. Throughout the colonial era, government and business interests dominated the historical and written record, leaving the voices of *contratados* marginalized, silenced, and forgotten in colonial-era documents. Even in historical reports that were critical of Portuguese colonial labor practices, the actual voices of individual forced laborers were largely absent. Balancing the historical record with the perspectives of *contratados* therefore becomes imperative to the revision of hegemonic accounts of forced labor during the colonial era.

Sadly, hegemonic narratives remain a problematic part of contemporary Angolan historiography in the independence era. While the colonial narrative emphasized an ideal of *Luso-tropicalismo* while ignoring the suffering and humiliation of Angolans, the post-independence, official narrative of the MPLA (Popular Movement for the Liberation of Angola) celebrates the liberation war while providing little space for dissent and diverse opinions. For example, in the public discourse, competing nationalist movements are often portrayed as nothing more than stooges of foreign aggression; their dystopic or critical perspectives on independence therefore become discredited within the discourse of the current MPLA nationalist narrative. Again, oral history provides an opportunity to collect and recognize these competing and dissenting postliberation voices and may help scholars to identify and interrogate new historiographical angles within the current Angolan context.

As an example of how oral history interrogates recently constructed histories of postindependence Angola, I would like to finish with material from a series of interviews that focus on the closing of Cassequel/Primeiro de Maio in 1991. Certainly Cassequel's closure mirrored failures across Angola, as central planning, war, and neglect ravaged once-productive enterprises. Like most nationalized enterprises in independent Angola, the centralized management structure had failed to maintain agricultural productivity. Annual harvests and sugar production declined significantly every year between 1976 and 1990 because of a lack of trained personnel, deteriorating equipment, the nonpayment of salaries, and the theft of company property.

At the time of its closing, approximately 4,000 workers were employed at Cassequel/Primeiro de Maio. Their memories of the former institution, preserved in oral history interviews I conducted in 2001 and 2006, have been complicated and conditioned by the ensuing humanitarian crises that followed Cassequel's dismantling. During the worst fighting of the 1990s civil war, the coastal region around Catumbela remained under government control and relatively safe. The government's initial plan after the closure was to turn over roughly 4,000 hectares of the former plantation to the former workers and recently arrived refugees.[1] As of 2006, however, there had been no concessions of legal title to the vast majority of land being rented by individual agriculturalists. The government agency that controls the land has granted concessions to Sonongal (the national oil company) to build a housing development for its workers on lands close to the city of Lobito. This arrangement has led to anger among agriculturalists who fear the loss of their land and livelihood. Since 1993, ADRA (Acção para o Desenvolvimento Rural e Ambiente), a local nongovernmental organization, has fought for recognition of the property rights due former workers of Cassequel/Primeiro de Maio. Many of the landless work as laborers for the region's large landowners, some of whom are high-ranking officers in the Angolan Armed Forces, which carved an airstrip and base out of Cassequel's sugarcane fields during the civil war.

The situation also has had dire humanitarian consequences. Locally the people who work for food are known by the Umbundu term *tchinhango*, which

1 Aart Van Der Heide, *Relatório da Avaliação do Projecto de Catumbela, Julho 1990*. (Benguela, Angola: ADRA (Acção para o Desenvolvimento Rural e Ambiente), 1990).

refers to the people and the labor system.[2] The standard payment in 2006 was a paltry 1 kilogram (2.2 pounds) of *fuba* [maize meal] per day. In the late 1990s, an ADRA study indicated chronic malnourishment and high infant-mortality statistics among residents. Although these statistics seemed to be improving by 2006, there was still widespread poverty and increasing fear about the lack of land titles.[3]

This poverty and the concentration of land ownership in the hands of a few, plus the widespread impression that the wealthy and well connected enjoy privileged access to government decision making, begs the question: Did the revolution deliver a better life? For many the answer is no, which explains why some former workers now remember aspects of colonialism with fondness. In the words of one respondent interviewed in 2001, "At least in those days we had enough to eat."[4] Another resident of Catumbela explains, "As an employee of Cassequel I had a normal life, because each of us had a salary, and we had an employees' cooperative where we received monthly food rations. Now after the war, the situation is very difficult, such that many die of hunger in Catumbela, we don't receive salaries, there is no food in the cooperative, the hospitals do not have medicines..."[5] It is still to be seen the extent to which Angola's peace dividend, the oil boom, and the opening of a new Cuca beer factory near Cassequel's old factory grounds will revitalize Catumbela and give former *contratados* and their descendants an improving quality of life.

When I conducted interviews in 2006, memories were also still fresh from Angola's decades long civil war, which continued almost uninterrupted between 1975 and the assassination of UNITA (National Union for the Total Independence of Angola) leader Jonas Savimbi in 2002. Salomão dos Santos remembers that after the initial honeymoon, when everything seemed "like a bed of roses," the situation quickly deteriorated into a brutal war without reason or end.[6] It was during this period that people remembered colonialism as a time of relative peace: "in spite of having to pay our taxes, the suffering was nothing like now. We had food, clothes, drinks, etc., but now we have nothing, neither food nor clothes, and only war. What kind of independence is this?"[7] One interviewee described the civil war as a kind of football game, in which

2 Author interview with Jeronimo Lua, June 9, 2006, Catumbela.

3 ADRA, *Relatório Annual 2006* (Benguela, Angola: ADRA (Acção para o Desenvolvimento Rural e Ambiente), 2006).

4 Author interview with Reinaldo Pereira Machado, July 17, 2001, Gama.

5 Author interview with Jeronimo Lua, June 9, 2006, Catumbela.

6 Author interview with Salomão dos Santos, Feb. 21, 2006, Balombo.

7 Ibid.

ordinary people were kicked back and forth between waring elites. Paulo Sapeque describes the intense poverty caused by the civil war: "We had hunger, all over people went about naked because they had no more clothes. Villages were destroyed, the beautiful houses of the colonists were destroyed, bridges were blown apart…UNITA stole whatever they wanted, wherever they went they massacred, raped, and killed."[8] The recent trauma remembered by this interviewee above underscores that there has not been a national reckoning or an opportunity for truth and reconciliation processes, as has happened in neighboring South Africa. As such, Angolan history remains splintered, ideologically-divided, and inherently unresolved.

As these final interviews demonstrate, emotion and circumstances ultimately affect what and how we remember the past.[9] Collectively, they demonstrate that Cassequel is and continues to be a contested place of memory within Angolan history. For some—namely, those who served as forced labor—it represents a tragic place, reminiscent of hard work and colonial humiliations; for others—namely, Portuguese and Angolan skilled workers—Cassequel evokes memories of comfort and pride on the one hand, and lost opportunities and bitterness toward independence on the other. A former mechanic remembered Cassequel as "a brilliant jewel that belonged to men of action, dreamers, and entrepreneurs."[10] Although perhaps tinged by nostalgia,[11] this memory reflects deeply held disappointment in the failed economic policies of independent Angola and what is perceived as the unfair vilification of Portuguese colonists. Consideration of these disparate memories and perspectives, and their recognition within the historiographical record, provides a rare opportunity to understand contemporary Angola in a more nuanced and inclusive spirit.

---

8 Author interview with Paulo Sapeque, April 14, 2006, Bailundo.

9 Raphael Samuel and Paul Thompson, eds., *The Myths We Live By* (New York: Routledge, 1990), 2.

10 Gonçalo Inocentes, *As Cheias do Rio Catumbela* (Lisboa: self-published, 2012), 168.

11 For more colonial nostalgia, see "Memórias Coloniais" edited by Pedro Aires Oliveira and Cláudia Castelo, *Cadernos de Estudos Africanos*, Nos. 9/10, Julho 2005/Junho 2006.

Appendix

Sociedade Agrícola do Cassequel: Dividends and profits, select years 1916–1971

Year	Dividends	Profits
1916	Esc. 142.500$00 (£31,667)	
1929	£26,670	£33,865
1931	£15,124	£43,002
1933	£14,723	
1934	£14,461	
1935	£14,250	
1936	£15,125	
1939	Esc. 58,674$34	
1940	Esc. 37,417$84	
1941	Esc. 62,833$20	
1943	Esc. 148,939$46	
1944	Esc. 146,654$12	
1945	Esc. 148.131$64	
1946	Esc. 213,563$89	
1948		Esc. 9.201.455$57 ($369,341.00)
1952	Esc. 589,198$55 ($20,493.86)	Esc. 18.894.795$04 ($657,210.00)
1954		Esc. 22.769.834$44 ($791,994.00)
1955		Esc. 22.864.816$01 ($795,298.00)
1957		Esc. 29.566.130$34 ($1,028,387.00)
1959		Esc. 29.293.596$76 ($1,018,908.00)
1961	Esc. 12.250.000$00 ($426,087.00)	Esc. 25.277.956$28 ($879,233.00)
1962	Esc. 409.360$00 ($14,239.00)	Esc. 19.954.790$79 ($694,080.00)
1964	Esc. 475,970$00 ($16,556.00)	Esc. 26,217,927$04 ($911,928.00)
1967	Esc. 16,412,415$00 ($578,775.00)	Esc. 21,882,074$88 ($771,660.00)
1969	Esc. 20,692,848$05 ($719,751.00)	Esc. 13,888,269$96 ($483,070.00)
1970	Esc. 24.511.196$95 ($852,563.00)	Esc. 16.192.834$92 ($657,101.00)
1971	Esc. 8.750.000$00 ($355,072.00)	Esc. 20.655.189$11 ($838,182.00)

SOURCE: SAC, *RELATÓRIOS*, VARIOUS YEARS, AC.

 | DOI 10.1163/9789004301757_009

Bibliography

Unpublished Primary Sources

Archives

Angola

Arquivo do Cassequel (AC), Catumbela, Angola (now housed in the AHBES)
Company Reports, various years 1913–1974
Correspondence, 1915–1974
Photographs
Arquivo Histórico (AH), Luanda
Caixas
Concelho do Huambo: 457, 466, 470, 472, 537, 540, 543, 544, 545, 548, 575
Districto de Benguela: 245, 1766, 1861, 1865, 1866, 1878, 1888, 1890, 2115, 3521, 3530, 5329, 5425, 5593
Códices
Benguela: 1887, 1966, 1968
Huambo: 1966, 1967, 1968, 1970
Lobito: 1937

Portugal

Arquivo Histórico do Banco Espírito Santo (AHBES), Lisbon
Sociedade Agrícola do Cassequel Collection
Caixas
Correspondence/Expediente
Órgãos Sociais e Administração
Arquivo Histórico Ultramarino (AHU), Lisbon
Gabinete do Ministro
Maços
Sala 6: 2,9, 192, 2827, 2894, 533, 546
Sala 12: 873, 3737
Gabinete dos Negócios Políticos
Ministro do Ultramar
Caixas
1 and 2
Repartição Central dos Negócios Indígenas
Maços
Sala 3: 1661, 1725, 2243
Arquivo Nacional de Torre do Tombo (ANTT), Lisbon
Arquivo Salazar

"Banco Espírito Santo," AOS/CO/FI-46
"Companhias Coloniais—Sociedade Agrícola do Cassequel," AOS/CO/UL-8
Arquivo Histórico-Parliamentar (AHP), Lisbon
Secção XXVIII, Caixa 48, n. 10 "Henrique Galvão"
Arquivo Mário Soares (AMS), Lisbon
Conselho da Revolução, 2975.028, 2975.031

United Kingdom

Public Records Office (PRO), London
Foreign Office (FO)
FO 367/1956, FO 371/7211, FO 371/8448, FO 371/11137, FO 371/11990, FO 371/12712, FO 371/13480, FO 371/21275, FO 371/21280, FO 371/31120, FO 371/39583, FO 371/80769, FO 371/90301, FO 371/90313, FO 371/109661

United States

United States National Archives (USNA), College Park, Maryland
POL 13 AFR, SNF, Box 2032
National Security Archive (NSA), http://www.nsarchive.org
"Soviet Ambassador to the People's Republic of Angola E.E. Afanasenko, Memorandum of Conversation with President of the Movement for the Popular Liberation of Angola, Agostinho Neto, 4 July 1975"
"Fidel Castro's 1977 Southern Africa Tour: A Report to Honecker"
Cold War International History Project (CWIHP), http://cwihp.si.edu
"Raúl Díaz Argüelles to the Armed Forces Minister Raúl Castro, 11 August 1975"
University of Washington Archives, Seattle, Washington
Gladwyn Murray Childs Papers, Accession No. 2208

Select Interviews

Angola

Francisco Swenda, Gama, 4 July 2001
Faustino Alfredo, Catumbela, 5 July 2001
Joaquim Hepolito de Andrade, Catumbela,10 July 2001
Germano Adelino Castrioto, Catumbela, 10 July 2001
Mário Santos, Catumbela, 13 July 2001
João Areias, Catumbela, 13 July 2001
Jorge Luíz Chingue, Gama, 16 July 2001
Evanisto Kaitangue, Gama, 17 July 2001
Daniel Gawes, Gama, 17 July 2001
Daniel Antóntio, Gama, 17 July 2001
Joaquim Segungondo, Gama, 17 July 2001
Alfredo Tomás, Gama, 17 July 2001

Reinaldo Pereira Machado, Gama, 17 July 2001
Julhete Luengo, Gama, 17 July 2001
António Fidalgo Galina Fortes, Catumbela, 18 July 2001
Maria Fatima, Catumbela, 20 July 2001
Paulino Muqunita, Catumbela, 31 July 2001
Dionisio Isaac, Catumbela, 31 July 2001
Domingos Marcelino, Catumbela, 31 July 2001
Senhor Pita Gros, Dombe Grande, 2 February 2006
Capinãlo Njinji, Bocoio, 14 February 2006
João Ndamba, Monte Belo, 17 February 2006
José Inácio, Monte Belo, 17 February 2006
Graciano Missão, Monte Belo, 17 February 2006
Augsotinho Carvalho, Monte Belo, 17 February 2006
Inocêncio Calei, Monte Belo, 17 February 2006
Adriano Ndalesi, Monte Belo, 17 February 2006
Alfredo Domingos, Monte Belo, 17 February 2006
Tchimbe Ngucika, Balombo, 21 February 2006
José Samuel, Balombo, 21 February 2006
Abel Quinta Kakumba, Balombo, 21 February 2006
João Kutakata, Balombo, 21 February 2006
Salomão dos Santos, Balombo, 21 February 2006
Inácio Boboleta, Balombo, 21 February 2006
Jacinta Cahomas, Balombo, 21 February 2006
Verónica Chilomba, Balombo, 21 February 2006
Justina Candeia, Balombo, 21 February 2006
Maria Naboano, Balombo, 21 February 2006
Justino Patrício, Cayengue-Mbola Kavulo (Balombo), 23 February 2006
Virgílio Chiquete, Cayengue-Mbola Kavulo (Balombo), 23 February 2006
Vasco Cafere, Cayengue-Mbola Kavulo (Balombo), 23 February 2006
Daniel Martinho Dovala, Cayengue-Mbola Kavulo (Balombo), 23 February 2006
Augusto Katchitiopololo, Bailundo, 12 April 2006
Rafael Kassoma, Bailundo, 12 April 2006
Paulo Sapeque, Bailundo, 12 April 2006
Francisco Segunda, Bailundo, 12 April 2006
Bento Samualanga, Bailundo, 12 April 2006
Justina Kalumbo, Bailundo, 13 April 2006
Cipriana Nduva, Bailundo, 13 April 2006
Cristina Vatchia, Bailundo, 13 April 2006
Augosto Lopes Katchilele, Chinguar, 18 April 2006
Félix Alberto Satuala, Chinguar, 18 April 2006

Bernarda Kabyndo, Chinguar, 18 April 2006
Constantina Baça, 18 April 2006
Dembue Nguguevula, Quilengues, 9 May 2006
Domingos Muculica, Quilengues, 9 May 2006
Chemi Pagador, Quilengues, 9 May 2006
Ngulengue Kaloko, Quilengues, 9 May 2006
Manuel Seguro, Quilengues, 9 May 2006
Ndumbakai Muhongo, Quilengues, 9 May 2006

Portugal

Engenheiro Octávio Almeda Rocha, Lisbon, 11 June 2001
Doutor José Manuel Pinheiro Espírito Santo, Lisbon, 30 August 2002
Catarina Rodrigues Silva, Lisbon, 29 August 2002
Doutor Carlos Verdete, Évora, 29 August 2002
Doutor Carlos dos Santos Moita, Lisbon, 5 February 2001

Published Primary Reports, Bulletins and Newspapers

Reports

Alto Comissariado da Província de Angola, *Regime Monetário e Bancário e Bancário da Província de Angola*. Lisboa: Imprensa Nacional, 1926.

Brito Capello, Guilherme Augusto de, *Relatório do Governador Geral da Província de Angola, 1887*. Lisboa: Imprensa Nacional, 1899.

Gomes Coelho, Guilherme, *Relatórios dos Governadores das Provincias Ultramarinas, Districto de Benguella, 1887*. Lisboa: Imprensa Nacional, n.d.

International Labor Office, *Report of the Ad Hoc Committee on Forced Labor*, Supplement No. 36, New Series of the International Labor Office. Geneva, 1953.

Laboreiro, Simão de, *A Circunscrição Civil Da Ganda Relatório do Administrador, 1914–1915*. Loanda: Imprensa Moderna, 1916.

Paiva Couceiro, Henrique de, *Angola (Dous annos de Governo Junho 1907–Junho 1909) Historia e Commentarios*. Lisboa: A Nacional, 1910.

Paulo Cid, Francisco de, *Relatórios dos Governadores das Províncias Ultramarinas, Districto de Benguella,1892*. Lisboa: Imprensa Nacional, 1899.

Sousa, José Napoleão do Sacramento, *Relatório da Alfândega de Benguela Relativo ao ano de 1915*. Lisboa: Imprensa Nacional, 1918.

Bulletins and Newspapers in the Biblioteca Nacional, Lisbon

A Defeza de Angola
A Redempção

A Reforma
A Voz d'Africa
Actividade Económica de Angola
Boletim da Agência Geral das Colónias
Boletim da Sociedade de Geographia de Lisboa
Boletim Oficial da Provincia de Angola
Diário de Luanda
Diário de Notícias
Expresso
Gazeta Agrícola de Angola
Jornal de Angola
Jornal de Benguela
Jornal do Comércio
Le Nouvel Observateur
Nô Pintcha
O Commercio de Benguella
O Distrio de Benguela
O Público (Lisbon)
O Século
Revista Colonia
Ultramar
Vitória Certa

Non-Portuguese Newspapers

Fact and Reports
Guardian (Manchester)
Financial Times (London)
The Times (London)
Times of Zambia

Books, Articles and Dissertations

Adas, Michael. *Machines as the Measure of Men: Science, Technology, and Ideologies of Western Dominance*. Ithaca: Cornell University Press, 1989.

Alberti, Verena. *História Oral a experiência do CPDIC* [Centro de Pesquisa e Documentação de História Contemporânea do Brasil]. Rio de Janeiro: Vargas, 1990.

Albright, David E.. *Communism in Africa*. Bloomington: Indiana University Press, 1980.

Alexandre, Valentim. *Velho Brasil Novas Áfricas: Portugal e o Império (1808–1975)*, Porto: Edições Afrontamento, 2000.

———. *O Império Africano Séculos XIX e XX*, Lisboa: Edições Colibri, 2000.

———. *Origens do Colonialismo Português Moderno (1822–1891)*, Lisboa: Sá da Costa, 1979.

———. "Portugal em África (1825–1974): Uma Perspectiva Global," *Penélope*, N.° 11, 1993, pp. 53–66.

———. "A África no Imaginário Político Português (Séculos XIX–XX)" , *Penélope*, N.° 15, 1995, pp. 39–52.

Alpers, Edward A. "'To Seek a Better Life': The Implications of Migration from Mozambique to Tanganyika for Class Formation and Political Behavior," *Canadian Journal of African Studies*, Vol. 18, No. 2, 1984, pp. 367–388.

Anderson, Anderson, Perry, "Portugal and the End of Ultra-Colonialism," *New Left Review*, No. 15, May/June 1962, pp. 83–102.

———. "Portugal and the End of Ultra-Colonialism 2," *New Left Review*, No. 16, July/August 1962, pp. 88–123.

Anonymous. *O cacau de S. Thomé: Resposta ao relatorio da missão Cadbury, Burtt e Swan Nas provincias de S. Thomé e Principe e de Angola em 1908*. Lisboa: Typographia d'A Editora, 1910.

Atkins, Keletso E. *The Moon Is Dead! Give Us Our Money! The Cultural Origins of an African Work Ethic, Natal, South Africa, 1843–1900*. Ann Arbor: University of Michigan, 1993.

Austen, Ralph A. *African Economic History Internal Development and External Dependency*. London: James Currey, 1987.

Axelson, Eric. *Portugal and the Scramble for Africa 1875–1891*. Johannesburg: Witwatersrand University Press, 1967.

Azevedo, J.M. Cerqueira de. *Subsídios para o Estudo da Economia de Angola nos Últimos cem anos*. Luanda: Imprensa Nacional, 1945.

Bailyn, Bernard. "The Idea of Atlantic History," *Itinerario*, Vol. XX, No. 1, 1996, pp. 19–44.

Ball, George W. *The Past Has Another Pattern*. New York: W.W. Norton & Company, 1973.

Ball, Jeremy. "'A Time of Clothes': The Angolan Rubber Boom, 1886–1902," *Ufahamu*, Vol. 28, No. 1, Fall 2000, 25–42.

Barbosa Casqueiro Richard. *A Cultura da Cana do Açúcar com Especial Referência ao Caso de Angola*. Instituto Superior de Agronomia, 1956.

Bastos, A.. *Monographia de Catumbella*. Lisboa, 1912.

Bastos, Viuva. et al., *A Escravatura em Mossamedes: Carta Aberta dirigida a S. Ex.ª o Presidente da Republica por um grupo de agricultores, industriaes e commerciantes de Mossamedes*. Lisboa: Typographia do Commercio, 1912.

Batalha, Fernando, *A Urbanização de Angola*. Luanda: Museu de Angola, 1950.

Bender, Gerald. *Angola under the Portuguese: the myth and the reality*, Berkeley: University of California Press, 1978.

Béthencourt, Alexandra de. *Fundação Ricardo do Espírito Santo Silva*. Lisboa: Fundação Ricardo do Espírito Santo Silva, 1999, p. 21.

Birmingham, David, "The Coffee Barons of Cazengo," *Journal of African History*, Vol. XIX, No. 4, 1978, pp. 523–538.

———. *Empire in Africa: Angola and its Neighbors*. Athens: Ohio University Press, 2006.

Breytenbach, Jan. *Forged in Battle*. Cape Town: Saayman & Weber Ltd., 1986.

———. *They Live By The Sword*. Alberton, South Africa: Lemur Books Ltd., 1990.

Brinkman, Inge (ed.). *Singing in the Bush: MPLA songs during the war for independence in south-east Angola (1966–1975)*. Koln: Rudiger Koppe Verlag, 2001.

Cadbury, William A. *Labour in Portuguese West Africa*. London: George Routledge and Sons, LTD., 1910.

Caetano, Marcello. *Os Nativos na Economia Africana*. Coimbra: Coimbra Editora, Limitada, 1954.

Capela, José, *O Vinho Para O Preto*. Porto: Afrontamento, 1973.

———. *O Imposto de Palhota e a Introdução do Modo de Produção Capitalista nas Colónias*. Porto: Afrontamento, 1977.

Carreira, António. *Angola Da Escravatura ao Trabalho Livre*. Lisboa: Editora Arcádia, 1977.

———. *Cabo Verde (Aspectos sociais. Secas e fomes do século XX)*. Lisboa: Ulmeiro, 1984.

Carreira, Iko. *O Pensamento Estratégico de Agostinho Neto Contribuição Histórico*. Lisboa: Publicações Dom Quixote, 1996.

Carvalho, Jerónimo Paiva de. *Alma Negra: Depoimento Sobre a Questão Dos Serviçais de S. Tomé*. Porto: Tipografia Progresso, 1912.

———. *A Desafronta: Defesa de um homem injustamente perseguido e caluniada*. Coimbra: Tipografia Literária, 1916.

Casimiro, Augusto. *Angola e o Futuro (Alguns Problemas Fundamentais)*. Lisboa: Livrolândia, LDA., 1957.

Casqueiro, Richard Barbosa. *A Cultura da Cana do Açúcar com Especial Referência ao Caso de Angola*. Instituto Superior de Agronomia, 1956.

Castelo, Cláudia. *Passagens para África: O Povoamento de Angola e Moçambique com Naturais da Metrópole (1920–1974)*. Porto: Edições Afrontamento, 2007.

Chabal, Patrick, ed. *A History of Postcolonial Lusophone Africa*. Bloomington: Indiana University Press, 2002.

Chatelain, Heli. *Folk Tales of Angola*. Boston, 1894.

Chikueka, Maria Chela. *Angola: Torchbearers*. Toronto: Chela Book Group, 1999.

Childs, Gladwyn Murray. *Umbundu Kinship and Character*. London: Oxford University Press, 1949.

Chomsky, Noam. *American Power and the New Mandarins*, New York: Pantheon Books, 1967.

Clarence-Smith, Gervase. *The third Portuguese empire 1825–1975*. Manchester: Manchester University Press, 1985.

———. "The Sugar and Rum Industries in the Portuguese Empire, 1850–1914," in Adrian Graves and Bill Albert, eds., *Crisis and Change in the International Sugar Economy, 1860–1914*. Norwich & Edinburgh: ISC Press, 1984, pp. 226–235.

———. "Mossamedes and its Hinterland, 1875–1915," Ph.D. Dissertation, University of London, 1975.

———. "Slavery in coastal southern Angola 1875–1913," *Journal of Southern African Studies*, 1976, Vol. 2, No. 2, pp. 214–223.

———. "O proteccionismo e a produção de açúcar na África Central e Equatorial (Angola, Moçambique, Zaire, Zimbabwe), 1910–1945," *Revista Internacional de Estudos Africanos*, N. 4 e 5, Janeiro-Dezembro, 1986, pp. 159–189.

———. "Cocoa Plantations and Coerced Labor in the Gulf of Guinea, 1870–1914," in Klein, Martin A., Ed., *Breaking the Chains: Slavery, Bondage, and Emancipation in Modern Africa and Asia*. Madison: University of Wisconsin Press, 1993.

———. "Runaway Slaves and Social Bandits in Southern Angola, 1875–1914," in G. Heuman, ed., *Out of Bandage, Runaways, Resistance and Marronage in African and the New World*. London: Frank Cass, 1986, pp. 23–33.

Clarence-Smith, Gervase and Moorsom, R. "Underdevelopment and Class Formation in Ovamboland 1845–1915," *Journal of African History*, XVI, 4 (1975), pp. 365–381.

Cleveland, Todd, "Rock Solid: African Laborers on the Diamond Mines of the Companhia de Diamantes de Angola (Diamang), 1917–1975," Ph.D. Dissertation, University of Minnesota, 2008.

Coelho, Guilherme Gomes. *Relatórios dos Governadores das Provincias Ultramarinas, Districto de Benguella, 1887*. Lisboa: Imprensa Nacional, n.d.

Coelho, Maria Antonieta Martins Rodrigues. "Rupture and Continuity: The State, Law and the Economy in Angola, 1975–1989." PhD diss, University of Warwick School of Law, 1994.

Cooper, Frederick. *On the African Waterfront: Urban Disorder and the Transformation of Work in Colonial Mombasa*. New Haven: Yale University Press, 1987.

———. "Conditions Analogous to Slavery," in Thomas C. Holt, Rebecca J. Scott, and Frederick Cooper, eds., *Beyond Slavery: explorations of race, labor, and citizenship in postemancipation societies*. Chapel Hill: The University of North Carolina Press, 2000, pp. 107–149.

———. *Decolonization and African Society: The labor question in French and British Africa*. Cambridge: Cambridge University Press, 1996.

Correia, Adérito and Sousa, Bornito de. *Angola História Constitucional*, Coimbra: Livraria Almedina, 1996.

Correia, Dr. Alberto Carlos Germano da Silva. "A Doença do Sono em Angola," *Revista Médica de Angola*, Vol. IV, N° 4, Agostto de 1923, pp. 159–175.

Costa, Eduardo. "A Administração civil nas nossas colonias africanas," *Boletim da Sociedade de Geographia de Lisboa*. Lisboa: Imprensa Nacional, 1903.

Couceiro, Henrique de Paiva. *Angola (Dous annos de Governo Junho 1907–Junho 1909) Historia e Commentarios*. Lisboa: A Nacional, 1910.

Cunha, J.M. da Silva. *O Trabalho Indígena Estudo de Direito Colonial* . Lisboa: Agência Geral do Ultramar, 1954.

———. *A Reforma do Código de Trabalho dos Indígenas*. Lisboa, 1954.

———. *O Sistema Português da Política Indigena. Subsídios para o seu Estudo*. Coimbra: Coimbra Editora, 1953.

Curtin, Philip D. *The Image of Africa: British Ideas and Action, 1870–1950*. Madison: University of Wisconsin Press, 1964.

Curto, José. "Alcohol and Slaves: the Luso-Brazilian alcohol commerce at Mpinda, Luanda, and Benguela during the Atlantic slave trade, c. 1480–1830 and its impact on the societies of West Central Africa," Ph. D. Dissertation University of California, Los Angeles, 1996.

Cushman, Mary Floyd. *Missionary Doctor—The Story of Twenty Years in Africa*, New York: Harper and Brothers, 1944.

Da Costa, Eduardo. *Estudo sobre a Administração Civil das Nossas Possessões Africanas*. Lisboa: 1903.

Da Costa, P. Cándido F. *Cem Anos dos Missionários do Espíritu Santo em Angola, 1866–1966*, Nova Lisboa, 1970.

Damas, Dr. Carlos. "Memórias: O Banco Inter Unido," *BES Actual: Revista Interna do Grupo Banco Espírito Santo*, n. 12, April 1999, pp. 30–32.

———. "José Maria do Espírito Santo e Silva, de cambista a banqueiro, 1869–1915," *Análise Social*, Vol. XXXVII, Outono de 2002, pp. 851–878l.

———. "Espírito Santo e os Windsor em 1940," *Grande Reportagem*, May 2002, pp. 97–101.

Dáskalos, Sócrates. *Um Testemunho para a História de Angola do Huambo ao Huambo*, Lisboa: Vega, 2000.

Davidson, Basil. *The African Awakening*, London: Jonathan Cape, 1955.

———. "Towards a New Angola," *People's Power in Mozambique, Angola and Guinea Bissau*, No. 9, July–September 1977, pp. 5–12.

Dias, Jill R.. "Black Chiefs, White Traders and Colonial Policy Near the Kwanza: Kabuku Kambilo and the Portuguese, 1873–1896," *Journal of African History*, XVII, 2 (1976), pp. 245–265.

———. "Famine and Disease in the History of Angola c. 1830–1930," *Journal of African History*, 22 (1981), pp. 349–378.

Dinis, José de Oliveira Ferreira. Secretário dos Negócios Indígenas da Província de Angola *Relatório do Ano de 1913*. Luanda, Angola: Imprensa Social, 1914.

———. *Populações Indígenas de Angola*. Luanda, 1918.

———. "A Evolução da Política Colonial Portuguesa," *Boletim da Agência Geral das Colónias*. Lisboa: Agência Geral das Colónias, Ano IV, Abril de 1928, No. 34, pp. 3–13.

———. "Da Política Indígena em Angola: Os impostos indígenas," *Boletim da Agência Geral das Colónias*. Lisboa: Agência Geral das Colónias, Ano V., Maio de 1929, N. 47, pp. 136–165.

———. "Contribuição para o Estudo de Demografia Indígena de Angola," *Boletim da Agência Geral das Colónias*, Ano VI, N. 58, Abril de 1930, pp. 32–53.

Diogo, Alberto and Da Costa Oliveira, Jorge Eduardo. "Regime Açucareiro," *Actividade Económica de Angola*, No. 61 a 63, Setembro/Dezembro 1961 e Janeiro/Agosto 1962, pp. 169–186.

Duffy, James. *Portuguese Africa*. Cambridge, Massachusetts: Harvard University Press, 1959.

———. *A Question of Slavery. Labour Policies in Portuguese Africa and the British Protest, 1850–1920*. Oxford: Oxford University Press, 1967.

Edwards, Adrian C. *The Ovimbundu under Two Sovereignities: A Study of Social Control and Social Change among a People of Angola*, London: Oxford University Press, 1962.

Egerton, F.C.C. *Angola without Prejudice*. Lisbon: Agency-General for the Overseas Territories, 1955.

Ellis, Stephen. "Writing Histories of Contemporary Africa," *Journal of African History*, Vol. 43, 2002, pp. 1–26.

Enes, António. *Moçambique: Relatório Apresentado ao Govêrno*. Lisboa: Agência Geral das Colónias, 1893.

Enes, António, e outros. "O Trabalho dos Indígenas e o Crédito Agrícola: Do relatório elaborado pela Comissão encarregada de estudar o problema de trabalho dos indígenas em 1899," *Antologia Colonial Portuguesa*, Vol. 1. Lisboa: Agência Geral das Colónias, 1946, pp. 25–55.

Esteves, Emmanuel. "O Caminho de Ferro de Benguela e o impacto econômico, social e Cultural na sua zonas de influência 1902–1952." Ph.D. Dissertation, Universidade do Porto, 1999.

Farinha, Luís. "Do Império Português à Descolonização: Henrique Galvão e o império." *História*. Ano XXII, Número 21, Janeiro 2000, pp. 18–28.

Faro, José de Sousa e. *Angola Como eu a vi em 1930–1931*. Lisboa: Imp. Da Armada, 1932.

Fernandes, Francisco Alfredo. *O Posto Administrativo Na Vida Do Indígena*. Lisboa: Publicações Europa-América, 1955.

Ferreira, Eduardo de Sousa. *Portuguese Colonialism in Africa: the end of an era The effects of Portuguese Colonialism on Education, Science, Culture, and Information*, Paris, 1974.

Ferreira, Manuel Ennes. *A indústria em tempo de guerra (Angola, 1975–91)*, Lisboa: Edições Cosmos Instituto da Defesa Nacional, 1999.

Ferreira, Vincente. *Estudos Ultramarinos*, Volumes I–IV. Lisboa: Agência Geral do Ultramar, 1954.

Fieldhouse, D.K.. *Merchant Capital and Economic Decolonization The United Africa Company 1929–1987*. Oxford: Clarendon Press, 1994.

Frankel, S. Herbert. *Capital Investment in Africa: Its Course and Effects*. London: Oxford University Press, 1938.

Freudenthal, Aida. "A Baixa de Cassanje. Algodão e revolta," *Revista Internacional de Estudos Africanos*, nos. 18–22, 1995–99, pp. 245–278.

———. "Angola," in A.H. de Oliveira Marques, ed., *O Império Africano 1890–1930*. Lisboa: Editorial Estampa, 2001.

———. *Arimos e Fazendas A transição agrária em Angola*. Luanda: Edições Cha de Caxinde, 2005.

———. "Os quilombos de Angola no século XIX: a recusa da escravidão," *Estudos Afro-Asiáticos*, Vol. 32, 1997, pp. 109–34.

Freudenthal, Aida, José Manuel Fernandes, Maria de Lurdes Janeiro, eds. *Angola no século XIX Cidades, Território e Arquitecturas*. Lisboa: Mem Martins, 2006.

Freyre, Gilberto. *Aventura e Rotina: Sugestões de uma viagem a procura das constantes portuguêsas de caráter e ação*. Rio de Janeiro: José Olympio, 1953.

———. *The Portuguese and the Tropics*. Lisbon: Executive Committee for the Commemoration of the Vth Centenary of the Death of Prince Henry the Navigator, 1961.

Gabriel, M. Nunes. *Angola. Cinco Séculos de Cristianismo*. Lisboa: Queluz, 1978.

Galvão, Henrique. *Informação Económica Sôbre Angola*. 1933.

———. "Exposição do Deputado Henrique Galvão, á Comissão de Colónias da Assembleia Nacional, em Janeiro de 1947." Arquivo Histórico-Parliamentar, Assembleia da República.

———. *Santa Maria: My Crusade for Portugal*. Cleveland: The World Publishing Company, 1961.

Garcia, Dr. José de Penha. "A assistência e a protecção aos indígenas na moderna política colonial," *Boletim da Agência Geral das Colónias*, Ano. 6, Junho de 1929, N. 48, pp. 16–39.

Geraldes, C. de Melo. *Alguns Aspectos do Problema da Mão-de-Obra Indígena na África Tropical*. Lisboa, 1930.

Gleijeses, Piero. *Conflicting Missions: Havana, Washington and Africa, 1959–1976*. Chapel Hill: University of North Carolina Press, 2002.

Grohs, Gerhard and Czernik, Godehard. "State and the Church in Angola 1450–1980" *International Studies on Contemporary Africa Series*, No. 3, Genève: Institut Universitaire de Hautes Etudes Internationales, 1983.

Guerra, Henrique. *Angola Estrutura Económica e Classes Sociais: Os Últimos Anos do Colonialismo Português em Angola*. 4.ª Edição. Lisboa: Edições 70, 1979.

Guimarães, Fernando Andresen. *The Origins of the Angolan Civil War Foreign Intervention and Domestic Political Conflict*. New York: St. Martin's Press, 1998.

Hailey, Lord. *An African Survey: A Study of Problems Arising in Africa South of the Sahara*. London: Oxford University Press, 1938.

Hammond, R.J. *Portugal and Africa 1815–1910 A Study in Uneconomic Imperialism* Stanford: Stanford University Press, 1966.

Harries, Patrick. *Work, Culture, and Identity Migrant Laborers in Mozambique and South Africa, c. 1860–1910*. Portsmouth, NH: Heinemann, 1994.

Harris, John H. *Portuguese Slavery: Britain's Dilemma*. London: Methuen & Co. Ltd., 1913.

Hastings, Adrian. *The Church in Africa 1450–1950*. Oxford: Clarendon Press, 1994.

Hatzky, Christine. *Cubans in Angola South-South Cooperation and Transfer of Knowledge, 1976*–1991. Madison: University of Wisconsin Press, 2015.

Heimer, Franz-Wilhelm, Ed. *Social Change in Angola*, München: Weltforum Verlag, 1973.

———. *The Decolonization Conflict in Angola, 1974–76: An Essay in Political Sociology*. Geneva: Institut Universitaire de Hautes Etudes Internationales, 1979.

Henderson, Lawrence W. *Angola: Five Centuries of Conflict*. Ithaca, N.Y.: Cornell University Press, 1980.

———. *The Church in Angola: A River of Many Currents*, Cleveland, Ohio: The Pilgrim Press, 1990.

Hendrickson, Hildi. "Bodies and Flags: The Representation of Herero Identity in Colonial Namibia," in Hildi Henrickson, Ed., *Clothing and Difference: Embodied Identities in Colonial and Post-Colonial Africa*. Durham: Duke University Press, 1996, pp. 213–244.

Heywood, Linda. *Contested Power in Angola, 1840s to the Present*, Rochester: University of Rochester Press, 2000.

———. "Porters, Trade, and Power: The Politics of Labor in the Central Highlands of Angola, 1850–1914" in Coquery-Vidrovitch, Catherine and Lovejoy, Paul E., *The Workers of African Trade*, Beverly Hills: Sage, 1985.

———. "Production, Trade and Power—The Political Economy of Central Angola 1850 1930," Ph.D. Dissertation, Columbia University, 1984.

Heywood, Linda and Thornton, John. "African Fiscal Systems as Sources for Demographic History: The Case of Central Angola, 1799–1920," *Journal of African History*, 29 (1988), 213–228.

Hopkins, A.G. "Imperial Business in Africa Part I: Sources," *Journal of African History*, XVII, I (1976), pp. 29–48.

Hudson Institute. *Angola: Some Views of Development Prospects*, 2 Volumes. New York: Hudson Institute, 1969,

Iliffe, John. *The Emergence of African Capitalism*. Minneapolis: University of Minnesota Press, 1983.

———. *Tanganyika Under German Rule 1905–1912*. Cambridge: Cambridge University Press, 1969.

Inocentes, Gonçalo. "As Cheias do Rio Fagulha," (Unpublished manuscript, 2012).

International Labour Organisation. *Conventions and Recommendations, 1919–1981*. Geneva: International Labour Organisation, 1982.

Isaacman, Allen. *Cotton is the Mother of Poverty: Peasants, Work, and Rural Struggle in Colonial Mozambique, 1938–1961*. Portsmouth, NH: Heinemann, 1996.

Jamba, Sousa. "The Idea of Angola," *Times Literary Supplement*, June 8, 2001, p. 12.

Jerónimo, Miguel Bandeira. *Livros Brancos, Almas Negras: A "Missão Civilizadora do Colonialismo Português c. 1870–1930"* Lisboa: Imprensa de Ciências Sociais, 2009.

Júnior, Miguel, ed. *A Batalha de Kifangondo 1975 Factos e Documentos* (Luanda: Mayamba Editora, 2013).

Katzenellenbogen, S.E. *Railways and the Copper Mines of Katanga*. Oxford: Clarendon Press, 1973.

Keese, Alexander. "Forced Labour in the 'Gorgulho Years': Understanding Reform and Repression in Rural São Tomé e Príncipe, 1945–1953" *Itinerario* Vol 38, Issue 01 (April 2014), pp. 103–124.

———."The Constrains of Late Colonial Reform Policy: Forced Labour Scandals in the Portuguese Congo (Angola) and the limits of reform under authoritarian colonial rule, 1955–1961" *Portuguese Study Review* 28:2 (2012): 186–200.

Laboreiro, Simão de, *A Circunscrição Civil Da Ganda Relatório do Administrador, 1914–1915*. Loanda: Imprensa Moderna, 1916.

Le Goff Jacques. *History and Memory*. New York: Columbia University Press, 1992.

Lippmann, Walter. *US War Aims*. Boston: Little, Brown and Company, 1944.

Macedo, José de. *Autonomia de Angola*. 2.ª Edição. Lisboa: Centro de Socio-Economia Instituto de Investigação Científica Tropical, 1988.

Magalhães, José Calvet de, *Portugal e as Nações Unidas*. Lisboa: Instituto de Estudos Estratégicos e Internacionais, 1996.

Mamdani, Mahmood. *Citizen and Subject: Contemporary Africa and the Legacy of Late Colonialism*. Princeton: Princeton University Press, 1996.

Mantero, Francisco. *A Mão-de-Obra Indígena nas Colónias Africanas*. Lisboa, 1924.

Marcum, John A. *The Angolan Revolution, Volume 1 The Anatomy of an Explosion (1950–1962)*. Cambridge, Massachusetts: The MIT Press, 1969.

———. *The Angolan Revolution, Volume II Exile Politics and Guerrilla Warfare (1962–1976)*. Cambridge, Massachusetts: The MIT Press, 1978.

Margarido, Alfredo. *A Lusofonia e os Lusófonos: Novos Mitos Portugueses*. Lisboa: Edições Universitárias Lusófonas, 2000.

Marques, João Pedro. *Sá da Bandeira e o Fim da Escravidão: Vitória da Moral, Desforra do Interesse*. Lisboa: Instituto Ciencias Sociais, 2008.

———. *The Sounds of Silence: Nineteenth-Century Portugal and the Abolition of the Slave Trade*. New York: Berghahn Books, 2006. Translated by Richard Wall.

Martins, Maria Belmira. *Sociedades e Grupos em Portugal*. Lisboa: Editorial Estampa, 1973.

Mata, Eugénia and Valério, Nuno. *História Económica de Portugal Uma Perspectiva Global*. Lisboa: Editorial Presença, 1994.

Matos, Norton de. *A Província de Angola*. Porto: Maranus, 1926.

———. *Memórias e Trabalho da Minha Vida*. Lisboa, 1944.

———. *A Nação Una*. Lisboa, 1953.

Maxwell, Kenneth, *The Making of Portuguese Democracy*. Cambridge: Cambridge University Press, 1995.

Mazula, Assahel Jonassane. *O Homem e o Trabalho*. Lisboa: Editora Gráfica Portuguesa, Lda., 1969.

Mbembe, Achille. *On the Postcolony*. Berkeley: University of California Press, 2001.

Mello, Lopo Vaz de Sampaio e. *Política Indígena*, Oporto: Magalhães & Moniz, Ltd, 1910.

Mendes, Afonso. *O Trabalho Assalariado em Angola*. Lisboa: Instituto Superior De Ciências Sociais e Política Ultramarina, n/d.

———. "Mão-de-Obra" in *Ultramar*, 4 (1961).

Meneses, Filipe Ribeiro de and Robert McNamara, "The Last Throw of the Dice: Portugal, Rhodesia and South Africa, 1970–74" *Portuguese Studies*, Vol. 28, No. 2 (2012), 201–215.

Milheiros, Mário. *Índice Histórico-Corográfico de Angola*. Luanda: Instituto de Investigação Científica de Angola, 1972.

Miller, Joseph C. "The Significance of Drought, Disease and Famine in the Agriculturally Marginal Zones of West-Central Africa," *Journal of African History*, 23 (1982), pp. 17–61.

———. *Way of Death: Merchant Capitalism and the Angolan Slave Trade 1730–1830*. Madison, Wisconsin: The University of Wisconsin Press, 1988.

Monteiro, Armindo. "O Problema das Transferências de Angola," *Boletim da Agência Geral das Colónias*, No. 7, Ano 7, Julho de 1931, pp. 3–134.

———. *As Grandes Directrizes da Governação Ultramarina no Período que Decorreu entre as Duas Guerras Mundiais*. Lisboa, 1942.

Moorman, Marissa. *Intonations: A Social History of Music and Nation in Luanda, Angola, from 1945 to Recent Times*. Athens, Ohio: Ohio University Press, 2008.

Moutinho, Mário. *O Indígena no Pensamento Colonial Português*. Lisboa: Edições Universitários Lusófonas, 2000.

Naturães. *Voz D'Angola Clamando No Deserto. Offerecida aos Amigos da Verdade Pelos Naturaes.* Lisboa: [Typographia Rua da Barroca, 1901] Edições 70, 1984.

Ndombasi, Tshingi Kueno. "Le Chemin de fer de Benguela 1903–1953: Le Capital Prive et la colonisations Portugaise en Angola," Ph. Dissertation, Universite Paris VII, 1996.

Neto, Agostinho. *Sacred Hope.* Translated into English by Marga Holness. Dar es Salaam: Tanzania Publishing House, 1974.

Neto, Maria. "In Town and Out of Town: A Social History of Huambo (Angola) 1902 1961" Ph.D. Dissertation, University of London, 2012.

———, "Comércio, Religião e Política no Sertão de Benguela: O Bailundo de Ekwikwi II," Fontes e Estudos: Revista do Arquivo Histórico Nacional, no. 1, November 1994, 101–118.

Nevinson, Henry W. *A Modern Slavery,* First published London, 1906. New York: Schocken Books, 1968.

Nevinson, Henry W. and Francisco Mantero. *Slavery In Portuguese Africa Opposing Views.* Northbrook, Ill.: Metro Books, INC., 1972.

Newitt, Malyn. *Portugal in Africa The Last Hundred Years.* London: C. Hurst & CO., 1981.

———. *A History of Mozambique.* London: Hurst & Company, 1995.

Nogueira, Franco. *Diálogos Interditos: A Política Externa Portuguesa e a Guerra de África,* 2 vols. Lisboa: Intervenção, 1979.

Okuma, Thomas. "The Social Response of Christianity in Angola," Ph.D. Dissertation, Boston University, 1964.

Oliveira, Jorge Eduardo da Costa. "Regime Açucareiro," *Actividade Económica de Angola,* N° 61 a 63, Setembro/Dezembro 1961 e Janeiro/Agosto 1962, pp. 169–187.

Oliveira, Mário António Fernandes de. *Alguns aspectos da administração de Angola em época de reformas (1834–1851).* Lisboa: Universidade Nove de Lisboa, 1981.

Oliveira, Pedro Aires. *Armindo Monteiro uma bigrafia polílica.* Lisboa: Bertrand Editora, 2000.

Oliveira, Ricardo Soares de. "Business success, Angola-style: postcolonial politics and the rise and rise of Sonangol" *Journal of African Studies* 45, 4 (2007), 595–619.

Parpart, Jane L. *Labor and Capital on the African Copperbelt.* Philadelphia: Temple University Press, 1983.

Parreira, Henrique Gomes de Amorim. "História do Açúcar em Portugal," *Anais da Junta das Missões Coloniais,* Vol. VII, 1952, pp. 210–309.

Pawson, Lara. *In the Name of the People Angola's Forgotten Massacre.* New York: I.B. Tauris, 2014.

Péclard, Didier. "'Eu sou americao': dynamiques du champ missionnaire dans le planalto Central angolais au XX siècle" in *Lusotopie,* 1998, pp. 357–376.

———. "Religion and Politics in Angola: The Church, the Colonial State and the Emergence of Angolan Nationalism, 1940–1961," *Journal of Religion in Africa,* XXVIII, 2 (1998), p. 160–186.

Pélissier, René. *História das Campanhas de Angola. Resistência e Revoltas 1845–1941.* 2 vols. Lisboa: Estampa, 1986–88.

———. *La Colonie du minotaure: Nationalismes et révoltes en Angola, 1926–1962.* Orgeval: Pélissier, 1978.

———. *Les Guerres grises: Résistance et révoltes en Angola, 1845–1941.* Orgeval: Pélissier, 1977.

Penvenne, Jeanne Marie. *African Workers and Colonial Racism: Mozambican Strategies and Struggles in Lourenço Marques, 1877–1962.* Portsmouth, N.H.: Heinemann, 1995.

———. "'We are all Portuguese!' Challenging the Political Economy of Assimilation: Lourenço Marques, 1870–1933," in Leroy Vail, Ed., *The Creation of Tribalism in Southern Africa.* London: James Currey, 1989, pp. 255–288.

———. "João dos Santos Albasini (1876–1922): The Contradictions of Politics and Identity in Colonial Mozambique," *Journal of African History*, No. 37, 1996, pp. 419–564.

Pereira, Dr. Pedro Teotónio. *Organização Corporativa.* Lisboa: Edições SPN, 1935.

Pirio, Gregory Roger. "Commerce, Industry and Empire: The Making of Modern Portuguese Colonialism in Angola and Mozambique, 1890–1914," Ph.D. Dissertation, University of California, Los Angeles, 1982.

Pitcher, M. Anne. *Politics in the Portuguese Empire: The State, Industry, and Cotton, 1926–1974.* Oxford: Clarendon Press, 1993.

Popular Memory Group. "Popular memory: theory, politics, method," in Robert Perks and Alistair Thompson, eds., *The Oral History Reader.* London: Routledge, 1998.

Portelli, Alessandro. "The Peculiarities of Oral History," *History Workshop*, No. 12, Autumn 1981, pp. 96–107.

Portugal, Ministério da Economia. *Colectânea de Legislação sôbre a Indústria Açucareira Desde 1848 até 1944.* Lisboa: Editorial Império, no date.

Prakash, Gyan. "Subaltern Studies as Postcolonial Criticism," *American Historical Review*, Vol. 99, No. 5, 1994, pp. 1475–1490.

Redinha, José. *Distribuição Etnica da Província de Angola.* Luanda: Centro de Informação e Turismo de Angola, 1965.

Rego, A.A. Fernandes. *A Mão-de-Obra nas Colónias Portuguesas de Africa.* Lisboa, 1910.

Reinsch, Paul Samuel. *Colonial Government: An Introduction to the Study of Colonial Institutions.* Freeport, New York: Books for Libraries Press, 1970; and Paul Samuel Reinsch, *Colonial Administration.* New York: The MacMillan Company, 1905.

Roberts, Andrew, Ed. *Photographs as sources for African History.* London: SOAS, 1988.

Rosa, Manuel Ferreira. "A Nova Orientação Educacional do Indígena," *Actividade Económica de Angola* N. 5, Marco de 1937, pp. 25–30.

Rosas, Fernando. *O Estado Novo nos Anos Trinta, 1928–1938.* Lisboa: Editorial Estampa, 1986.

———. *Portugal entre a Paz e a Guerra 1939–1945.* Lisboa: Editorial Estampa, 1995.

Ross, Edward Alsworth. *Report on the Employment of Native Labor in Portuguese Africa*. New York: The Abbott Press, 1925.

Salgado, R. Ribeiro. *A Evolução do Comércio Especial Ultramarino*. Lisboa: Agência Geral das Colónias, 1939.

Samuels, Michael A. "A Failure of Hope: Education and Changing Opportunities in Angola under the Portuguese Republic" in Chilcote, Ronald H., Ed., *Protest and Resistance in Angola and Brazil*, Berkeley: University of California Press, 1972.

———. *Education in Angola, 1878–1914: A History of Culture Transfer and Administration*, New York: Teachers College Press, 1970.

Santos, Maria Emília Madeira. *Nos Caminhos de África Serventia e Posse*, Lisboa: Instituto de Investigação Científica Tropical, 1998.

Santos, Oliveira. "Reply to the Accusations Addressed to the League of Nations by Mr. Edward A. Ross Against the Portuguese in Angola," Libsoa: Imprensa Nacional, 1930.

Scott, James. *Weapons of the Weak: Everyday Forms of Peasant Resistance*. New Haven: Yale University Press, 1985.

Sender, John and Smith, Sheila. *The Development of Capitalism in Africa*. London: Methuen, 1986.

Shapiro, Martin F. "Medicine in the Service of Colonialism: Medical Care in Portuguese Africa 1885–1974." Ph.D. Dissertation, University of California, Los Angeles, 1983.

Silcox, L.M. *The History of Chissamba Retold*, Toronto: Canada Congregational Women, 1916.

Silva, Fernando Diogo da. *O Huambo. Mão-de-Obra Rural no Mercado de Trabalho de Angola*. Luanda: Fundo de Acção Social no Trabalho em Angola, no date.

Silva Rego António da. *O consciente e o inconsciente na colonização portuguesa*. Benguela, 1965.

Soares, Mário. *Portugal's Struggle for Liberty*. Translated by Mary Gawsworth. London: George Allen & Unwin Ltd., 1975.

Sociedade de Geografia de Lisboa, *Elementos para a resolução dos Problemas Coloniais*. Lisboa: Tip. Da Cooperativa Militar, 1913.

Soremekun, Fola. "A History of the American Board Missions in Angola 1880–1940," Ph.D. Dissertation, Northwestern University, 1965.

———. "Trade and Dependency in Central Angola: The Ovimbundu in the Nineteenth Century," in Palmer, Robin and Parsons, Neil, Eds., *The Roots of Rural Poverty in Central and Southern Africa*. Berkeley: University of California Press, 1977.

Sousa Ferreira, Eduardo de, *Portuguese Colonialism from South Africa to Europe*. Freiburg: Aktion Dritte Welt, 1972.

Sousa Lara, Luiz de. *A Indústria do Açúcar na Economia do Império Conferência Realisada na Sociedade de Geografia em 6 de Março de 1936*. Lisboa: Sociedade de Industrial de Tipografia, 1936.

Spies, F.J. du Toit. *Operasie Savannah. Angola 1975–1976*. Pretoria: S.A. Weermag, 1989.

Telo, António José. "O Fim do Ciclo Africano do Império" , in *Portugal na Transição do Milénio*, Lisboa: Fim de Século, 1998, pp. 327–355.

Torres, Adelino. *O Império Português Entre o Real e o Imaginário*. Lisboa: Escher, 1991.

Tucker, John T. *Drums in Darkness*, New York: Doran Company, 1927.

———. *The Land of the Blacksmith Prince*. London: World Dominion Press, 1933.

———. *A Tucker Treasury*. Winfield, British Columbia: Wood Lake Books, 1984.

Uralov, K. *A Justa Causa de Angola*. Moscovo: Edições da Agência de Imprensa Nóvosti, 1976.

Urquhart, Alvin W. "Patterns of Settlement and Subsistence in Southwestern Angola," National Academy of Sciences—National Research Council, Report No. 18, 1963.

Uys, Ian, *Bushman Soldiers: their Alpha and Omega*. Germiston, South Africa: Fortress Publishers Ltd, 1993.

Vail, Leroy and White, Landeg. *Capitalism and Colonialism in Mozambique A Study of Quelimane District*. Minneapolis: University of Minnesota Press, 1980.

———. "Forms of Resistance: Songs and Perceptions of Power in Colonial Mozambique," Africa Seminar, University of Cape Town, 20 September 1983.

Van Onselen, Charles. *Chibaro African Mine Labour in Southern Rhodesia 1900–1933*. Johannesburg: Ravan Press, 1976.

Vilhena, Ernesto Jardim de. *Questões Coloniaes: Discursos e Artigos*. Lisboa, 1910.

Welty, Susan. "Slavery Is Not Dead," *Negro Digest*, Vol. IV, No. 6, April 1946, pp. 57–60.

Wheeler, Douglas. "The Portuguese in Angola 1836–1891: A Study in Expansion and Administration," Ph.D. Dissertation, Boston University, 1963.

———. "The Portuguese Revolution of 1910," *Journal of Modern History*. Vol. 44, June 1972, pp. 172–94.

———. *Republican Portugal, a political history, 1910–1926* (Madison, 1978).

———. "Aqui é Portugal!: The Politics of the Colonial Ideal during the Estado Novo, 1926–1974," in *Portugal na Transição do Milénio*, Lisboa: Fim de Século, 1998, pp. 375–405.

———. "José Norton de Matos (1867–1955)," in L.H. Gann and Peter Duignan, Eds., *African Proconsuls Europeans Governors in Africa*. New York: The Free Press, 1978, pp. 445–463.

———. "The Galvão Report on Forced Labor (1947) in Historical Context and Perspective: Trouble-Shooter Who Was 'Trouble'," *Portuguese Studies Review* (Vol. 16, no. 1, 2008), 115–152.

Wheeler, Douglas and Christensen, C. Diane. "To Rise with one Mind: The Bailundo War of 1902," in Franz-Wilhelm Heimer, Ed., *Social Change in Angola*, München: Weltforum Verlag, 1973, pp. 53–92.

Wheeler, Douglas and Pélissier, René. *Angola*. London: Pall Mall Press, 1971.

Wilensky, Alfredo Héctor, translated by Frank R. Holliday. *Trends in Portuguese Overseas Legislation for Africa*. Braga, Portugal: Pax, 1971.

Worger, William. *South Africa's City of Diamonds: Mine Workers and Monopoly Capitalism in Kimberley 1867–1895*. New Haven: Yale University Press, 1987.

Wright, George. *The Destruction of a Nation: United States' Policy Towards Angola since 1945*. London: Pluto Press, 1997.

Wylie, Diana. *Starving on a Full Stomach: Hunger and the Triumph of Cultural Racism in Modern South Africa*. Charlottesville: University Press of Virginia, 2001.

Index

www.ingramcontent.com/pod-product-compliance
Lightning Source LLC
Chambersburg PA
CBHW071444230926
51846CB00001B/330